TECHNIQUES OF THE SELLING WRITER

TECHNIQUES OF THE SELLING WRITER

By

Dwight V. Swain

UNIVERSITY OF OKLAHOMA PRESS
NORMAN

Excerpt from *The Lost World* by Sir Arthur Conan Doyle is re-printed by permission by the Estate of Sir Arthur Conan Doyle and John Murray Ltd.

Library of Congress Catalog Card Number: 73–7419

ISBN: 0–8061–1191-7 (paper)

13   14   15   16

*For Joye,
who cared*

Foreword

Be warned in advance that we here shall deal with one topic and one only: writing.

By writing, I mean the process of creation as applied to fiction . . . the conjuring up of original stories out of the nether reaches of your mind.

My purpose is to help would-be fiction writers learn how to carry out this process less slowly and less painfully. The devices set forth all are used, consciously or otherwise, by selling writers.

This is because said devices have proved effective in making stories enjoyable and/or enticing to readers. The selling writer, as a commercially-oriented professional, can't afford to write copy that *isn't* enjoyable and/or enticing.

Since they're primarily tools, these techniques have little bearing on literary quality or the lack of it. No writer uses all of them. No writer can avoid using some of them. How well they serve will depend on you yourself.

They are, in brief, tricks and techniques of the selling writer. They're all this book has to offer.

❖ ❖ ❖

It would be fitting, at this point, to give personal credit to all the people who helped show me the literary ropes in years gone by. But such a list would of necessity run too long, for it would include each and every writer of each and every book and magazine I ever read . . . plus the many friends who taught me about assorted joys and the enemies who taught me about trouble . . . plus the editors like Ray Palmer and Howard Browne and Bill Hamling who pushed and poked at me and bought my stories

. . . plus such colleagues as Ned Hockman (who, though I've worked with him on fifty fact films, still can show me new tricks about how to put together a motion picture) and Foster-Harris (who knows all that there is to know about plotting and about how to be an inspiration) and the late great Walter S. Campbell, founder with Foster-Harris of the University of Oklahoma's courses in Professional Writing . . . plus, above all, my students, who for a dozen years now have backed me into corners and made me figure out ways to say things so that they make sense to someone who *hasn't* already sold a million words of copy.

Truly, one and all, I'm grateful.

D.V.S.

NORMAN, OKLA.

Contents

TECHNIQUES OF THE SELLING WRITER

CHAPTER 1

Fiction and You

A story is experience translated into literary process.

You need to know only four things in order to write a solid story:

how to group words into motivation-reaction units;

how to group motivation-reaction units into scenes and sequels;

how to group scenes and sequels into story pattern;

how to create the kind of characters that give a story life.

This book tells you how to do these things; these, and many, many more. In detail: step by step. The tricks are here . . . the tools, the techniques, the devices. You'll find them in Chapters 2 through 9.

Are these things hard to learn?

Not at all.

At least, not if you take the job a step at a time, so that you understand *why* you do each thing, as well as *how.*

Then why do so many people find it difficult to learn to write?

They fall into traps that slow them down and hold them back.

Eight traps, specifically:

1. They take an unrealistic view.
2. They hunt for magic secrets.
3. They try to learn the hard way.
4. They refuse to follow feeling.
5. They attempt to write by rules.

6. They don't want to be wrong.
7. They bow down to the objective.
8. They fail to master technique.

Every one of these traps is a major hazard. Therefore, before we get down to specific skills, let's consider each in detail.

Reality and the writer

Can you learn to write stories?
Yes.
Can you learn to write well enough to sell an occasional piece? Again yes, in most cases.
Can you learn to write well enough to sell consistently to *Redbook* or *Playboy* or Random House or Gold Medal?
Now that's another matter, and one upon which undue confusion centers.
Writing is, in its way, very much like tennis.
It's no trick at all to learn to play tennis—if you don't mind losing every game.
Given time and perseverance, you probably can even work yourself up to where Squaw Hollow rates you as above-average competition.
Beyond that, however, the going gets rough. Reach the nationals, win status as champion or finalist, and you know your performance bespeaks talent as well as sweat.
So it is with writing. To get stories of a sort set down on paper; to become known as a "leading Squaw Hollow writer," demands little more than self-discipline.
Continued work and study often will carry you into *American Girl* or *Men's Digest* or *Real Confessions* or *Scholastic Newstime*.
But the higher you climb toward big name and big money, the steeper and rougher your road becomes.
At the top, it's very rough indeed. If you get there; if you place consistently at *Post* or *McCall's* or Doubleday, you know it's because you have talent in quantity; and innate ability that sets you apart from the competition.
Now this doesn't seem at all strange to me. The same principle

applies when you strive for success as attorney or salesman or racing driver.

Further, whatever the field, no realist expects advance guarantees of triumph. You can't know for sure how well you'll do until you try. Not even a Ben Hogan, a Sam Snead, or an Arnold Palmer made a hole-in-one his first time on the links. To win success, you first must master the skills involved. A pre-med student isn't called on to perform brain surgery.

Good—that is, salable—stories presuppose that you know how to write, how to plot, how to characterize, how to intrigue readers; how to make skilled use of a hundred tools.

A book like this one shows you these basic tricks and techniques.

What you do with those devices, however; how well you use them, is a thing that must ever and always depend on you: your intelligence, your sensitivity, your drive, your facility with language.

Your talent.

But before you shrug and turn aside, remember just one point: In writing, more than in almost any other field, initiative is the key. Ernest Hemingway had to write a first line and a first story too. So did John Steinbeck and Edna Ferber, Faith Baldwin and Pearl Buck and Frank Yerby and Erle Stanley Gardner. Each followed the same path. Each linked desire to knowledge, then took his chances.

Try it yourself. You may prove more able than you think.

The hunt for magic secrets

Observe Fred Friggenheimer, a non-existent beginning writer.

This morning, the postman brings Fred a shiny new Mephisto Supersonic Plot Computer.

This device has cost Fred twenty-five dollars. Its value, in terms of the benefit he can derive from it in his efforts to write better stories, isn't twenty-five cents.

Unfortunately, novices in the field of fiction often tend to a child-like faith in magic keys or secret formulas.

No such key exists. There isn't any formula or secret.

At least, no single secret.

That's worth remembering. No one can call his shots as a writer until he abandons his dreams of magic keys and, instead, looks reality straight in the eye.

What is reality?

Reality is acknowledging the complexity of fiction. It's accepting the fact that both you and I are human, and that we must crawl before we walk, and that the journey of a thousand miles begins with a single step.

Corollary: A lot more steps must of necessity follow Number One.

Thus, four boys in Friend Friggenheimer's town last night stole the chalice from a church. Caught, they reveal that they've been reading up on witchcraft and want to try to evoke Satan.

Fred reads about the incident in his morning paper. It intrigues him. "Here," he tells himself excitedly, "is a story!"

Fred's wrong. The theft is an incident. With skilled handling and the development of a point of view and dynamic characters and complications and climax and resolution, it quite possibly may build into a story. But for now, it remains an incident and nothing more.

A story is a complex thing. Its materials demand skill in their manipulation.

Story components, in turn, don't stand alone, nor yet hang in a vacuum. There's no such thing as plot, per se, or character, or setting.

Neither is story merely words or language . . . let alone style, or symbol, or imagery, or structure.

The experts do us badly here. Too often, they give the impression that a single player makes a ball team.

Take Fred's friend George Abercroft (like Fred, he's really non-existent), a specialist in story structure. Organization is the important thing, he says. Learn pattern, and it will solve your every problem.

But a superior architect may prove a poor carpenter; and you the writer must execute your works as well as plan them.

The specialist in character, in turn, sneers at plot as if it were a dirty word . . . conveniently forgetting that it's impossible truly to delineate character sans situation.

Ignoring content, the stylist prays to Flaubert and performs assorted sacred rites with language . . . as if the garment were more important than the wearer.

So many specialists . . . so many out-of-focus answers.

And each authority is dangerous to the very degree that he's correct, because that's also the degree to which he distorts the actual picture. Put four such specialists to work as a group, designing a woman, and she might well turn out like the nightmare of a surrealistic fetishist, all hair and *derrière* and breasts and high French heels.

So . . . no magic key. No universal formula. No mystic secret. No Supersonic Plot Computer.

It's enough to plunge a man to the depths of despair.

—Not to mention frustration.

Yet there's another way to look at your dilemma, and that way just may point you to salvation.

Consider: Do you really want to succeed just because you possess a magic secret?

For if there were some super-trick, some mysterious formula to puff away creative problems, then it stands to reason that said trick must be as difficult to perform as the Indian rope illusion, multiplied by Cagliostro and carried to the nth power, with Paracelsus, Apollonius of Tyana and Madame Helena Blavatsky thrown in. Otherwise, 999 writers would already be using it and the world would be blessed with a great deal more good fiction.

Denied such thaumaturgy, a beginner like our friend Fred Friggenheimer finds his task made both easier and harder. Instead of one secret, he must master dozens, hundreds . . . devices, procedures, bits of craftsmanship and rules of thumb and gimmicks.

And that brings us to a further hazard.

Must you learn the hard way?

Mabel Hope Hartley (that's not her real name), queen of the love pulps thirty years ago, is another of Fred's acquaintances. Old and tired now, she turns out just enough confessions to support herself.

Mabel tells Fred that a writer needs no help or guidance. Published stories, she claims, should be his textbooks, for what

secrets can there be to writing when every detail is spread before you on the printed page?

True enough, as far as it goes. But how many of us can correctly note and/or interpret everything we see? —And let no man
say me nay who hasn't tried to figure out the recipe for creole
gumbo from what his taste buds tell him. A whiff of perfume is
no sure clue to the scent's formulation. Just because you've
walked on carpets doesn't mean you're qualified to weave one.
Art conceals art, in writing as elsewhere. The skill of a skilled
writer tricks you into thinking that there is no skill.

So it might be just as well to take the sneers of our imaginary
Mabel Hope Hartley with several grains of salt. Mabel's merely
confused about the issues, because she did her own studying
without benefit of text or teacher—reading, rereading, writing,
rewriting, struggling, failing; sweating, swearing, pacing the
floor, experimenting, straining; wrestling with her work night
after night in agonies of despair or of frustration; battering at
the wall of authorial success till her square Dutch head was
bloody.

Next question: Is Mabel's procedure a good one?

It's a moot question, really. Often you have no choice but to
play by ear. The tune exists only in your own head, so you doodle till you achieve the effect you want.

But in many areas this may prove a wasteful process. Earlier
travelers have already noted landmarks and drawn maps of sorts.
"Do this," they say, or "Don't do that."

Short cuts are ever welcome, in a business as complex as this
one. So, most of us seize upon such rules with gratitude . . . attempt conscientiously to apply them.

Certainly Fred Friggenheimer does.

And that's where he runs into trouble.

Why?

Because often rules—arbitrary rules, at least—conflict with an
infinitely more vital element: feeling.

Emotion and the writer

All your life you've lived with feelings . . . inner awarenesses,
pleasant or painful, that rose in you when you bumped a knee or

bit a lemon, kissed a girl or soothed a hurt child. The Marine Band playing "The Halls of Montezuma" brought one type of emotion . . . a guitar and "La Paloma" another. Your father's death, your sister's marriage, snowflakes drifting down, the smell of wood smoke, angry words, soft whispers, a scornful laugh, the comedian whose pants fall down, puppies' warm cuddlesomeness . . . to one and all of them, you react.

With feelings.

In some of us, these feelings are more intense than they are in others; and, they're aroused by different stimuli and situations. The slight that brings this woman to fury is passed by unnoticed by her neighbor. Fred Friggenheimer is more aware of certain nuances than is George Abercroft . . . more sensitive to subtleties of sensation and of impulse: overtones, undertones, implications. *You* pity the sharecropper's bony, sway-backed horse; *I* pity the cropper; *our friend* pities himself, that he should be forced to face the fact of such degradation.

In other words, each of us experiences and responds to life differently, in a manner uniquely and individually his own.

Now all this is ever so important to a writer.

Why?

Because feeling is the place every story starts.

Where do you find feeling?

It springs from the human heart.

As a writer, your task is to bring this heart-bound feeling to the surface in your reader: to make it well and swell and surge and churn.

Understand, feeling is in said reader from the beginning. You give him nothing he doesn't possess already.

But emotion, for most people, too often is like some sort of slumbering giant, lulled to sleep by preoccupation with the dead facts of that outer world we call objective. When we look at a painting, we see a price tag. A trip is logistics more than pleasure. Romance dies in household routine.

Yet life without feeling is a sort of death.

Most of us know this. So, we long wistfully for speeded heartbeat, sharpened senses, brighter colors.

This search for feeling is what turns your reader to fiction; the reason why he reads your story. He seeks a reawakening:

heightened pulse; richer awareness. Facts are the least of his concern. For them, he can always go to the *World Almanac* or *Encyclopedia Britannica*.

Further, Reader wants this sharpening of feeling because he needs it, emotionally speaking. Otherwise, why would he bother with your copy?

Now, let's look at the other side of the coin:

Where do stories originate?

In you, the writer.

Why do you write them?

You too have feelings . . . feelings that excite you, the way the witch-cult excited Fred Friggenheimer.

An emotional need comes with these feelings: the need to communicate your excitement to others. So, where another man similarly excited might let his tension go in talk, or get drunk, or chop weeds in his garden, you write a story . . . put down words with which you seek to re-create the feelings that seethe inside you.

That is, you *hope* the words re-create those feelings.

And then?

For some fortunate souls, that's all there is to it. So talented are they . . . so sensitive, so perceptive, so completely attuned to themselves and to their audience . . . that they intuitively grasp everything they need to know of form and structure, style and process. They write, readers read, the world hails them as geniuses. . . . A happy state.

However, don't let the thought of such ability depress you. Though I've heard for years about these awesome figures, I've yet to meet a living, breathing writer who hadn't worked—and worked hard—for everything he got.

Most writers learn by doing. Practice, trial and error, train them. It's as if our friend Fred were to go home tonight to his wife Gertrude with a joke to tell.

Listening, she stares at him blankly. "What's so funny about that?"

Fred tries again. And maybe, this time, he gets the point across: Gertrude laughs.

Tomorrow, a new joke comes along. So, Fred tries to remember what he did before, so that he can present this story to Gertrude in such a manner that she'll laugh first time round, without benefit of follow-ups or explanations.

If his plan succeeds, he tucks the procedure away in the back of his head. From here on out, for him, it will constitute a cornerstone of verbal humor. He's found himself a rule to follow.

It's the same with writing. By trial and error, you learn that some things work and others don't . . . then incorporate that knowledge into rules-of-thumb.

Failure to develop such rules says merely that the man concerned is incapable of learning by experience. No matter how hard he tries, his time is wasted.

Where's Fred to find these tools . . . the specific bits and tricks he needs?

Here Mabel Hope Hartley scores. As she says, the devices are all right there before his eyes, in every published story . . . more of them than any one man can ever hope to master. Even though Fred lives to be a hundred, he'll still learn new twists each time he sits down to read or write.

But in order to reach that stage, Fred—and you—first must master fundamentals, so that he knows what to look for.

The trouble with rules

No writer in his right mind writes by a set of rules.

At least, not by somebody else's rules.

Why not?

Because rules start from the wrong end: with restriction; with form; with mechanics; with exhortation about things you should and shouldn't do.

Where *should* you start, then?

With feeling. *Your own* feeling.

A story is like a car that runs on emotion. The author's feeling is the gasoline in its engine. Take away its fuel, and even the shiniest, chrome-plated literary power plant is reduced to so much scrap iron.

Feeling first takes form *within you.* If you haven't got a feeling, you can't write about it, let alone arouse it in somebody else.

The self-taught writer holds a small advantage here, perhaps. Lacking formal training, he tends to be unaware of technique as

a thing separate and apart. Intellectualization of art is alien to
his thinking. First, last, and all the time he deals with what he
feels: Dick's love for Janice . . . the hatred Vincent turns on
Tom . . . the mother's anguish when Elsa runs away. Skill, to
him, is simply a tool to help convey feeling. No feeling, no writing.

A novice like Fred Friggenheimer, on the other hand, may assume that rule counts for more than story. So, he admires his plot
because it so perfectly follows the formula laid down by the
Mephisto Computer.

In so doing, he ignores the gasoline of feeling. Then he wonders why the car won't run.

That's why the first *real* rule of successful story-writing is . . .
find a feeling.

Or, if you prefer a different phrase: Get excited! Hunt till you
uncover something or other to which you react. With feeling.
The more intensely, the better.

Maybe it's a girl that turns you on . . . a gyroscope . . . a god
. . . a gopher. A disaster . . . a moment of truth . . . a funny
fragment. A color . . . an odor . . . a taste . . . a bar of music.

For me, once, it was an electroencephalograph, a machine that
measures brain waves. Because it fascinated me; because I felt
so strongly about it, it ended up as a paperback novel. —You'll
agree, I think, that no one can get much farther out than that.

After you find your feeling, rules come in handy . . . help
you to figure out the best way to capture in words whatever it is
that so excites you. But the feeling itself must always remain
dominant. Though rules may shape your story, you yourself must
shape the rules.

Beware, too, of the other man's rule. He sees the world
through different eyes.

Thus, George Abercroft is an action writer. "Start with a fight!"
is his motto. And for him, it works.

But Fred Friggenheimer's witch-cult yarn, as he conceives it,
puts heavy emphasis on atmosphere. The fight he tries to stick
in like a clove in a ham at the beginning, following George's
rule, destroys the mood—and the story.

Even with your own rules, indeed, you must be careful. Because somehow, subtly, they may not apply to this explicit situation.

"There is really no such thing as *the* novel," observes novelist Vincent McHugh. "The novel is always *a* novel—the specific problem, the particular case, the concrete instance."

And again: "The novel is not a form. It is a medium capable of accommodating a great variety of forms."

Feelings differ. So do the stories that spring from them.

General rules imply that all are the same.

Be very wary, therefore, of anything that says, "Reject this feeling." Search instead for the kind of guidance that tells you, "Here's a way to do the thing you already want to do . . . to use effectively the impossible situation, the outlandish incident, the offbeat character."

How do you tell whether a rule is good or not, in terms of a specific problem?

Answer: Find out the reason the rule came into being. What idea or principle stands behind it?

"The man who knows *how* will always find a place in life," says the adage, "but the man who knows *why* will be the boss."

Arbitrary rules restrict and inhibit you.

Knowing why sets you free.

Take George's rule about starting every story with a fight. It's born of George's markets—men's magazines in which the emphasis is on fast, violent action, with blood on page one an absolute must.

If Fred only realized that fact, he'd ignore George's rule when he himself writes a mood-geared story.

Projected, this principle means that a writer should have theories on every phase of writing—how to get ideas, how to plot, how to build conflict, how to bring characters to life, how to create the right feelings in a given reader.

And, he should think through and take note of the *why* behind each and every how. Otherwise, how can he discover the procedures most effective for and best suited to him, in terms of his own temperament and tastes?

Nor does it matter whether these theories are right or wrong in the view of objectivity or the critics. Their purpose is only to provide one particular writer with working tools and orientation.

Universality is no issue. If an approach works for you, that's all that counts. Writing a story, any story, is a very personal, very individual business. No one else can fight the battle for you. You must win or lose all by yourself, alone in the solitude of your psyche, working out of the depth and breadth of your own feeling.

Which brings us to another interesting question: If feeling is indeed the issue, where do you find it?

Or, more specifically, what kind of a person is the writer?

Your right to be wrong

You start with an urge to write, and that's really all you need.

That's all, that is, so long as you don't let other things get in the way.

What other things?

They go by so many names. But they all boil down to one issue: the fear of being wrong.

To write successfully, you have to have the nerve to look at something in a new way and say, "This fascinates me. Look what I've done with it!"

Looking at anything in a new way takes nerve.

Why?

Because other people may see it from a different angle.

Whereupon, out of disagreement may spring disapproval. A husband may scoff, "Look who thinks she can write!"

Or a boss may shoot you down: "Young man, I pay you to do a job, not ride a hobby!"

Or a neighbor—"You'd think that woman would clean up her kids a little if she's got so much time to spare."

Or an editor—". . . nor does rejection necessarily imply any lack of merit."

Or a friend—". . . so we're all so proud of you—even if it *is* just a Sunday School paper."

Or a relative—"Honestly, Gladys, you can't imagine what they said when they found out you write those awful confessions!"

Or the pastor—"Just ask yourself, Sam: Do you want your children to know their father wrote a book like this?"

Or the critics—"This work lacks even ordinary competence."

"A stylistic mishmash." "The characters are caricatures at best." "A shallow and empty story, without insight or compassion."

So many voices, all singing the same song: "What makes you think that *you* could ever write anything worth reading?"

Voices like that sap your courage. They drain away your spirit. They make you want to run and hide, or lock a mask over your thoughts and feelings . . . and never, never, never write again.

Don't listen to them.

"A writer who is afraid to overreach himself is as useless as a general who is afraid to be wrong," mystery specialist Raymond Chandler once warned.

"I cannot give you the formula for success," says Herbert Bayard Swope, "but I can give you the formula for failure: Try to please everybody."

What qualities and/or conditions are most valuable to a writer?

Spontaneity. Freedom. The opportunity for unstudied, impulsive roving through the backlands of his mind.

Which are most detrimental?

Inhibition. Self-censorship. Restraint.

(Inhibition of feeling, that is—*not* inhibition of behavior. Becoming a writer doesn't automatically license you as a libertine, or grant you a permit to appear roaring drunk at high noon in the public square.)

In this world, all of us want to be right, on the one hand; to avoid being wrong, on the other. So, we search for certainty.

To that end, too often we put on blinders . . . shut out those thoughts and feelings and interpretations which don't conform to those we hear expressed by others, lest we find ourselves borne down by frowns of disapproval.

Rules for writing constitute one such set of blinders . . . designed to help us never to be wrong.

Is it so bad to want to win acceptance?

Of course not. But hem a writer in with rules, and in spite of himself he unconsciously weighs each new thought against the standard of the rule, instead of bouncing it around in free association until other thought-fragments, magnetized, cling to it.

To be a writer, a creative person, you must retain your ability to react uniquely. Your feelings must remain your own. The day you mute yourself, or moderate yourself, or repress your proneness to get excited or ecstatic or angry or emotionally involved . . . that day, you die as a writer.

Why should this be so?

The answer lies in . . .

The snare of the objective

There are two types of mind in this world . . . two approaches to the field of fiction.

One type is that of the objectivist, the man who sees everything analytically. Three things warp his orientation:

a. He depends on facts.

b. He distrusts feelings.

c. Therefore, he tries to write mechanically.

This man may have an inclination to create. But he's the product of an educational system that focuses on facts the way a Mohammedan zeros in on Mecca; and, in his case, the education took.

Now there's nothing wrong with facts as such. Educators of necessity seek a common ground on which to reach their students.

But one of the characteristics of a fact is that it has a record of past performance. That's what makes it a fact: Phenomenon X behaved and/or existed in thus-and-such a manner yesterday, last week, last month, last year. So, we have reason to anticipate that it will behave and/or exist the same way tomorrow.

This means that to deal with facts, you must devote a great deal of attention to analysis of their track records. What did they do in previous encounters, and how did they do it? They're like cases in law: Past history dominates. First, last, and always you check precedents.

If this were as far as the matter went, there wouldn't be any real headache. But the educators refused to let it go at that. Facts were easy to present. Knowledge of them was easy to test. In many areas they were of great practical use. Centering attention on them obviated the complications that went with dealing with each student as an individual.

So, educators in the lead, an entire society plunged into wholesale fact-worship.

When you glorify one thing, it's generally at the expense of something else. In this case, the "something else" was feeling.

Now a feeling is about as opposite to a fact as you can get. At best, you might describe it as a sort of internal driving force, like electricity in a motor. You can't see it or hear it or smell it or taste it or touch it. It reveals itself to the outside world only in overt behavior, as a reaction. Even measuring its intensity, by any objective standard, remains a problem not at all satisfactorily resolved.

As if that weren't enough, feelings differ from moment to moment and person to person. They're the ultimate variable—utterly unpredictable, oftentimes; poker with everything wild.

Faced with this unpredictability of feelings, this refusal of an element to behave in neatly ordered fashion, the educators responded with varying degrees of uncertainty, suspicion, outrage.

—Feelings all, of course, you understand; but acceptable, because they were housed in the right people.

Being human as well as frustrated, the educators took the obvious course of action: They taught generations of children to depend on facts.

—And, as a corollary, to hold all feelings suspect.

Result: a population trained to feel guilty every time it discovers that emotion prompted an action.

What happens when a man conditioned to such a mode of thinking decides he wants to create something?

Naturally enough, he approaches it as a problem in fact-finding.

That is, he looks to stories already written . . . studies them . . . attempts to dig out the common denominators that they share.

From this survey, he deduces rules. Then, he tries to write stories of his own that fit these regulations.

A story, thus, is for him an exercise in mechanics . . . a sort of juggling of bits and pieces; a putting together of a literary jigsaw puzzle. Seeing the product but not the process, viewing the end result rather than the dynamic, forward-moving forces that brought it into being, more often than not he ends up with something limp and inert. For though he may have skill, he's at heart a thinker, a logician. It never occurs to him to *feel* about his story. If it did, he'd thrust the thought aside, because he has no faith in feeling. He's afraid to trust it.

Now this is a dangerous distortion of attitude in any circumstances, even though you still may be able to function satisfactorily enough in spite of it so long as your job is merely to saw boards or sew seams or mix premeasured chemicals.

In a creator, however, such a pattern looms as utter and complete disaster.

Why?

Because the creator automatically is doomed to failure if he assumes that past and precedent can provide him with certainty and guarantee success.

No such certainty does or can exist—not in writing, nor in life itself. No matter how carefully we plan and prepare for tomorrow, tonight may find us frozen as solid as those famed Siberian mammoths, refrigerated for centuries like giant sides of beef by a blast of frigid air so sudden and so devastating that they died with buttercups still in their mouths.

Incidentally, science and the objectivists haven't yet figured out just what happened that day.

The only true certainty in life, so far as we know, is death— at least, what we call death.

As a writer, to deal with this world, you must accept it and your own ever-so-finite limitations as they are. Facts are something you have to take for granted. But you don't worship them, for your security, your certainty, is in yourself.

In your feelings.

Feeling, indeed, is what drives you forward. Wrapped up in your story, you face the future, not the past. The tale you tell excites you. You write out of the thrill of that excitement. Everywhere, you see new possibilities, new relationships. "What if—?" is your watchword. The rules, when you think of them, are incidental.

Which all is merely another way of saying that the writer is subjective more than objective; that his inner world is more important to him than the external one. Intuitively, he knows that "plot" and "character" and "setting" and all other analytic elements of the craft, taken apart from story, are just that: analytic; which is to say, dead, in the same way that any part of a dissected laboratory specimen is dead.

Because most readers read to feel, not analyze, they love the work of the subjectivist-turned-writer.

For precisely the same reason, they ignore the fiction of the non-creator, the analyst.

Does this mean that you write as Jack Kerouac is alleged to, with no heed for technique; no attempt at revision or correction?

No, indeed. The picture of "pure" creator versus "pure" objectivist is an exaggeration. No such creatures exist. Always, the issue is a matter of degree and emphasis. The writer puts heavier stress on the emotional entity we call *story* because he feels, and isn't afraid to trust his feelings. That is all.

The successful writer also has intelligence as well as talent; far too much intelligence to rely on spontaneity alone.

But he does *separate* logic from emotion; critical judgment from creation. So, though feeling is the wellspring of his work, over and over again along the line he pauses . . . sits back . . . subjects his plans and copy to reappraisal.

That reappraisal is based on the rule-of-thumb testing that is the shrewdest, most practical application of the past experience we call principle. Each story teaches him new tricks . . . brings him new tools, new techniques. Insight continually grows in him, and so does understanding. So, he improves as he goes along . . . seldom falls into the same trap twice.

That procedure; that separation of frames of mind; that alternating between creation and critique . . . it's the most effective way to learn, in any creative field. It uses rules as a checklist, not a blueprint. Feeling dominates; not logic.

Thus, it encourages spontaneity and takes advantage of it in the initial excitement of storytelling.

Then, later, it spots story flaws and pins down points of error.

Do I make myself clear? Communication of feeling—*your* feeling—demands skill as well as heart.

To win that skill, you have no choice but to begin right where you are—this very moment.

Ordinarily, that means you start a long way down the ladder.

You first have to be willing to be very, very bad, in this business, if you're ever to be good. Only if you stand ready to make mistakes today can you hope to move ahead tomorrow.

Writing as a creative act

As Pasteur once observed, chance favors the trained mind.

Feeling tells you what you want to say. Technique gives you tools with which to say it.

Facility lies in knowing at once what to do next, and so doing it more quickly than somebody else.

To know what to do next, you must master process . . . an ordered, step-by-step presentation of your materials that pushes emotional buttons in your reader, so that he feels the way you want him to feel. It's a way of going about things; an answer to your "how-to" questions.

For example?

"How do you make description vivid?" "How do you build conflict?" "How do you tie incidents together?" "How do you decide where to start your story?" "How do you make a character interesting?" "How do you insure that a story is satisfying to your readers?"

Or, if you'd rather: "*By what steps* do you make description vivid?" "*By what steps* do you build conflict?"

Often, these questions overlap, for process operates on all levels. Some processes are simple, some complex; some basic, some specialized. The steps you take to make a character easily recognizable may be quite definite and explicit. "How do you create a hero with whom your reader can identify?" is likely to prove a good deal more involved. That is, it requires more steps, and must take into account more variables. It may even demand a combining or interweaving of several rudimentary processes.

Must a writer know all these processes?

That depends on the writer, and his level of aspiration—the kind and quality of writer that he wants to be. Many successful writers get by with only a few skills, well handled. Others have more tricks up their sleeves than they can use. The general rule is to do the best you can with what you've got at the given moment.

Fortunately, too, in writing, most of us do many things effectively by instinct. Years of reading have given us a feeling for what's right and what isn't, and old habits turn out to be correct. So the amount you have to learn really is rather limited.

In fact, if you try to learn too much, or strain too hard, it probably means that you're fascinated with technique for its own sake, rather than as a tool to help you tell a story. You may be endeavoring to write mechanically, without sufficient excitement over your ideas.

Which processes are most important?

The ones *you* need most, at this specific moment.

Which stories are best to study?

The ones which intrigue *you*.

Aren't some better than others?

Of course. But any story, taken as a whole, is a hodgepodge of good and bad. To study some so-called classic as a model, unless you first cross your fingers and then take each sentence with a teaspoonful of salt, is to lay yourself wide open to all sorts of confusion. For in Sentence A, you find, Classic Author performs admirably. In Sentence B, he botches things.

Why?

Because he has blind spots, even as you and I.

A particular flaw may reflect a private weakness. Or it may mean that this individual writer is sloppy or ill-trained. Or that the phone rang at the wrong moment, or that his wife called him down to dinner.

Thus, an entire story may make most entertaining reading, even when reprinted as a textbook model. But it covers too much ground to be truly useful. "Standard" procedures (an exaggeration and a misnomer if ever there was one!) are modified by the demands of the story situation, the writing situation, and the tastes and competence of the writer himself.

—And that's even ignoring the fact that a story rated as a model by a given writer or editor or teacher or critic may not be anything resembling the right model for *you*.

You can't take it for granted that any fragment of any story is ideally handled until you've analyzed it from all angles. Techniques, by and large, are explicit and specific. You learn them from examples that isolate the point under examination . . . eliminate as many variables as possible.

To what degree are the processes outlined here subject to modification?

As before noted, you don't write fiction by the numbers. Each person goes about it in a different way. Some plan and some don't. Some plod and some don't. Some think and—not necessarily regrettably—some don't.

Thus, there's no one right answer to any writing question. You do different things in different ways at different times. Not only are we safe in saying that you seldom would write a line the same way on two successive days; we also can state flatly that both lines written could very well be "right."

Or wrong.

The problem, you see, is much like that in ball-playing. No matter how good a batter you are, you can't guarantee in advance that you'll hit a given pitch . . . because the material fights back and no two curves break just alike.

Mood also enters. You change, and your way of handling your material changes with you. In the long run, you learn rules only to deviate from them.

How do you master all the varied techniques?

By writing stories. Which is to say, by being willing to be wrong.

Then, having been wrong, you check back through your stuff for process errors . . . places where you skipped over steps, or went off the path, or started with the road map upside down.

Do that enough times, on enough stories, and eventually you'll learn.

Won't exercises give the same result less painfully?

Regrettably, no; at least, not in my experience. The man who cottons to exercises generally isn't cut out to be a fiction writer. He's certainty-oriented; reaching out for a sure thing.

Most potentially successful writers have little patience with such. They're too eager to get on with their own stories; too intoxicated with their own euphoria; too excited over their ideas.

Exercises excite no one. Palpably artificial, only tenuously related to the difficulties that beset you, they turn writing into drudgery for anyone.

So buckle down and forge yourself a kit of techniques out of the iron of your own copy. Each story will give you more experience to translate into literary process. Each trick mastered will free you just a little more from your feelings of inadequacy and frustration.

Finally, your excitement soars, unshackled, and to your own amazement you discover that somehow, in spite of everything, you've turned out to be a writer.

What's the first step?

There's the world of words to master; an important world, too, with laws and protocol all its own.

No doubt you'll want to violate those laws, in many cases. But half the fun of sinning lies in knowing that it's sinful.

To that end, let's move on to Chapter 2, and there take a look at language and its regulations.

The Words You Write

A story is words strung onto paper.

"God forbid that I should set up for a teacher!" cried Italy's master playwright of the eighteenth century, old Carlo Goldoni.

Even more so, saints preserve us from that writer with the effrontery to proclaim himself a grammarian.

Most writers paragraph for effect, punctuate on impulse, and let split infinitives and comma splices fall where they may. Omnivorous reading substitutes for systematic study. Syntactic nomenclature is a thing they learn only if, somehow trapped into teaching others the craft, they find themselves in need of terms to describe the errors of their students.

None of which in any wise prevents their writing adequate or better than adequate copy.

In other words, this is a business in which the star performers play by ear, and who cares? So long as a man's writing is itself clear and accurate and specific, no holds are barred. And anyone who needs instruction in the traffic laws of the English language has wandered into the wrong field.

Yet words are vital to a writer, no matter how askance he looks at grammar. Some work for him; some against him. And some just clutter up the landscape.

If you're just starting, you need to know which words do what, and why.

Specifically, it's desirable that you learn three things:

1. How to choose the right words.
2. How to make copy vivid.
3. How to keep meaning clear.

Taking first things first, let's begin with . . .

How to find the right words

What are your essential jobs, in actually writing copy? They are:

    a. Selection.
    b. Arrangement.
    c. Description.

What's the issue in *selection?*
As a writer, you provide peepholes through which your reader may look into the lives of other people. So, you must decide:

    Who is to be viewed?

Do we deal with doctor, lawyer, merchant, chief? What specific individuals?

    When do we observe these characters?

At what moment, what period, what time of their lives? Or, as the old gag phrases it, do infants have more fun in infancy than adults do in adultery?

    Where do we catch these people?

Are they afield? On the street? At the office? In church? Homebound? In the living room? The bedroom? The bathroom?

    What are they doing?

Are they working? Playing? Loving? Hating? Worshipping? Sinning? Learning? Forgetting?
—And, closely related, *what* does your reader notice as your people go about these multitudinous activities? Does he see sunrise, or mudhole? Beauty, or blemish? Is he caught by the smell of frying bacon, or the rasp of saw teeth biting into a pine board, or the smoothness of velvet beneath his fingers, or the taste of a sucked anise drop? A bellow of rage, or an eyelash flicker?

    Why does he notice?

What makes this detail important to him and to your story?

How does your reader see all this?

Is he looking at it objectively? Subjectively? Through the eyes of you, the writer? Through those of your hero? Those of your villain? —Or is this the viewpoint of the familiar innocent bystander, lining up for his turn at getting hurt?

These are more or less weighty decisions, every one. For, ever and always, you the writer must *select*.

Simultaneously, you *arrange* events for your reader, in what you fondly hope will prove effective order.

Do you move from cause to effect?

Or backward, from effect to cause?

Do you present your story in strict chronological order, as the events involved transpire?

Or, do you resort to some sort of frame or flashback, some device of recollection?

Order does make a difference. Show a gun, then a coffin, then tears, and you put your focus on heartbreak. If coffin comes first, then tears, then gun, the issue may be vengeance.

So, you *arrange*.

Then, you bring your material to life.

With *description*.

To live through a story . . . experience it as vividly as if it were his own . . . your reader must capture it with his own senses.

How do you put perfume on the page? The tiger's roar? The whisky's bite? The warm spring air? The earth? The blood?

With words: description.

But simply written, of course? With short words, short sentences, short paragraphs, and so on?

Well, maybe. Simplicity is a virtue, within reason. But Proust sometimes wrote in sentences literally hundreds of words long. Ionesco makes all language a paradox. A current paperback novel—an original, not a reprint—includes such words as *ubiquitous, relegated, nebulous, modulated,* and *ebullient.* Einsteinian concepts and beyond are standard fare in the science-fiction pulps.

So?

Few of us read voluntarily about the primer-level doings of Dick and Jane. Simplicity is a virtue in writing, true; but never the primary virtue.

What is?

Vividness.

How about brevity?

It's important too. Within reason.

Within reason?

Who, just learning this business, knows where or when or how to be brief? In the wrong place, brevity can destroy you.

So?

As in the case of simplicity, brevity is never the heart of the issue. Vividness is.

Making copy come alive

How do you write vividly?

You present your story in terms of things that can be verified by sensory perception. Sight, hearing, smell, taste, touch—these are the common denominators of human experience; these are the evidence that men believe.

Describe them precisely, put them forth in terms of action and of movement, and you're in business.

Your two key tools are nouns and verbs.

Nouns are words that name something: *dog, boat, pencil, man, telephone, grass, chair.*

Verbs are words that tell what happens: *gulp, whirl, jump, choke, smash, slump, snore.*

The nouns you want are *pictorial* nouns: nouns that flash pictures, images, into your reader's mind.

The more *specific, concrete,* and *definite* the noun . . . the more vivid the picture.

The noun *rhinoceros* flashes a sharper, more meaningful picture to your reader than does the noun *animal.*

But *animal* is sharper and more meaningful than *creature.*

In the same way, consider *bungalow* versus *house* versus *building* . . . *starlet* versus *girl* versus *female* . . . *Colt* versus *revolver* versus *firearm* . . . *steak* versus *meat* versus *food.*

The more specific you get, the more vivid you get. *Kim Novak* draws an even sharper picture than *starlet; tenderloin* or *chateaubriand* than *steak.*

—Assuming, that is, that your reader knows precisely what *chateaubriand* means. If he doesn't, all your efforts have only confused the issue further . . . which just might offer a lesson to those among us who would rather write *hirsute* than *hairy*, *collation* than *chow.*

How do you determine a given reader's degree of understanding?

Despite endless gobbledygook about psychological testing, market analysis, and the like, for most of us, ordinarily, the answer may very well be summed up in two principles: (1) You guess; and (2) you hope.

Beyond that, who really knows? Sure, you try to familiarize yourself with the patterns and attitudes and limitations of your readers, but that still doesn't mean that you can't miss a mile. I've gotten away with Thorstein Veblen references in a pulp detective story, and I've been shot down for using the word *clue* in an adult education film; so you'll pardon me, I trust, if I remain just a wee bit dubious of definitive answers where this point is concerned.

But as Mark Twain once observed, the difference between the right word and the almost right word is as the difference between lightning and the lightning bug. So *do* strive for that right word!

Broadly speaking, the thing you need to avoid is the general as contrasted with the particular (*reptile* creates a less vivid image than does *rattler*); the vague as contrasted with the definite (*them guys* is less meaningful than *those three hoods who hang out at Sammy's poolroom*); and the abstract as contrasted with the concrete (to say that something is red tells me less than to state that it's exactly the color of the local fire truck).

Obviously, all this is a matter of degree and, in many instances, categories overlap. If we want to generalize about such generalizations, however, we're probably safe in saying that abstraction, especially, offers hazards, for it expresses quality apart from object.

Thus, *love* is a noun denoting a quality. But for most of us, said quality exists meaningfully only when its object is considered. Love means one thing when you speak of how a patriot feels about his country . . . another, if the issue is a young mother's reaction to her baby . . . another, if your subject is a nun who kneels in prayer before the image of the Virgin Mary . . . another, if you listen to a shy high-school boy try to tell his girl friend how he feels about her . . . another, when discussed by the lantern-jawed prostitute sitting next to you at a bar.

So, talk about the individual instance every time! Which is to say . . . work with nouns that are specific and definite and concrete.

One further observation: The singular of a noun is almost always stronger than the plural. Cattle (plural, please note) may create an image of sorts as they mill restlessly. But for vivid impression, nail your picture down to some individual animal, at least in part—the bellow of a mossy-horned old steer, the pawing of a bull, a wall-eyed cow's panicked lunge.

The reason for this, of course, lies in the fact that every group is made up of individuals, and we really falsify the picture when we state that "the crowd roared," or "the mob surged forward," or even "the two women chattered on and on." And while such summary may constitute a valid and useful verbal shorthand, it doesn't give a truly accurate portrait.

So much for nouns. Now, what about verbs?

The ones you want are the *active* ones—the verbs that *show* something happening. Walk wide around the others!

Specifically, the verb *to be* is weak, in all its shapes and forms and sizes.

Why?

Because it describes existence only—a static state.

Your story stands still in any sentence that hangs on such a verb. Nothing happens. The situation just "is," and for its duration your reader must in effect mark time, shifting wearily from one foot to the other while he waits for the story to get back under way. "She was unhappy" may be true enough; but where does it go? What's "she" doing? What specific behavior reveals the unhappiness and hints at remedial action to come?

"Sam *was* in the chair" states its case in even drearier terms than "Sam *sat* in the chair." Incorporate a bit of action into the picture, and impact sharpens: "Sam *slumped* in the chair," or

"Sam *twisted* in the chair," or "Sam *rose* from the chair," or "Sam *shoved back* the chair."

To repeat: *Active* verbs are what you need . . . verbs that *show something happening*, and thus draw your reader's mental image more sharply into focus. For a vivid, vital, forward-moving story, cut the *to be* forms out of your copy every time you possibly can. "The trooper *was pounding*" is never as strong as "The trooper *pounded*." And when you get down to a really passive approach, such as "The table *was pounded upon* by the trooper"—well!

Worst of all *to be's* forms is the past perfect tense. You can recognize it by the word *had*—a red flag of danger in your story every time.

For *had* describes not just a static state, but a static state *in the past*: "He *had traveled* far that day." "I never *had realized* how much I loved her."

Each *had* makes your story jerk, because it jars your reader out of present action and throws him back into past history.

Perhaps the jerk is only momentary, as when a lazy writer sticks in a bit of exposition: "John stared at her. He *had always wondered* why she took the attitude she did. Now, she left him no choice but to force the issue."

Here the jerk, the shift backward, is hardly noticeable. But throw in enough such, enough *hads,* and your story grinds to an aching, quaking halt. Forward movement stops. Your reader finds himself bogged down in history.

This is the kiss of death. No one can change what's already happened. To waste story time on it is, at best, an irritation. What your reader wants is present action—events that have consequences for the future; characters shaping their own destinies. If he doesn't get this sense of forward movement, he turns to another, more skillfully written yarn.

But isn't past history sometimes vital in developing your story?

Of course. We'll discuss how best to handle it when we deal with flashback techniques in Chapter 4. For now—get out your blue pencil and eliminate those hads!

—At least, eliminate as many as possible, within the bounds of common sense. Sure, you'll need some for legitimate purposes:

as transitional words to help you move in and out of the afore-
mentioned flashback situations, for example.

In other cases, however, simple rephrasings will solve the
problem.

Thus, a few paragraphs ago, we mentioned that one John "had
always wondered," and so on. Yet the line would read better
—and cut the offending *had*—if we said, "Why did she take the
attitude she did? It was time to get to the root of it."

In general, the trick is to bring the past forward into the present, so that you describe what happens in *past* tense instead of
past perfect.

To that end, translate recollection into action, or link the two
tightly together. If your heroine once *had loved* your hero, make
that fact an issue in the here-and-now: "He held her shoulders
rigid. 'Do you love me?' 'You're being ridiculous!' 'You used to.
At least, you said you did.'"

Or perhaps:

"Her eyes were still the same, Ed decided. Her eyes, and her
mouth.

"Thoughtfully, he wondered how she might react if he tried
to kiss her, the way he did that long-gone night there by the
river."

A little practice on this kind of thing works wonders. Try it!

So much for verbs. What else is there?

Pronouns: words that substitute for nouns—*he, she, it, they,
we,* and so on.

What is there to say about them?

Watch your antecedents!

That means, be sure that each pronoun refers back to the
right noun.

"This time, the girl asked Jane to loan her a dollar for lunch.
Sighing, she gave it to her."

Like *who* gave *what* to *whom?* Or, are you becoming as confused as I am?

So much for pronouns.

Adjectives are words that modify nouns . . . help you to nail
down meaning more precisely. When you describe someone's
face as a "*gaunt, hewn* caricature," the adjectives differentiate

it markedly from a *chubby* face, a *sour* face, a *babyish* face, or what have you.

Same way, *blonde* is a rather general category. You narrow it when you make the gal a *brassy* blonde, or a *raucous* blonde, or a *hard-faced* blonde, or a *blowsy* blonde.

How about a brassy, raucous, hard-faced, blowsy blonde?

Yes, you can run anything into the ground if you really try!

So much for adjectives.

Adverbs? They modify verbs . . . describe the manner in which an act is performed: *angrily, wearily, animatedly, gloomily, delightedly, smilingly.*

It does get a little tiresome, doesn't it?

Remedy: Wherever practical, substitute action for the adverb.

"*Angrily,* she turned on him"? Or, "Her face stiffened, and her hands clenched to small, white-knuckled fists"?

"*Wearily,* he sat down"? Or, "With a heavy sigh, he slumped into the chair and let his head loll back, eyes closed"?

Vividness outranks brevity.

At least, sometimes.

So much for adverbs.

To live through your story, experience it, your reader must capture it with his own senses.

He may see it more clearly if it bears a perceptible relationship to something he has experienced before. —That is, if it's *similar* or *in contrast* to some phenomenon out of his own past.

Comparison, the books call it. Metaphor. Simile.

You use it when you refer to a hoodlum as a "shambling gorilla of a man," or to a dancer as a "sprite," or to a tank as a "mechanized avalanche of steel." The surf on the beach may be white and thick as cotton candy; or cotton candy as airy and evanescent as surf on a sunny beach.

Used skillfully, it's another excellent device to help make your copy come alive.

A matter of meaning

What's in a name?

A good deal more than Shakespeare gave it credit for in his famed remark on roses, apparently. Else why would Hollywood rechristen the Gertie Glutzes of this world, prior to launching them into stardom?

In the same way, there's a good deal more in any word than meets the eye.

The issues involved are somewhat less than simple, as any semanticist will be happy to explain to you in three or four brief volumes. But for our purposes here, we can get by nicely with just one key fact: People's feelings come out in the words they use.

The way the experts describe this is to say that the words in question have both *denotation* and *connotation.*

Denotation means the word's "actual" or "dictionary" meaning.

When, *in addition* to this "actual" meaning, a word implies or suggests something further, the things it implies or suggests are its connotations.

These connotative or implied or associated meanings frequently hold overtones of approval or disapproval; and too often, the overtones outweigh the word's "actual" meaning.

Take a word like *propaganda.* In simplest terms, it *denotes* information, put forth in a systematic effort to spread opinions or beliefs.

Thus, whether it's classed as good or bad *should* depend on whether you agree or disagree with the opinions or beliefs in question. But in practical terms, and on a grass-roots level, the very word has acquired *connotations* of falsehood, distortion, dishonesty, and misrepresentation. Consequently, to label any material as "propaganda" is to put a blighting negative stamp on data and cause alike.

Strike, steed, politician, student, Okie, soldier, stenographer—they're just words, apparently, with reasonably clear-cut denotations. But such are their connotations—and the connotations of thousands of other words, to boot—in large segments of the population as to create a distinct hazard for the writer. For if he fails to take account of their implications, their emotional overtones, he can alienate a host of readers without even being aware of what he's doing. Let him describe the wrong character as *sullen* or *wanton* or *coarse* or *ineffectual* or *finicky,* and he may unwittingly damn the man far worse than if he had called him a thief.

So beware! Pay attention not just to words as words, but also to the feelings they mirror when people use them.

* * *

Where do scripts go wrong, language-wise, beyond the points already covered?

Here I have no comprehensive answers, let alone data that can be classed as definitive. But awkwardness does develop in certain special areas often enough to be worth mentioning.

Thus,

a. Sentence structure grows monotonous.
b. Subject and verb are separated.
c. Adverbs are placed improperly.
d. Words and phrases are repeated inadvertently.
e. Correct grammar becomes a fetish.
f. Meaning isn't made clear instantly.

There are more, of course; too many more. But these will do for a start.

The solution to each problem is largely a matter of common sense.

Take monotonous sentence structure, for example.

It demands little genius to recognize that too many short sentences, or long sentences, or simple, or complex, or periodic, or loose, or what-have-you sentences are likely to grow tiresome.

The answer, obviously, is to introduce variety—variety of length, form, style, and so on. Many a tired old declarative sentence (*He stalked off without a word*) has been given a lift via rearrangement of its elements (*Without a word, he stalked off*) . . . rephrasing (*Grim, wordless, he stalked off*) . . . addition of some bit of action (*Pivoting, he stalked off*) . . . or of color (*Face a cold mask of menace, he* etc.), or the like.

On the other side of the fence, beware variety for variety's own sake. The moment syntactical acrobatics attract attention to themselves, they also detract from your story; and that's a sure road to disaster.

Why do subject and verb become separated?

My guess is that occasionally we all tend to get tangled up in the maze of our own thinking. How else can you account for some of the monstrosities you see in print?

Here's an example from a student manuscript: "The girl, in spite of her confusion and the hazard offered by the razor-edged shards of glass from the shattered window, somehow broke free."

Girl is the subject in the above sentence; *broke* the verb. Yet they're separated by twenty words of modification, and the separation renders the sentence distracting and confusing.

Is the separation needed? Or could our reader perhaps survive a different version: "Confusion seemed to overwhelm her in that moment. The razor-edged shards of glass from the shattered window offered an added hazard. Yet somehow, the girl broke free."

The lesson here is, don't try to cram too much into one sentence; and the issue lies less in length than it does in content. Any time you feel the need to explain some aspect of your basic sentence, take pause. Odds are that what's bothering you really calls for an *additional* sentence or two or three, so that you can keep your developing line of thought straight and clear and simple.

Improper placement of adverbs grows from a failure to understand placement's effect on impact, probably.

To get maximum effect, put adverbs at the beginning or end of the sentence: "*Angrily,* he walked away." Or, "He walked away *angrily.*" Though special cases may justify "He walked *angrily* away," or the like, most often the effect of the modifier upon the reader is lost.

Unintentional repetition of words or phrases is the product of careless copy-reading.

Thus, in one line, your hero "moved *blindly* up the sagging staircase." Three lines later, "*Blinded* by the leaping flames," your heroine falls. Which is a natural enough mistake, but one that should be corrected as a matter of routine.

What about the occasions when you *want* repetition, in order to achieve a particular effect?

Three's the charm, as the old folk-saying has it. If the same word appears twice, it looks like an accident. But the third time (and after, if you don't carry the device to absurdity) your reader assumes it's intentional and for a reason: "It was a day for color. Not just one color, but many. The color of Sandra's lips. The color of Ed's worn blazer. The color of sea and sand and sky."

Grammar as a fetish?

To keep rules in proper perspective, violate them by design only.

That is, make them tools for manipulation of your reader's emotions. If that takes sentence fragments, non-punctuation, stream-of-consciousness, and one-word paragraphs, by all means use them. Winston Churchill blazed the trail for all of us when he spoke his mind to the purists who insisted that no sentence end with a preposition: "This is one rule up with which I shall not put!"

So, deviate if you must. But do it with malice and by intent, not accident.

And, most of the time, stay within the rules. Your readers will feel more at home that way!

Our sixth and final point is all-encompassing, of course.

It's also the most important of the lot: Meaning *must* be made instantly clear. If your reader has to read a sentence twice to make sense of it, you're in deep trouble.

I can't overemphasize this point. Oh so many would-be writers denounce the stupidity of readers who won't or can't understand. But what do all the screams accomplish? Stupid or not, the reader still gropes and fumbles and, finally, gives up, unless the idea gets through.

That incredible, pompous, egocentric gem from the pen of a "literary" novelist, "I write. Let the reader learn to read," would be funny, were it not so ridiculous as to be tragic. To refuse to write so that a mass audience can understand you, and then rage because that same audience rejects you, is about on a par with insisting that grade-school youngsters learn their ABC's from college physics texts. Most professionals accept it as their job to devise ways to communicate with their readers, regardless of said readers' level. After all, if you feel too superior, you can always go hunt a different market!

* * *

And so it goes with words and language. They're tools. All your writing life, you work with them . . . using them to tie your reader to your story.

This book will touch on words and the use of words a hundred times, in a hundred different contexts. And it still won't say one one-hundredth of what needs to be said.

But for now, let's assume that you're properly impressed with words' significance, and therefore stand ready to move on to a related but somewhat more involved aspect of the subject . . . the application of language to the manipulation of reader feelings.

Is that important?

I won't kid you. It's the foundation stone on which you as a writer stand or fall.

CHAPTER 3

Plain Facts about Feelings

A story is a succession of motivations and reactions.

The preceding chapter tells you how to communicate with your readers.

With words.

What should you as a fiction writer communicate?

Feelings.

＊　＊　＊

Feeling is a thing you build through manipulation of motivation and reaction. To handle it properly is a matter at once both simple and complex. *How* and *why* intermesh. Problems arise that involve orientation, psychology, chronology, procedure.

Once you're made aware of basic principles, however, application becomes well-nigh instinctive: easy and natural as breathing.

The key is to understand completely where each and every step fits in.

What are these steps?

1. You decide what's good and what's bad.
2. You give your reader a character for a compass.
3. You create a story world.
4. You inject an element of change.
5. You draw motive power from cause and effect.
6. You pin down development to motivation and reaction.

7. You make motivation-reaction units shape emotion.
8. You measure copy length with tension.
9. You learn to write in M-R units.

Here we go!

How to tell good from bad

How do you decide whether a thing is good or bad? —Everything *is* good and/or bad, you know, in varying degrees and depending on circumstances.

Take a rainstorm, for instance. Is it good or bad?

How about a bombing raid? A strike? A seduction? A divorce? A marriage? A cigarette? A chocolate bar? A job?

Now it doesn't matter whether you're living with the above-mentioned phenomena, or merely writing about them. In either case, before you can answer any queries intelligently, you need two things:

a. The specific instance.
b. A yardstick.

Thus, in the case of our rainstorm, we must consider such items as how much rain, how severe a storm, where, when, and so on. Specifics all. Added together, they constitute the specific instance.

Every story deals with a specific instance: this girl, that boy, the murder down the block, old Mrs. Martin's death, the wife-swapping of those couples out on Little River. A story that attempts to stay at the level of generality is both impossible and a self-contradiction.

But no matter how specific you get; no matter how tightly you nail your topic down, the data have no meaning until you find a yardstick—a standard by which to measure and, above all, evaluate them.

Because we're men, humans, we consider each phenomenon that touches us in terms of its immediate and/or ultimate effect on man.

Opinion as to what constitutes man's welfare varies markedly from time to time and place to place, however. St. Augustine

hews to one line, Adolf Hitler to another. And as for Norman
Mailer—!

In the case of our rainstorm, are we to view it through the
eyes and feelings of carnival owner or farmer? Power-company
trouble-shooter or umbrella salesman? Housewife-with-a-batch-
of-clean-clothes-to-hang-out, or housewife-looking-for-an-excuse-
not-to-wash-today? The issue is never the event itself; never
what happens. A thing matters only insofar as it relates to and
affects and is judged by people. *Meaning* and *significance* are
virtual synonyms in this context. We decide how significant a
thing is by the way a particular somebody behaves when faced
with a specific instance.

In other words, a thing isn't just significant. It's significant to
somebody.

Next question: *Which* somebody?

Most of us draw our conclusions about the good, the true, and
the beautiful according to how the specific event involved affects our individual situation. The bombing raid is rated by
whether we or our enemies are on the receiving end. The strike,
by our personal attitudes toward unions. I view seduction one
way if I'm the seducer; another, if it's my sister or wife or daughter who's seduced. Chocolate bars are good, if I'm hungry; bad,
if I'm trying to reduce; and so on.

Thus, all value judgments are, in the last analysis, highly personal. We can never be sure where the individual stands until
we check him out in detail. —Which last may not prove the
easiest task in the world, incidentally, as witness government's
periodic failures in security screening. The secret thought walled
up within the human mind still stands well-nigh impregnable
against external onslaughts.

But if the individual is the yardstick, how does he make his
evaluations? Does he go by intelligence and logic?

Well, hardly. I may marry because a girl dances like a dream
. . . divorce because her snoring gives me nightmares . . . take
or quit a job on no better grounds than the company's coffee-
break policy . . . and smoke up a storm in the face of tons of
research findings and the dire predictions of my physician.

So, again, how does the individual make his value judgments?

He responds to facts with feelings.

What is a fact?

A fact is data upon the interpretation of which we (or a considerable number of us, at least) agree. It's a consensus of opinion: The world is round, the United States has 200,000,000 population, certain disorders of the pancreas result in diabetes, sirloin steak ordinarily proves more tender than round.

What is a feeling?

A feeling is private interpretation of data. It's a man's uniquely personal and individual response to his world: I love this woman, I pity that dog, I hate hot cereals, I'm sad or happy or confused. Most often welling unbidden, without benefit of intellect or logic, it's a subjective awareness of the ebb and flow of inner tensions, expressing itself in a reaction.

"Reaction" is convenient verbal shorthand for "I desire to behave in a particular way." —I may not act, you understand. But the impulse is with me. If, magically, all my restraints and inhibitions were to vanish, I'd embrace the woman, soothe the dog, throw out the cereal, weep or laugh or throw a temper tantrum.

Behavior, in turn, seldom stands neutral. It confirms or denies, moves you forward or back. All reactions, all feelings, boil down to "This is good," or "This is bad." You like peach pie, or you dislike it. You're pleased with your new office, or displeased. You enjoy parties, or they make you uncomfortable.

Facts exist independently, outside people. But they have meaning and/or significance only as we have feelings about them; react to them. Seven inches of rain in a night is a fact, so long as you merely see an item about it in the paper. Let it wash through your living room and ruin two thousand dollars' worth of furnishings, and it takes on true meaning and significance for you. For significance, remember, starts within the individual, in feeling. Beauty still rests in the eye of the beholder. Evil is a thing that lurks in the hearts of men.

Things don't have feelings. Events don't. Places don't. But people do. And things and events and places can *create* feelings in people . . . trigger an amazing range of individual reactions. Let a harmless snake slither across a room—even in circumstances which make it impossible for the snake to be dangerous—and someone screams. Does he scream at the snake? No. He screams at his own feelings. In the same way, we "know" that most baldness is incurable, that aspirin is aspirin, that no soap will make an ugly woman beautiful. But we go right on spending fortunes annually for baldness cures and brand-name aspirin and beauty soaps.

Indeed, in the largest sense, all objectivity is an outrageous myth. To assume that finite minds can successfully catalogue the infinite is in itself presumptuous, and indicative of infinite ego. Our whole pattern of life demonstrates how tightly we're shackled to the limitations of our species; how closely confined by our very humanness. Boy turns to girl instinctively. We talk of communicating with extraterrestrial beings when we can't even converse meaningfully with a chimpanzee. The scientist takes it for granted that human life is more important than that of the laboratory animals he uses in his research.

What does all this say?

Merely that each of us has an orientation to the world . . . a built-in polarity, an emotional compass. Though we bow down before that useful tool, the concept of objectivity, most of the time our feelings still tell us which man to trust, which girl to marry; the car to buy, the price to pay, the faith to believe in, the candidate to vote for.

Understand, these feelings of ours may tell us wrong as well as right, as any woman knows when her husband first glimpses her new twenty-dollar hat. They offer no guarantee of intelligence or morality or taste. But they do at least give us an intimately personal guide, a standard.

Take away a man's feelings, by lobotomy or otherwise, and he's reduced to a human vegetable.

Persuade him to mistrust those same feelings—via an objectivist education, perhaps—and he bobs like a chip on the sea of life: drifting, aimless, without force or focus.

For as we earlier implied, each of us is by nature an egocentric sun around which a private world revolves. I know where I stand, so everything else falls into place because it's in a set relation to me.

In fact, that's the way it *should* be, unless we stand ready to give up all sense of purpose and direction.

Which brings us, next, to the matter of what bearing all this has on your story.

The focal character: your reader's compass

How do you make readers care about what happens in your story?

—They *must* care, you know. Otherwise, they won't read!

So, how do you make them care?

You give them a stake in what happens. You put them in a position where they stand to win or lose, emotionally.

To that end, you center your story on a character who stands to win or lose also, so that your readers can feel for him or against him.

A story recounts events. But those events can't or won't stand alone. They need to be explained, interpreted, evaluated, made meaningful.

Above all, they must be translated into feeling.

What that means is that a story is essentially subjective, not objective. Consequently, it needs to be as strongly oriented as a person.

What is orientation?

Originally, *to orient* meant to cause to face the east, as in building a church so that its altar stood at the east end. Later, the term was broadened to include any activity which made clear to somebody what his proper relationship was to a given situation.

Thus, to orient means to point somebody in the right direction.

In story, that somebody is the reader.

"To give the reader an experience is only a part, not the whole, of the writer's function," observes critic Edmund Fuller. "It is giving us evaluated experience that distinguishes the great or the good writer, whether the evaluation be spelled out specifically, or whether it is tacit in the total context of characters, actions, and conditions that he sets before us to represent his world. (It is always the writer's world that we enter in art—never the objective world.)"

But though this evaluation of experience is the writer's task, and though it is the writer's world the reader enters, there are all sorts of opportunities for confusion. Too often, the writer falls into the trap of writing about *things*—about sex, about violence, about scenery, about war, about domestic bliss or discord. Historical fact or clinical detail overwhelm him. The implications and evaluations, tacit in his thinking, never quite reach the reader.

In brief, although his work may on the face of it be cast rigidly in story form, it isn't actually fiction. For a story is never really *about* anything. Always it concerns, instead, someone's *reactions* to what happens: his feelings; his emotions; his impulses; his dreams; his ambitions; his clashing drives and inner conflicts. The external serves only to bring them into focus.

Or, as the old rule-of-thumb has it, "Every story is somebody's story."

So, enter an individual who, for our purposes, shall be termed the *focal character*.

This figure is precisely what his title indicates: the person on whom the spotlight focuses; the center of attention; the man whose reactions dominate the screen.

The focal character has three main functions:

    a. To provide continuity.
    b. To give meaning.
    c. To create feeling.

What about *continuity?*

Given half a chance, events in a story tend to hang in space, like so many screams in the night. The focal character is a continuing factor to link them into a cohesive whole and tie them to past and future, even though the action moves from 2000 B.C. to A.D. 2000, from New York to San Francisco, and from music hall to morgue. Our attention is on him and his reactions, first and foremost, so everything else falls into place.

He also gives *meaning* and significance to whatever happens. —Meaning, remember, is always a conclusion you and I draw about something from the way a particular somebody behaves when faced with a specific instance. If that somebody is our focal character, and if he lets go a scream of horror or a gurgle of delight at the sight of the crown jewels or tomorrow's headlines or a hot-pastrami sandwich, then we have grounds for assuming that something about the item in question is uniquely significant *to him*. Therefore, until something happens to change our minds, we'll deal with such fragments with the same degree of attention or consideration he shows . . . use them to measure and judge all the story's dimensions.

As a reader, thus, my attitude toward the rainstorm we cited earlier will be determined by whether the rain helps or handicaps the focal character. Whether a setting is colorful or drab . . . whether an incident is important or inconsequential . . . whether another character is good or bad—each point will be judged and interpreted with the focal character's reactions as a guide.

At the same time, your reader judges and interprets the focal character himself.

It's in this judging of the focal character that we enter the area of said focal character's third function . . . the creation of *feelings*.

What kind of feelings?

Favorable feelings or unfavorable feelings. Feelings for or feelings against.

It's impossible to exaggerate the importance of these feelings. The biggest single reason that a focal character exists is to evoke them.

Why?

Because your reader needs someone on whom to pass judgment.

It works this way: Sneering, our focal character pours a glass of beer over the head of the saloon's crippled swamper, a harmless, helpless, half-bright type.

Instantly, without volition, your reader bristles with feelings of hostility and outrage.

Or again: A murderous bully threatens our unarmed focal character with instant death unless he pours the beer over the swamper. Instead, the focal character throws the beer into the bully's face.

Like magic, your reader's heart hammers with a different kind of feeling. Excitement races through him and he reads on eagerly, thrilling to the stiff-necked courage laid out before him on the page. Unconsciously—perhaps in spite of himself—he passes judgment on the focal character, just as he did before.

Why does your reader judge the focal character?

Because he can't help doing it; can't restrain himself. Convictions, feelings, are part of him—his most inner being. When he bumps into the right stimulus, they come boiling forth, reaffirming their own existence in heightened tension and speeded pulse.

If your reader *doesn't* judge, count on it that the focal character is too bland and innocuous and uncommitted to be worth writing about.

Without some character of whom he can approve or disapprove, in varying degree, your reader will have no stimulus to feeling.

Without feeling, he won't care what happens in your story.

If he doesn't care, he stops reading.

And you're dead.

*   *   *

Even while your reader judges, however, his feelings merge with those of the focal character.

That is, he lives through the story with him.

"When you understand the feelings of one of the characters in the moving picture," says psychiatrist David Fink, "you are copying his tensions. You are feeling in yourself something of what he feels in the fictional situation. You are understanding the story with your own muscle tensions and with the spasms of your intestines and with your own glandular secretions. Without these reactions, the show would have no meaning. Without these reactions, nothing in life would have meaning."

So, your reader's feelings *about* your focal character, plus the focal character's own feelings as communicated to said reader, unite to bring the story itself to life. Together, they provide the sense of purpose and direction that a good story needs.

Without a focal character, your reader is in the position of a city boy plunked down in the middle of some mountain fastness in backwoods Colorado or Montana. He's completely free to travel, but he doesn't know which way to go.

The boy is, in a word, disoriented. Until he finds a landmark, or a tree to climb, or a compass to point him north, or a stream or an Indian guide to follow, he's in deep trouble.

Double that in spades for your poor reader. He stands confronted by a story world fully as baffling to him as are the Rockies to the tenderfoot.

People move through this story world. Events transpire. Situation and scenery change.

Yet somehow, it remains drab and empty to your reader, without significance or excitement, because he has no home base from which to judge it. He simply doesn't know where he stands.

What he needs is merely a light in the window to guide him— a contemporary version of those old Hollywood story-conference clichés, "Which is our ball team?" and "Who do we cheer for?"

He needs, indeed, a focal character whose actions reveal to him which end of the gun he's on . . . whether he's cat or mouse, wife or other woman, winning or losing coach, good guy or bad.

Does this mean that the term "focal character" is a synonym for "hero"?

Not unless Sammy Glick is a hero in Budd Schulberg's *What Makes Sammy Run.* Or Macbeth. Or Dracula. Or Elmer Gantry.

Thing is, "hero" has come to have connotations of the positive and desirable in our thinking. A focal character may prove the opposite, yet still intrigue us even as we loathe him.

Therefore, he may—ordinarily will—be the hero. But not always.

Are "focal character" and "viewpoint character" the same?

A viewpoint character is someone through whose eyes we see all or part of a story. In effect, we get inside his skin.

He is *not* necessarily the person around whom the yarn revolves, however. Sherlock Holmes is a focal character; the viewpoint is Watson's. In Dashiell Hammett's *The Maltese Falcon,* Sam Spade is the focal character . . . the viewpoint, author-objective.

On the other hand, François Villon is both focal character and viewpoint character in Robert Louis Stevenson's *A Lodging for the Night.* Same for Mark Twain's Huckleberry Finn, Walter Huff in James M. Cain's *Double Indemnity,* Mickey Spillane's Mike Hammer, and an infinity of others.

So, a focal character *may* be a viewpoint character; but then again, he may not.

But definitely, he *will* be the central and most important character, because he's the one who determines your reader's orientation.

Isn't it possible to write a story without a focal character?

Of course it is. But the penalties frequently are much the same as might descend upon our city boy if we were to give him a gimmicked compass, whose needle points in one direction one moment, in another the next. The lack of a strong central figure to cheer for or throw rocks at takes the steam out of the story. Direction, continuity, and perspective all tend to disintegrate.

In William March's *Company K,* for example, each chapter is from the first-person viewpoint of a different member of a World War I infantry unit. The writing is superior, individual episodes hold considerable interest, and the author eliminates possible confusion in advance by explaining the whys and wherefores of his procedure in the opening episode.

But the unity a focal character would give just isn't there. The book ends up as a series of sketches rather than a novel. The all-encompassing montage of war the author attempts is reduced to a blur by sheer diffuseness.

How do you present a focal character most effectively, so that maximum meaning and feeling are conveyed?

An intriguing question. To answer it, we first need to give attention to that fascinating microcosm which we term . . .

The story world

You need to remember three key points about the world in which your story takes place:

a. Your reader has never been there.
b. It's a sensory world.
c. It's a subjective world.

Each of these items is of quite crucial importance. To build a story world is to play God in a sort of private Genesis. You can understand the issues best if you consider them as they relate to the world of reality—the world in which you and your readers move from day to day.

Thus, our own world is a vast, echoing, drafty place, in which it's easy to get lost. No matter how much you travel, there always are new corners to explore . . . odd alleyways you haven't seen before.

Equally, you dare assume little about your reader's background. He may not be familiar with the jungles of Mount Kenya, or the rush of commerce along Singapore's Raffles Place, or Chicago's South State Street in those blocks sleazy with decay, or even the garish tastelessness or slick contemporary note struck by the living room of the house next door. So, the only course is to paint each setting before said reader's very eyes, in full color and sufficient—not to mention pertinent—detail to bring it completely alive for him.

Next question: How do you bring a setting to life?

The answer, of course, lies in the human animal himself. His world is a sensory world—a world of green grass and white houses . . . purring kittens and thundering trucks . . . Chanel No. 5 and curling wood smoke . . . fresh cold orange juice and hot crisp bacon . . . silk's rich smoothness and the harsh grit of volcanic ash.

So, you build your story world of these same sensory impressions—the seen, the heard, the smelled, the touched, the tasted. Emphasis is on the vivid image and the impactful figure of speech.

Then, with analogies, you link it all to the familiar, even if it costs you an extra word or two or three. It will be worth it. Someone who's never smelled the lunar pits now may come to realize that they have a parallel in the acrid, sulfurous, flaming smoke that belches from the shaft of an exploding mine.

Finally, and perhaps most important of all, you consider the frame of reference in which this world exists.

Here is where you relate all that has gone before to your reference point, your focal character.

You do this by presenting your material *subjectively,* as your focal character receives it.

Why?

Because each of us, on the basis of his goals and attitudes and past experiences, reacts to his environment in his own unique and private way. The manner in which I see things depends as much or more on my own mood as it does on the external stimulus—the place or person or event. One man shudders at slum dirt; another bristles at the sullen hostility that pervades each grime-stained, gutter-stinking door front; another relaxes, unaware of filth or fear, because here he's at home in his own world.

The words a writer uses to describe a setting must mirror such feelings. Your very phrases distinguish a thing you like from one you dislike, all efforts at objectivity notwithstanding.

And so you build your story world—a moody, subjective bailiwick, brought to life so vividly with sensory images that each and every reader automatically finds himself transported there, no matter how limited his experience.

But don't relax, even then. Your job is just beginning. For the story world, far from being static, is an ever-changing place.

Story equals change . . .

A story records change. It sets forth the details of how your focal character moves from one state of affairs and state of mind to another.

Take the typical mystery. It begins with your hero somehow plunged into jeopardy via murder. It ends when he brings the killer to justice and, in so doing, eliminates the peril.

Between those two points is movement—a duality of movement, in point of fact. External, physical movement carries Hero through assorted clashes with Villain, until one or the other is defeated. Parallel with this runs a thread of internal emotional movement. Most often, it's presented introspectively—at least in part in thoughts or feelings. Sometimes, however, it's merely implied, or demonstrated in physical terms.

This internal movement reveals the continually fluctuating levels of tension that eddy through Hero in the course of the external struggle. Too, here are the categories of reactive feeling—such items as shock and grief and rage and panic and grim resolve, and a host of others so complex that they really can't be labeled.

A love story? We begin with boy wants girl; we end with boy gets girl. Between lie an infinity of possible physical complications, with emotional turmoil to match.

And so it goes. In fantasy, heroine *becomes* witch; in science fiction, spaceman *battles* monster; in domestic romance, wife *improves* husband; in western, marshal *cleans up* town; in business novel, executive *wins* top post.

In each and every case, however, one thing stands out: Somebody *does* something. The situation, the state of affairs, at the end of a successful story is not the same as it was at the beginning. And neither is the focal character's state of mind. In greater or lesser degree, he's revised his evaluations, his attitudes, his ideas of who is good and what is bad and how to deal with specific kinds of trouble. His future is different than it would have been had the story not taken place. If nothing else, he's relieved of uncertainty as to just how his problem will work out!

Why is this factor of change so vital?

The answer lies in your reader's attention span. Boredom attacks in seconds when no new stimulus—for which read, "change" —impinges on him. If you want proof, see how long—or, rather, how briefly—you can force yourself to concentrate fully on a given object or fixed point. There's no story in a static situation. A still life will never hold your reader. Word photography isn't enough.

But change alone isn't enough either, if your goal is a successful story. What you seek isn't action for its own sake, but those specific changes that affect story development. The things that happen must move your character along toward his goal, closer and closer to the place you want him to go.

Concretely, you want external developments that will lead him to feel—and therefore behave—in a **constructive** manner where the story problem is concerned.

Shall we contrast this with much of the gobbledygook that passes for complication in beginners' stories? —At dinner one evening, Hero orders steak. But the waiter warns him against it . . . persuades him to try oysters instead. After eating them, Hero feels a bit queasy. Oysters, he decides, always seem to upset his stomach. He'll avoid them in the future.

Now, you do have change here. There's a switch both in the hero's state of affairs (an external force, the waiter, leads him to change his original order for steak) and in his state of mind (feeling illish, he decides not to eat oysters again). But unless his queasiness and/or his decision not to eat any more oysters have marked bearing on the rest of the story, you've merely wasted time, space, and effort.

On the other hand, suppose a love-story hero drops by to surprise his sweetheart.

He does indeed—she's in the arms of another man.

Shaken, Hero tells her off, or punches his rival's nose, or decides to go call Margie, or leaves town in a blind rage, cursing the fickleness of all women.

Have changes taken place? Yes. Do they affect the rest of the story—its development, its outcome? Yes. Is your focal character's state of mind changed by it? Indeed it is, even if only in terms of never again taking too much for granted.

Does this mean you must eliminate all your pet fragments, on grounds that they contribute too little?

On the contrary. The issue, ever and always, is to *make* them important to the development of your story. If you want a brilliant example of what I'm talking about, get hold of a copy of Clifton Adams' *The Dangerous Days of Kiowa Jones* and read Chapter 4. It concerns a sunset.

Generations of editors have screamed imprecations at writers who dragged in lengthy descriptions of such natural phenomena. Now, here's a sunset that occupies the better part of a chapter. Yet everyone loves it.

Why?

Because Br'er Adams, a skilled hand and then some, has motivated its inclusion; has made it a matter of vital importance to his hero; has centered a life-and-death struggle on it.

And there, in a nutshell, is the whole issue involved in the duality of story movement. External events have no meaning in themselves, no matter how bland or how violent they may be. Their inclusion or exclusion per se is completely inconsequential. They aid in story development only as someone has feelings about them and reacts to them.

Therefore, we *must* have change in both the external world, your focal character's state of affairs, and his internal world, his state of mind. Neither can stand without the other. Only as they interact, meshing like finely tooled gears, will your story roll forward.

Precisely how does this interplay, this dual movement, take place?

That's a question that calls for more detailed analysis of the patterns of causation that rule the story world.

. . . equals cause and effect . . .

There's a story about a Chinese who sought to divorce his wife for infidelity when she gave birth to a child with obviously Caucasian features. The judge granted the decree . . . on grounds that two Wongs don't make a white.

Or consider the light switch. You flip it. A lamp comes on, and all's right with the world.

In the same way, you pull the trigger, and your gun fires. You put a coin in a slot; a candy bar comes down the chute. You overeat; your weight goes up.

We expect things to proceed in an accustomed fashion, a fashion that makes sense to us. When they don't, we're upset. If you take out a cigarette and *it* starts to smoke *you*, you have a right to be surprised.

"Science is based upon the belief that the universe is reliable in its operation," says scientist and science writer Anthony Standen. People like the idea that there's a reason behind everything that happens . . . a cause for every effect, as we so glibly put it. It gives us a sense of security; a nice, tidy feeling that everything is in order and that we're in control so far as understanding is concerned, even if not physically.

So, in idle conversation—and sometimes, unfortunately, even in that not so idle—we act as if cause and effect link together at a one-to-one ratio. Each cause, we imply, brings about a single effect. Each effect results from a single cause.

Actually, our world seldom operates quite this simply or neatly. The situations with which reality presents us more often

than not prove nightmarishly complex. When a traffic patrolman
makes out an accident report, he checks items ranging from type
of pavement to weather, from presence or absence of stop signs
to time of day, from speed of vehicle to alcoholic content of
drivers. Similarly, an ulcer may be described as the result of too
much hydrochloric acid in the stomach—but just why is that ex-
cess acid there? Tell a psychiatrist that you slugged your wife
because she bought a new mink coat, and he'll have a field day
lecturing you on displacement, repressed hostilities, and veiled
aggressions.

Now most of us realize all this, of course. The weird chains
of reasoning set up in TV headache-tablet commercials intrigue
us and whet our curiosity far more than they convince us. But
we lack time or energy to debate the logic of the casual. It's
easier to stick with our fictions and stereotypes and oversimpli-
fications, that's all—just as in other days it was easier to take it
for granted that you'd sail off the edge of the world if you
cruised too far, or that the cows had gone dry because the old
witch-woman down the road had hexed them, or that the sun
was really Apollo driving a golden chariot across the sky.

Further, these same fictions and stereotypes and oversimpli-
fications are perfectly legitimate as tools for living. Perhaps it
isn't entirely correct to say that cars cause smog, or poverty
causes crime, or carelessness causes accidents. But the complex
is like Medusa. It can paralyze us. Sometimes we just can't wait
for all the evidence to come in before we act. Even a wrong assumption may guide us adequately until Ultimate Truth reveals
itself.

So we talk, however loosely, in terms of cause and effect.

How does this cause-effect pattern relate to change?

Change means simply that something happens—a woman
bursts into tears, a plane explodes in mid-air, the cover comes
off a book, it rains this particular afternoon. It's an event in a
vacuum, as it were, presently unlinked to anything before or
after.

When we talk about cause and effect, on the other hand, we
aren't just saying that something happens—but that it happens
because something else happened previously; that *in consequence* of Event Number 1, Event Number 2 comes to pass.

A useful concept, all in all. It helps give meaning to our world. But before we can get maximum mileage from it, for story purposes, we must carry it just a bit further, so that we understand it as it applies to people.

. . . equals motivation and reaction

Scene: a schoolroom. A tack, point up, rests on the teacher's chair. She sits down, then abruptly rises with a cry of anguish.

Here illustrated we have a specialized type of cause-effect pattern which we term motivation-reaction. It is cause and effect applied to people. Cause becomes *motivating stimulus* . . . effect, *character reaction*.

What is a motivating stimulus?

Anything outside your focal character to which he reacts.

What is a character reaction?

Anything your focal character does in consequence of the motivating stimuli that impinge upon him.

More specifically?

A character may react *to* anything . . . from the world coming to an end to a puppy's snuffling; from a breath of fresh air to the thunder of jet bombers overhead. He may react *by* anything . . . from dropping dead of shock to feeling a momentary pang of doubt; from smiling, ever so slightly, in his sleep to signing the order that sends a million Jews to the gas chamber.

A motivating stimulus may come to you on a level at which you aren't even consciously aware of it . . . at night, for example, when the temperature drops unexpectedly, chilling you in your sleep because your covers are too light.

You may react just as unconsciously, without waking, by huddling into a cramped fetal ball in an effort to defeat the cold.

And so it goes. Someone pulls a gun; you stop short. A girl casts a sidewise glance; you start forward. The clock strikes; you get up. The music ends; you sit down. There's a whiff of perfume; you straighten your shoulders. A skunk blasts at you from beneath the porch; you cringe into your coat. Each time, one motivating stimulus; one character reaction.

Together, they constitute a motivation-reaction unit. Each unit indicates some change, however small—change in state of affairs; change in state of mind.

Properly selected and presented, each one moves your story a step forward. Link unit to unit, one after another, and your prose picks up momentum. Strength and impact build. Before you know it, the sentences race down the page like a fast freight hurtling through the night. The situation cannot but develop!

That is, it cannot if you also understand such technicalities as . . .

The pattern of emotion

On this particular night the house is dark when you get home. A note on the hall table tells you that your wife has left you for another man.

You stare at the message stupidly at first, numb with disbelief. Then, in intermingling waves, shock washes through you, and horror, and pain, and rage, and grief. Falling into the nearest chair, you curse aloud. Only then, in spite of all your efforts to control yourself, the curses change to a strange sort of laughter. And even while you laugh, you find, tears somehow are coursing down your cheeks.

What has happened?

    a. You have received a motivating stimulus.

This is the note. It points up a change in your state of affairs, your situation.

    b. This change in state of affairs causes changes in your state of mind.

Your emotional balance, your equilibrium, is shattered. Feelings, ordinarily neatly restrained and disciplined, break loose in a surging chaos.

    c. These feelings take the overt form of observable reaction.

You fall into a chair. You curse, you laugh, you cry.

And there is the pattern of emotion. It's the mechanism which creates feeling in your readers, and then helps them keep those feelings straight.

Its secret lies in the *order* in which you present your material . . . a strictly *chronological* order, so that one item follows another exactly as they occur in point of time. Never is any doubt left as to which element comes first, or which is cause and which effect.

To that end, you pretend that only one thing can happen at a time: Your bridge partner studies his own hand, *and then* he looks across at the dummy, *and then* he eyes your opponents, *and then* he frowns, *and then* he tugs at his ear lobe, *and then* he twists in his chair, *and then* he puffs at his cigarette, *and then* he smiles wryly, *and then* he says, "Think you're pretty smart, don't you?" *and then* he plays the ace.

He does *not* do all these things at once, the way it really happened.

Now I grant you that I am, to a degree, exaggerating here. It's entirely legitimate for you to write, "Frowning, he twisted in his chair," or "Puffing at his cigarette, he eyed Steve's cards briefly." But *in general* you avoid all hints of simultaneity, of events that take place at the same time.

The reason you do this is rooted in the very nature of written communication. For in writing, one word *follows* another, instead of being overprinted in the same space.

Which makes it impossible truly to capture on paper the fact that a man breathes and sweats and scowls and digests his dinner all at the same time.

Furthermore, any attempt to present simultaneity rather than sequence is bound to confuse your reader.

Why?

Because simultaneity obscures the cause-effect, motivation-reaction relationship that gives your story meaning to him.

(You can *say* that things happened simultaneously, you understand. But in point of fact you emphasize sequence, chronological order: "After that, everything happened at once. Hans swung the bottle, and Melville, ducking, whipped out his knife. Across the room, Scarne slashed at the rope that held the chandelier. The next instant, the brackets gave way," and so on.)

To repeat, then, you present your material so that one thing follows another in strictly chronological order.

In terms of constructing a motivation-reaction unit, that order is this:

a. Motivating stimulus.
b. Character reaction.
   (1) Feeling.
   (2) Action.
   (3) Speech.

Next question: *Whom* do you motivate? *Who* does the reacting?

The answer, of course, takes us back to your focal character. He's the man on whom the spotlight shines. He's the center around which the action revolves. He's the orientational figure whose feelings give meaning to the events that transpire within your fiction's framework. Everything in your story, everything, relates to him.

Especially, this pattern of emotion.

The pattern itself isn't at all difficult to handle. The big thing to remember is that motivation *always* precedes reaction. Our world would turn topsy-turvy indeed if the teacher first jumped and cried out . . . *then* sat on the tack! Even worse, to have motivation follow reaction is to invite your reader to make his own interpretation of said reaction and, on the basis of it, then to refuse to believe the motive *you* assign. —Though even if he accepts it, as a matter of fact, its displacement from normal order will jar him at least slightly. "Far across on the hillside, a shot rang out. John stiffened," reads not too badly. "John stiffened when a shot rang out far across on the hillside," is awkward.

Given enough such minor jolts, your reader will develop a vague dissatisfaction with your copy. He may remark only that it's "jerky, sort of." But you've lost him.

Back to reaction. It breaks down into three components, you will note: feeling . . . action . . . speech.

These components' order too is set. Feeling precedes action, and action, speech, because feeling provides the drive for both the others. Without some such inner force, some source of motive impulse, there would be no overt behavior to reveal your focal character's state of mind.

Feeling, it might be well to point out too, is *not* the same as thought. Let a car horn blast behind you, and your heart leaps without conscious mental process.

In a word, you *feel*.

As a matter of fact, you probably jump also. That is, you *act*, and that action is an involuntary and well-nigh automatic process. Later, you may get around to speech, to snarling at whoever honked. But feeling comes first, and then action.

Behind this sequential order lies the fact that feeling is beyond the control of the person feeling. You don't *decide* to feel a particular way; you just *do*.

Action, in turn, can be to a degree controlled. And where speech is concerned, control is almost absolute.

Thus, speech demands conscious thought; a certain amount of organization. Action's demands are lower . . . closer to the instinctive: An old friend unexpectedly appears. Incoherent, you still embrace him. A car runs down your child. You race toward him, not even able to cry out.

Or, you enter an office for a job interview. You care what happens, so you already have feelings—uncomfortable feelings, negative feelings, resentful feelings that you're being studied like a paramecium under a microscope. But the personnel manager, far from appreciating your unease or asking you to sit down, merely leans back and considers you with cold, wordless disdain.

"Who're you?" he snaps finally.

His tone—the whole situation, for that matter—is a unit of motivation. In spite of all you can do, panic races through you.

Panic is feeling.

Like magic, sweat slicks your palms and soaks your armpits and trickles down your spine. Your collar is suddenly too tight, your clothes are too small. You twist and choke.

Actions, one and all.

All this time, you also grope desperately for words—words that just won't come.

"I—I—" you mumble inanely.

"Young man, I asked your name. . . ."

Shall we draw a kindly veil, and trust that we've made it clear that feeling precedes action, and action precedes speech? —And, of course, on a larger basis, that motivating stimulus precedes character reaction?

Time out for a few questions:

Must all three reaction components—feeling, action, speech—be included every time?

Of course not, as almost any fragment of dialogue will demonstrate. Here, Jill is the focal character:

"Hi, Jill!" he called. "How's it going?"

"Just fine, thanks."

"Hi, Jill!" he called. "How's it going?" is the motivating stimulus.

Jill's character reaction, in turn, spelled out, might read like this:

> *Feeling:*   A glow of warmth at his friendliness crept through Jill.
> *Action:*   She smiled.
> *Speech:*   "Just fine, thanks," she said.

Because they're so obvious, however, the writer doesn't feel it necessary to detail feeling and action. So speech alone carries the ball.

Alternatively, action might have been dropped . . . feeling and speech left in:

> *Motivating stimulus:*   "Hi, Jill," he called. "How's it going?"
>
> *Character reaction:*
> *Feeling:*   A glow of warmth at his friendliness crept through Jill.
> *Action:*   (NOT STATED)
> *Speech:*   "Just fine, thanks."

. . . And so on, through all the various possibilities.

Are there any particular hazards to leaving out one or two of the reaction components?

Primarily, there's the danger that you'll confuse your reader . . . especially when the feeling component is the one you leave out. To make clear the meaning a given action or speech is supposed to convey often requires interpretation only feeling can provide. *He turned away* is action that might fit feelings ranging from boredom to helplessness, from preoccupation to scorn, from hurt to rage. "Kiss me, darling!" could mirror passion, anguish, tenderness, contempt, or what have you.

Please don't misunderstand, however. I'm *not* recommending that you always use all three components; but, rather, that you develop your sensitivity to clarity, balance and the terse to the point where you can manipulate your materials with a nice skill and discrimination.

How much time should elapse between motivation and reaction?

When you start to sneeze, you snatch for your handkerchief *right now*. Not tomorrow. Not next week.

The same way, think of each stimulus your focal character receives as a demand for *immediate* action. Don't summarize, grouping a dozen or a hundred M-R units together. Break the package down to its individual components.

Are you tempted to write, "He got up"? Maybe that single sentence is exactly the one you need. But then again, maybe you'd do better to open as your character floats through a dark and misty private world. Then, suddenly, sound breaks in upon him: a clanging, strident cacophony, so loud that it seems it must surely split his skull. He flails wildly, lurching up out of the mists and darkness into a grubby, dawn-gray scene: his own room, with the alarm clock jangling beside him.

And so on. The thing to remember is that any motivation or reaction can be fragmented into smaller bits; and, generally, you'll achieve a greater sense of reality in your copy by using the littlest pieces. It's like a magician performing a coin trick. See it as a unit and it seems a miracle. But if you do it in slow motion, a step at a time, it becomes a completely understandable exhibition of manual dexterity.

In the same way, your copy should leave the impression of a continuing stream of reality, in which effect follows cause like a burnt finger jerking back from a hot stove. Even if the reaction is merely to stare numbly, it should start now, not five minutes after the stimulus to shock is past and gone. *No time* should elapse between. If it does, odds are that you've broken the flow by leaving out additional motivation-reaction units that should be included.

To what degree does each motivation-reaction unit stand alone?

To no degree. True, well-constructed units can be pulled out of context and analyzed as here. But this is for purposes of study only. In any actual story, what your focal character feels and does and says in his reaction will in turn link to the world outside him.

Sometimes there'll be a direct relation, a counterreaction: Bickham fires a shot. His opponent fires back.

In other cases, the situation merely provides observation of further external change: Bickham squirms forward a fraction, peering. Though still showing no awareness of him, the tyrannosaur has moved a bit closer.

Or, on occasion when the heightening of suspense through delaying action is an issue, there may not even be external change: Bickham studies the distant hillside. There still is no sign of life.

*　*　*

A story is a succession of motivation-reaction units. The chain they form as they link together is the pattern of emotion.

As a helpful step in learning how to forge such a chain successfully, it might be wise to probe a bit deeper into the nature of the motivating stimulus.

The motivating stimulus

A motivating stimulus is anything outside your focal character to which he reacts.

For a motivating stimulus to do its job well, it must have:

  a. Significance to your character.
  b. Pertinence to your story.
  c. Motivity to your reader.

A stimulus is *significant* to the degree that it presents the external world as your character experiences it. Although we may not view it through his eyes, the picture we receive of it must reflect his state of affairs and state of mind. A woman who goes to church to flirt with the man in the next pew zeros in on one set of stimuli. Her neighbor, come to check on the styling of other parishioners' clothes, reacts to a different group. A friend that seeks spiritual uplift and enrichment approaches with values that draw her attention to things that, to her, mirror such uplift and enrichment.

Yet all three sit side by side within the sanctuary. It's merely the stimuli they note which make the difference.

It is, in brief, a matter of *selection*.

Or consider a tiny mountain lake. Thickly wooded slopes sweep down to the water's edge along half its shore line. Sheer cliffs rise gray and forbidding on the far side. Two camping trailers and a tent stand in a patch of clear ground down close to the narrow south beach, where a rutted dirt road terminates. There are children at play . . . women cooking . . . a man who bait-casts a hundred yards or so off to one side.

The road, in turn, leads away from the lake, around a spur of brush, then off along the edge of a meadow thick with wild-flowers—columbine, trillium, bellwort, violets.

Now a pickup truck approaches, bouncing noisily along the road. Far away across the meadow, behind a hillock and almost in the shadow of another spur of brush, a pair of bear cubs frolic under their black-furred mother's watchful eye. Close to the center of the lake, a rainbow trout jumps, and the bait-caster on shore pauses, rod poised like some sort of long, strange, quivering, insectile antenna.

What will your focal character notice about this scene? To what specific fragment will he react? Is his lens fixed on the trout? The bears? (And if so, which one?) The blonde child peering from the tent? The approaching pickup? The sound of the pickup's motor? The gray rock faces of the cliff? The columbine? The bellwort? The big, raw-boned woman in Levis who hunkers by the fire, poking sullenly at her frying bacon with a stick?

It's hard to overemphasize the importance of your focal character's—and your—choice. For to a very considerable degree, your readers will draw their conclusions as to the meaning of the focal character's reaction on the basis of context—that is, the stimulus or motivation that provokes it.

Especially is this true if said reaction is objectively written, non-introspective, physical reaction.

Thus, a film editor may place a close-up of an actor's face directly after a shot of an actress lying dead in a coffin. Invariably, the audience will thereupon interpret the actor's expression, however blank, as one of grief.

But suppose, instead, that our editor cuts the self-same reaction shot in after a frightening scene—one in which a madman lunges at the camera with an ax, let's say.

This time, the audience will promptly declare the actor to be registering fury, or horror, or courage, or shock, or what have you.

Do you see the issue? The right reaction is the direct product of the right stimulus. Choose the correct fragment of motivation and you control the direction of your story. If you want a particular reaction, pick a stimulus that will evoke it. A good external motivation makes your character's consequent behavior completely logical to your reader.

Conversely, the *wrong* motivating stimulus is the meaningless or ambiguous one. It bores or confuses or irritates the reader. Worse, it may become a false plant, a false pointer . . . prepare him for something that isn't going to happen; head him down the wrong road.

For unconsciously, your reader takes it for granted that every stimulus in your story is brought in for a purpose. If a gun, or a car out of gas, or a loose board in the porch floor is introduced, he assumes that you'll pay him off for noting it by giving it a function later. Not to do so will net you the same brand of deserved resentment you'd draw from your wife if you were to have her bake a cake for a party which you secretly knew had been canceled. For you to focus on a mysterious redhead or a scream in the night or a stolen wallet and then not have it influence the course of your story can only make you the target for reader outrage.

So, how do you emphasize the significance of a stimulus properly?

You use the technique of the motion-picture close-up. That is, you direct and control your reader's attention by telling him what you want him to know and that only . . . just as the film director hammers home the importance of a trembling hand or an open door or a shattered doll by filling the screen with it to the point that it dominates everything else past all ignoring.

To this end:

(1) You choose the effect you want this particular stimulus to create, in terms of motivating your focal character to desired reaction and, at the same time, guiding your reader to feel with him.

(2) You pick some external phenomenon—thing, person, event—that you think will create this effect.

(3) You frame this stimulus so as to pinpoint the precise detail that highlights the point you seek to make.

(4) You exclude whatever is extraneous or confusing.

(5) You heighten the effect, by describing the stimulus in terms that reflect your focal character's attitude.

By way of illustration, let's go back to our scene at the mountain lake. Our focal character lies high on a rocky, wooded slope with a pair of binoculars. His purpose is to rescue an abused child whom he believes to be a prisoner in the camp below. The effect we seek to achieve at the moment is one that will excite such intense feelings of compassion and outrage in our focal character that he'll be blinded to everything except the absolute and urgent necessity of going ahead with the rescue, regardless of personal peril.

Note, now, how sharply this choice of effect limits us; how strongly it turns us away from most of the potential motivating stimuli laid out below. Meadow, bears, trout, truck, landscape—all must be abandoned, because they offer little chance for the specific kind of stimulus we need: a goad to compassion and to outrage.

Is there anything that offers more potential? Of course: the child herself—the little blonde girl peering from the tent. She'll be our motivating stimulus.

How to highlight the point we want to make? —Well, suppose the child's been beaten . . . punished for trying to run away, perhaps. Bring her up big in the binoculars, all anguished, tear-streaked face. And, since kids do cry for a variety of reasons and even our focal character knows it, maybe we should black one of her eyes—an ugly, swollen bruise, rich with blues and purples.

Is the child sucking a thumb or a lollipop? Blowing her nose? Playing with a puppy? No. All such are extraneous, introduce possibly conflicting notes, and thus shatter the unity of the effect. So, we'll avoid them.

On the other hand, perhaps it would be worth while to give her a rag doll to clutch to her ragged breast. A *broken* rag doll with the stuffing coming out, to draw a nasty parallel with her own condition and thus strengthen unity of effect.

Then, on to description, phrased in terms to reflect your focal character's attitudes, his mood. And here we come to an important point, already stated but worth beating on a bit.

For all we know, this child is a brat, a hateful little monster. She received her black eye when she climbed to the roof of one of the camping trailers in direct defiance of her mother's orders, then lost her balance and fell. In fact, she'd probably have fractured her stupid skull if she hadn't landed on another youngster, breaking his arm. That's why the pickup truck is bouncing along the road; the father had to take the other child to town to get the fracture set. Meanwhile, Little Miss Noxious has succeeded in floundering into the lake. It was the third time, and the rags she now wears are the only clothes her distracted maternal parent can find for her. Also, flailing in the water, the dear child lost the handsome new ten-dollar doll her father bought her for her birthday. So the rag doll is one she stole from the little girl of a poverty-stricken family down the line.

Now all the above and more may be true. However, for our purposes here, the important thing is that the focal character doesn't see it that way . . . and always, we describe in terms of *his* state of affairs and state of mind. So though our little darling be Miss Lucrezia Borgia, Jr., our story will present her with strong overtones of Little Eva.

So how *does* the focal character see her, maybe?

Agnes' face came into focus, then. The blonde hair was matted, the worn plaid dress in rags. She'd been crying too, apparently, for there were tear-streaks on her grime-smudged cheeks. Dark circles rimmed the great, frightened, little-girl eyes, and when she turned her head to the left a fraction, a bruise came into view, all ugly blues and purples, swelling shut the lids, as if she were a grown man slugged in a barroom brawl.

Miller lay very still, his knuckles white on the glasses. . . .

A motivating stimulus, and the start of the focal character's reaction. One approach, out of an infinity of possible approaches. Each of us would do it differently—differently each minute, even—for each of us can only be himself as he is at this moment.

Are all motivating stimuli this lengthily or this tightly drawn?

Of course not; no more than all shots in a movie are close-ups.

Thus, the scene on the lake might begin:

Motivating stimulus:	The lake lay like a drop of icy rain, caught in a cleft of a thin green leaf.
Character reaction:	
Feeling:	(NOT STATED)
Action:	Hunkering down in a clump of spruce high on the mountainside, Miller considered it carefully.*
Speech:	(NOT STATED)
Motivating stimulus:	The camping trailers stood at the lake's south end, Godden's tent beside them. . . .

. . . and so on.

Thing is, close-ups are *emphasis shots,* shots to make a point. They hit the hardest, count the most.

When you're trying to make a point, it's best if you don't miss the target. Right?

To that end, don't hesitate to frame tightly and move in close . . . *if* you feel it's necessary.

Back to our lesson: If the focal character dislikes something, you bear down heavily on its undesirable features in your description; and vice versa.

Thus, if he sees a girl through love's haze, you never get around to mentioning her harelip or off-color glass eye.

Or, you stress her positive points: her tenderness, her well-turned ankles, the glow of affection that lights up her face.

---

* *Carefully,* in this instance, is a good example of a word with connotations to color apparently objective description. It implies importance and/or strong interest (Why consider anything "carefully" if the item considered isn't somehow vital or otherwise intriguing?) and hints at danger: The situation apparently makes caution advisable.

Or, you do both.

If the focal character fears the villain, on the other hand, you focus on that gentleman's cruelty, his cunning, his viciousness, his lightning-fast reflexes, his heavy thews, the knife-scars he bears as tokens of the night he crippled three Moros running amok on Palawan.

So much for *significance*. It's precisely as simple and as complex as that.

There remain two other vital characteristics of the effective motivating stimulus: pertinence, and motivity.

The *pertinent* stimulus is one relevant to the matter at hand, the immediate issue.

But don't stop there. Always, the matter at hand itself has a function: to move your story forward . . . to develop the situation in the path you want it to take.

To that end:

(1) The pertinent stimulus must show some change in the external world—your focal character's state of affairs.

(2) This *external* change must be such as logically to evoke some change in his *internal* world also—his state of mind.

(3) This internal change must reasonably lead him to behave in the manner you want him to in order to move the story forward.

Consider the scene at the mountain lake. Our purpose was to motivate our focal character to proceed with his adventure. So, we presented an external stimulus thus:

Agnes' face came into focus, then. The blonde hair was matted, the worn plaid dress in rags,

and so on.

Whereupon, the focal character reacted:

Miller lay very still, his knuckles white on the glasses. . . .

Now suppose we changed the stimulus just a trifle:

Agnes' face came into focus, then. The blonde hair was smooth and neatly combed, the worn plaid dress clean even though in rags. She was laughing, and even at this distance the blue eyes seemed to dance with life. Hugging the battered doll to her, she looked down and spoke to it fondly.

The reaction?

Miller lay very still. Then, slowly, his hands relaxed and the color came back to his whitened knuckles. . . .

Thus, Miller again is motivated; again reacts, showing feeling. But this feeling is different from the one before. It points the scenes that follow in a potentially different direction.

And that's the test of pertinence. Not just, "Is this stimulus relevant to the immediate issue?" but also, "Does it keep the story itself on target, moving toward the twin goals of outcome and total effect I want it to achieve?"

So much for *pertinence*. It demands merely that you view each M-R unit in the perspective of the story as a whole.

But it's one thing for a story to move forward; another for it to seem to your reader as if it were so moving. Those motivating stimuli which help to induce this feeling that your story isn't standing still may be said to have *motivity*.

To be motive, a stimulus must spur your focal character to action. Instead of letting him rest on his laurels, it jerks him up and boots him in the pants.

To that end:

(1) The motive stimulus is one which demands response.
(2) The response demanded is of such a nature as to keep your focal character active.

Too many variables are involved to warrant making these points more explicit. In general, however, what you need is the stimulus that demands adjustment on the focal character's part. Fluffy white clouds aren't enough; a thunderhead that makes him race for cover may be. Beads of moisture forming on a cold glass don't call for action; the glass slopping red wine onto a snowy tablecloth does.

—Though of course fluffy clouds or beaded glass may do very well if they're in such context as to make imperative immediate, active response from your focal character.

Understand, please: This is *not* an appeal to eliminate all mood and color. The sense of movement isn't the only, or even necessarily the most important, element in your story. Motivity is a matter of degree and pacing, not an absolute. You'll always have a host of stimuli that ignore it.

However, your story may sag if you forget about it altogether. Beware the habitual or "file-and-forget" type of thing! Better that a girl's eyes challenge your character, or an alarm bell ring, or a man seize him by the wrist. For then he'll have to decide just what to do about it, and act; and that's what makes for a sense of movement.

So much for *motivity*, and for the motivating stimulus itself.

Now, what's on the other side of the fence? What, specifically, is involved when your focal character reacts?

The character reaction

A character reaction is anything your focal character feels, thinks, does, or says in consequence of a motivating stimulus that impinges on him.

To this end, it must be:

   a. Significant.
   b. Pertinent.
   c. Motive.
   d. Characteristic.
   e. Reasonable.

All our observations on the vital importance of careful selection and description of motivating stimuli apply equally to character reaction.

In addition, we may say that a reaction is properly *significant* only when it reflects precisely the image you seek to create. It must capture the exact shadings and nuances of mood. Tenderness can be a thing of infinite gradation, and so can cruelty, or rejection, or lust. If you try to draw a picture of your character as behaving in a kindly manner and, in addition, inadvertently leave the impression that he's somewhat of a fool for so behaving, the bit may do more harm than good.

Why does a reaction confuse? Most often, because you the writer haven't made up your mind as to precisely the effect you seek to achieve. You *must* decide, definitely and concretely: Is your character stupid, or stuporous, or at loose ends? Is he defeated, or merely faking defeat?

Then, your decision made, you must implement it with the right reaction—*demonstrate* your character's character and state of mind in terms of the thing or combination of things he feels or thinks or does or says.

Above all, make it your rule that if a reaction is in any way confusing, it must be clarified or left out.

What about the *pertinent* reaction?

It's the one which links the character to the story as you have conceived it. It moves him down the road you want him to follow. If the situation and your concept demand reckless courage, he'll behave differently than he would if you'd planned the scene for laughs or pathos.

The *motive* reaction? Insofar as practical, let your character respond *actively* to whatever happens to him. —It's even possible to make a character quite actively passive, you know: "Joe stood very, very still" . . . "Sam forced the tension from his muscles; breathed deeply in one last grim, raw-nerved effort to relax" . . . "Limp, silent, Helen let the sound wash over her in sleekly ululating waves."

Equally important, the motive reaction often is designed to bring about further change in the world outside your character: Hero's fingers let go of the coin; his antagonist's eyes flicker as it falls. Heroine's foot depresses accelerator pedal; car picks up speed; traffic cop kicks motorcycle forward.

A *characteristic* reaction is one that's in keeping with your character's known character. The Milquetoast doesn't suddenly slug a gorilla. The strong silent type doesn't burst forth with flowery speeches. Is your character phlegmatic? Volatile? Sullen? Tender? Weak? Passionate? Irritable? You pays your money and you takes your choice. But whatever he is, it will have a bearing on each of his reactions.

Reasonable means that your focal character's reaction should make sense in terms of the motivating stimulus he's received. Unless he's been established earlier as some sort of nut, he doesn't burst into tears over a fancied slight, or knife a friend for an inconsequential five-minute delay, or accept unwarranted abuse from petty tyrants.

In other words, you should *not* show him overreacting, under-reacting, reacting incongruously, or the like, within the frame of reference of situation, stimulus, and character.

So, how would your character react? In view of his motivating stimulus, what will he do?

There should be no problem if you lead your reader step by step. Link motivation and reaction tightly enough, and he can't help but understand how your character feels.

Which means only that *you*, first, must see each motivating stimulus as your focal character sees it . . . with *his* background, *his* attitudes, *his* dynamics and insights.

Then, you let him react *in character*.

If you're a girl and like a boy, your reaction to a pass will be different than if you loathe him.

Said reaction also will differ according to what specific kind of girl you are . . . your habitual reaction to passes.

If you chance on a holdup, you'll react one way if you're an honest citizen; another, perhaps, if you're an ex-con on parole.

Well, it *sounds* easy, anyhow.

But it still doesn't tell us just how far to go.

The problem of proportion

Life is an unending succession of motivation-reaction units. Your lungs lack air; you draw a breath. Your stomach empties; you search for food. The sun grows hot; your sweat glands ooze. Every minute, every hour, every day, your whole system works to maintain that unique internal balance physiologists know as homeostasis.

Yet in any story, some parts are presented in greater detail than are others. Here, whole chapters are devoted to action that takes place in fleeting minutes. There, a lapse of years may be passed over in a sentence.

So, how do you decide how much attention to give each element, each segment? How long should you write a given passage? Or how short?

Answer: You write to fit.

To fit what?

Feelings.

How do you measure feelings?

You check them with an emotional clock.

There are, you see, two kinds of time in this world: chronometrical, and emotional. One, you measure with a watch; the other, with the human heart.

Chronometrical time is objective. It offers sixty seconds to every minute, sixty minutes to every hour. And your minutes and my minutes and the Greenwich Observatory's minutes are pretty much the same.

Emotional time, by way of contrast, is relative, subjective, and based on feelings. In no two of us is it precisely the same.

The late Albert Einstein summed up the situation where emotional time is concerned, in a capsule comment on relativity: "When a man sits with a pretty girl for an hour, it seems like a minute. But let him sit on a hot stove for a minute, and it's longer than an hour."

What gives emotional time so wide a range?

Tension.

If you're relaxed, time races by. If you're tense, it stands still.

What's behind tension?

Fear: the fear that something will or won't happen.

Take a birthday picnic. The sky's blue, the temperature perfect, the food superb, your wife loving, your daughter doting; and all the while, in the back of your head, you think small, pleasant thoughts of how well things have worked out for you through this past year.

You're relaxed, happy, unafraid. Time races by.

But suppose, instead, that this is another, not-so-happy day. You pace the floor in a shabby hospital lounge that smells of fear and phenol, waiting for word to come down as to whether your youngest child will live or die. Panic rides you; draws your belly into a chill, rock-hard knot. The seconds drag by like hours; the minutes pile up in eons. Each footstep, each distant whisper, makes your nerves jump. Your tongue grows thick with too much smoking. Your eyes burn. Your clothes feel dirty, rumpled. Even though you shaved less than an hour ago, your beard is stubble rasping on your knuckles. . . .

Because tragedy is in you; because you live with the specter of a loved one's death, tension rides high and time stands still.

In writing, you translate tension into space: The more tense the situation as your focal character experiences it, the more words you give it.

Why?

Because your reader needs a clear and simple standard by which to judge the degree to which an event is important or inconsequential.

Wordage, length, gives him a yardstick with which to make this measurement. If you describe a thing in tremendous detail, he figures there must be something important about it. If you dismiss it with an aside, he takes it for granted that it holds no profound significance.

The issue is never words for words' own sake, however. On the contrary. Words are merely the tool you use to make crystal clear the reasons why your character is experiencing fear and tension in the first place.

To understand this properly, look first at the nature of danger.

Danger is objective. It's something that exposes you to the possibility of injury, loss, pain, or other evil.

A speeding bullet may be a danger. Same for a typhoid germ . . . a new neighbor . . . an old rival . . . a flash flood . . . a roller skate on the darkened front steps.

Fear is subjective. It's an individual's feeling-response when he perceives danger.

No one can translate danger into fear until he becomes aware that said danger exists. The speeding bullet may strike you dead while you stand relaxed and carefree, laughing. The typhoid germ enters your system undetected, while you think only about how good the water tastes. The new neighbor appears friendly; the old rival, a dead issue.

So, you feel no fear.

But suppose you *do* recognize the danger. —Perhaps you glimpse the marksman as he brings up his gun. Or it dawns on you as you drink that the water came from the contaminated well. Or you catch the glance that passes between your neighbor and your wife. What then?

Then, fear may come . . . a subjective alarm signal that puts you on an emotional war footing . . . mobilizes all your resources of energy and alertness for self-preservative effort.

That mobilization involves a multiplicity of glandular and muscular reactions. The common term for it is tension.

How does all this apply to story?

As always, the key factor is your focal character. Your story centers on him and his developing situation: the changes in external circumstance that we call state of affairs; the changes in internal attitude referred to as state of mind.

Any change in state of affairs brings with it the potentiality of danger.

Why?

Because it forces your focal character to readjust . . . to revise his behavior to fit the new situation. Face him with an unfamiliar girl or boss or car or drink, or inject a new element into an existing relationship, and he must decide how to act where it's concerned.

So?

The new behavior he chooses may not work out. His attempted readjustment may only plunge him into trouble.

Consciously or unconsciously, he knows this. Therefore, to a greater or lesser degree, he fears . . . even though he might deny any hint of such, and declare his state merely one of alertness or interest or attention.

Enter tension.

Note where this puts the issue: not in the event, but in the character's reaction to that event; not in external circumstance, state of affairs, but in the affected person's attitude, his state of mind.

Thus, your character's external stimulus, his change in state of affairs, may be notice of a promotion, or a telegram announcing a million-dollar inheritance, or a pretty girl begging him to kiss her. It still can generate fear and tension in him.

Why?

Because it forces him to choose a course of action—one of many, quite possibly.

If he chooses wrong, the results may be disastrous. Yet you never can know for sure, in advance, whether the choice you make will be the right one.

Take the matter of the pretty girl, for instance. Your character's first reaction is to kiss her, enthusiastically.

And yet . . . should he, really? Isn't it a bit out of line for any girl, let alone a pretty one, to come to a young man begging kisses? What's her motive? Why has she chosen him, among all the men available? Is she trying to compromise him? To make another man jealous? To pull off some wild publicity stunt at his expense? Can she be emotionally disturbed—?

The possibilities are well-nigh infinite. So, your character hangs teetering on the brink of action—reconsidering his situation, re-evaluating his position, trying to decide whether or not the game is worth the candle.

In brief, he faces a change in state of mind, and it bothers him. Whichever road he takes, he'll never again be quite the same. Let him succumb to the girl now, without loss, and tomorrow he'll be a fraction bolder—and not just in regard to girls, either.

Let him succumb with disastrous results, and he may turn timid or bitter or even vicious. Let him withdraw, turn down his chance, and the result may be self-righteousness or self-contempt.

Now not all situations in which your character finds himself will demand major soul-searching. Neither will all motivating stimuli that impinge upon him. The biggest part of life is always routine. Habit takes care of it.

Further, not all hazards that face your character will, to the same degree, prove pertinent; story-related. A soldier may sleep through a barrage which, by any objective standard, puts him in a position of total jeopardy. But you, writer, give it only casual mention because battle, at this point, isn't the issue.

Then, our soldier receives a Dear John letter, reacts to it with a plunge into deep depression, and loses his will to fight.

You thereupon devote page after page to detailing his every stimulus and reaction, because this is a love story and your character's state of mind where his girl is concerned is its core and heart, the crucial issue.

Always, the points you bear down on are those that influence the development of your story.

The time you need detail is when your focal character's state of mind changes.

The place to summarize is where no such change takes place.

The trick is to keep asking yourself, "How does my character feel about the changes that are taking place in his world, his state of affairs?"

If his course of action is clear-cut and non-dangerous; if his state of mind remains smooth and untroubled—then summary is permissible.

If, on the other hand, he's in a spot where all his efforts seem to come to naught, and disasters pile up, and he's forced repeatedly to ask himself, "What should I do now to avert this catastrophe that threatens to engulf me?"—then pour on the detail!

(Incidentally, it should here be noted that it isn't necessarily necessary to go inside a character's head in order to indicate change in his state of mind. While introspection is, at times, a useful tool, the objectivist school of writing as exemplified in Hemingway and Hammett has clearly demonstrated that it's quite possible to show what's going on by detailing behavior and appearance.)

To what degree can you afford to summarize?

Here a little judgment helps. Obviously, you often can get away with more in a long story than a short one; and skill in handling makes a tremendous difference. But in general, you may bridge almost any amount of time or space, *so long as your character's problem and state of mind remain essentially the same.*

Thus, a gigantic "fact"—a war fought, a country swept away, a decade passed—may be presented as a single unified motivating stimulus. Whereupon, your character's reaction—one small feeling, a sadness at such waste—may suffice to bridge the gap, because his original problem and state of mind have remained virtually the same through it all.

Or, to put it in different words, externals have changed; but you're still dealing with the same old story, of how your particular character deals with his private danger.

Why use so much detail at moments of crucial change?

Partly, as previously noted, to impress your reader with the event's importance.

Partly, to give proportion to your presentation . . . lay it out not on a plain or plateau, but in peaks and valleys. —More of this later.

Partly, to build up the scene and milk it dry of every drop of drama. —More of this later, too.

But above all, you use detail to make it absolutely clear to your reader precisely *why* your character does as he does . . . the pattern his thought and feelings follow; the strengths and weaknesses of his logic.

A portion of that *why* is subjective . . . a matter of your character's character. But another segment is more or less objective: external factors which influence your character's degree of tension and hence the amount of detail in which you present the incident.

Five aspects of this objective segment are:

    a. Necessity of readjustment in your focal character, and thus necessity of change in his state of mind.
    b. Degree of change.
    c. Immediacy of change.
    d. Difficulty of decision.
    e. Difficulty of action.

Thus, you may or may not feel threatened when a guest points out to you that you've erred in serving chablis at room temperature rather than chilled. But a sentence of life imprisonment, for most of us, makes readjustment an absolute necessity.

In the same way, the degree of threat you feel when you catch your wife kissing your best friend is unlikely to prove as intense as that which you experience if you find the two in bed together.

Immediacy? A falling safe demands one brand of readjustment and change in state of mind; the fact that you must remember to renew your lease next month, another.

Where difficulty of decision is concerned, most of us would have little trouble were we to have to choose between exposure as braggart and white liar, and murder of the person who would expose us. But would your choice be as easy if you discover that your dead father has embezzled bank funds, and you now must decide whether to devote your life to repaying the loss, as a matter of principle, when no one will ever know the truth if you keep silent?

Again, *deciding* what to do may be easy, with a Bengal tiger on the loose. But *doing* it may prove a trifle harder.

And so it goes. Each and every factor must be considered, if your copy is to maintain proper balance. Given a minor tension, you may decide that the change in state of mind involved is so slight that you can afford to ignore it, gloss it over. A major change, on the other hand, demands detailing . . . a subtle change, perhaps even more, simply because it's harder to make clear and believable.

One thing, however, is certain: Few aspects of writing are more vital. Overplay your tensions, or underplay them, or ignore them, and almost certainly your story will fail to satisfy.

Difficulties, in turn, generally reflect an effort to get too much mileage from a given M-R unit. To clarify anything, or build up its importance, demands fragmentation. Break down your material into smaller and smaller units! Spell out each flicker of meaning or feeling. Detail each nuance. If you don't know why your character stopped trading at one grocery and switched to another, go back and consider concrete instances, and the trivia that made those instances significant. Probe beneath the generalizations. Pinpoint the impolite clerk, the bad eggs, the nasty cashier, the thumb on the scales. Or even the scuttling cockroach, the penny overcharge, the tiny overemphasis on "sir" or "ma'am." Be petty and finicky and gimlet-eyed. Get down to specifics. Deal on a bedrock level with each individual motivating stimulus and character reaction.

* * *

By way of recapitulation, then . . .

    a. Summarize facts and mechanics.

    b. Detail that which is so emotionally pertinent that it holds the potentiality of creating tension or otherwise changing your focal character's state of mind.

Writing the M-R unit

How do you go about writing a motivation-reaction unit?

    a. Write a sentence *without* your character.

    b. Follow it with a sentence *about* your character.

Like this:

Now, with a roar, the red Jag picked up speed, careening recklessly as it hurtled down the drive and out onto the highway.

Stiff-lipped, Brad turned from the window and ground out his cigarette.

Our focal character here, let's assume, is the gentleman y-clept Brad. The first sentence—the one *without* Brad, the one in which he isn't mentioned—is of course a *motivation* sentence. It describes what it is that your character is going to react to, and it does so in terms precise enough to make it plausible that he react in the manner you wish.

Most important of all is the fact that your character does *not* appear anywhere in the sentence, either by noun or pronoun.

This is especially true while you're still a beginner, getting the feel of this device. For example, you do *not* fall into the trap of writing, "Now, *Brad saw* the red Jag pick up speed," etc.

The reason you shouldn't do this is that it's very, very easy for the inclusion of *any mention* of your character in a motivating sentence to transform said sentence into one of reaction; or, at least, to mix the whole thing up to the point where there's a feeling of clutter to the sequence. —Whereas what you want is something that confuses your reader not at all . . . external circumstance pure and simple, state of affairs to motivate your focal character. You even make it a point to watch your language: "careening recklessly" is the terminology of an outside observer —onlooker, not driver.

The second sentence, in turn, is a *reaction* sentence. That is, it's *about* Brad. It describes how he behaves *in consequence of* the action that takes place in Sentence 1. His state of mind is made clear by the use of the phrase "stiff-lipped," and the fact that he "grinds" out his cigarette.

Another example? How about a love story:

Dave's hands were very sure, very skillful.

A strange, raw-edged sort of panic gripping her, Sue pushed him away.

Sue is our focal character. Sentence 1, external to her, provides motivation, in the form of Dave's action. Sentence 2 shows how she reacts. We even tell how she feels—"A strange, rawedged sort of panic gripping her . . ."

By now, someone no doubt is complaining that the onesentence limitation isn't valid.

He's right, of course. Often two, or three, or even more sentences may be needed in order to present a given motivation or reaction with proper impact. So what we're really dealing with is what might be termed one *unit* of motivation and one *unit* of reaction.

Thus, take Example 1. That first, motivating sentence leans over a bit on the cumbersome side. Breaking it up and elaborating might make it stronger:

> Now, with a roar, the red Jag picked up speed. Careening recklessly, it hurtled down the drive; then, with a scream of protesting tires, fishtailed out onto the highway.

More vivid, right? Easier to read! And we've even eliminated the implication of simultaneity conveyed by the "as" of the original version.

Brad's reaction can stand a little attention, too:

> Stiff-lipped, Brad turned from the window. "I've had it!" he snapped, grinding out his cigarette. "The little bitch can go to hell!"

Yet though extra sentences may sharpen up your copy, there still are virtues to the one-sentence rule. When you're just learning, for example, you tend to kid yourself that you need a lot more verbiage than really is essential. Given half a chance, some of us would feel it necessary to mention that fury seethed within Brad; that his blue eyes grew bleak; that muscles knotted at the hinges of his jaws; that his nostrils flared and his fists tightened and his face flushed. As the saying goes, the kitchen sink would be there too if we could only figure out a way to get it through the door!

Even more important is the issue of confusion. The moment you get two sentences in a unit, there's also the danger that you'll give your reader the impression that there are two (or more) motivations in a row, or two (or more) reactions.

Here's a sample:

> Stiff-lipped, Brad turned from the window. He snapped, "I've had it!" He ground out his cigarette.

The problem is that each new declarative sentence with your character as subject tends to appear to constitute a fresh reaction, unless you handle it carefully. The moment you say something like, "He got up. He crossed the room. He opened the window. He peered out," your reader gets the feeling that all's not well . . . classifies the passage as jumpy and jerky.

Now such choppiness is acceptable for effect, upon occasion. But overworked, it can destroy you.

The thing that bothers your reader, though he's seldom aware of it, is the absence of anticipated sentences of motivating stimulus. Your construction makes him feel as if they should be present. But they aren't there.

A reconstruction will show you what I mean:

> He got up.
> "Steve, wait!" The girl sounded just a little frightened now.
> He crossed the room.
> Fingers unsteady, she plucked at the throat of her dress. "Please—I mean—oh, I feel so weak, so faint. . . ."
> He opened the window.
> Rain-freshened evening air eddied into the room, bringing with it a rattle and drone of traffic noises.
> He peered out.

Each of your character's actions now is motivated, even though the writing is rough and awkward. And high time! Confusion is a luxury you simply can't afford. So, see to it always that your line of M-R development is kept absolutely straight and clear and to the point.

Does this mean that every choppy passage demands insertion of motivations or reactions?

Not necessarily. Often, the answer is merely to juggle words or sentence structure until you achieve a surface unity; an impression of continuity that draws apparently divergent elements into a single motivation or reaction.

For example: "Getting up, he crossed the room, opened the window, and peered out."

Simple, eh? You shouldn't have any trouble with that . . . even though you surely will!

To maintain the flow of mounting emotional intensity in your copy, continue to alternate sentences (or, if need be, larger units) of stimulus and response, cause and effect, motivation and reaction:

Motivation	*Reaction*
Hot for the kill, two huge beetles bore down upon Kyla from behind, narrowing the gap that separated them from her with every slithering step.	
	Haskill drew back . . . whipped up his light-lance.
Running full tilt, the slim girl burst from the shadows now, the coleoptera close at her heels.	
	Tight-lipped, Haskill triggered a searing purple beam from the lance.
The foremost beetle drew into a writhing ball under the ray's impact, rolling crazily through the rubble.	
	Pivoting, the spaceman ran after Kyla . . . caught her by the arm and half-dragged her with him toward the avenue.
The rustle of coleopteran wing-sheaths rose instantly as if on signal—a furious fluttering, loud as the rasp of branches in a storm-tossed forest, closer and closer.	
	Haskill spun about; again brought up the light-lance.
The coleoptera broke before the threat, rushing for cover in a frantic scramble.	

. . . and so on, step by step, as your character—and your reader
—live through the rising action of the scene.

Note also that such rising action is an interaction, actually.
For just as your focal character reacts to his external motivation,
so the world outside reacts to him. Whatever he does will have
an effect on others.

❋   ❋   ❋

So much for the M-R unit . . . the concept of motivation and
reaction as it applies to fiction. Deceptively simple at first
glance, it sometimes poses problems of choice that are little less
than fiendish.

Fools will sneer at the motivation-reaction pattern as mere
mechanics; or, with equally unhappy results, will attempt to use
it as a mere mechanical device.

Clods will snatch at the first motivation that comes to hand,
then pair it with a painfully obvious reaction.

Literary nit-pickers will drag forth a thousand instances in
which master craftsmen have achieved brilliant effects while
appearing to ignore completely every precept here set forth.

(After all, shouldn't any of us be able to duplicate the feats
of a professional marksman the first time we get a gun in our
hands?)

Writers with better sense will recognize the M-R unit for what
it is: a tool, infinitely valuable, whose use they must master so
completely that its skilled manipulation becomes automatic and
instinctive. How well it serves them will depend on their own
sensitivity, their choice of materials, their insight into character,
and their talent at deciding which bits to build up and which to
subordinate.

How do you least painfully achieve such mastery?

The best way, I suspect, is to write in whatever manner
comes easiest for you, paying no attention to any rules whatever.

Then, go back over your copy and check to make sure that
each reaction is motivated; that each motivating stimulus gets a
reaction; and that ineptitude in use of language has not in any
way confused the issue.

Do this conscientiously on a hundred pages of copy, and on the hundred-and-first there'll be few errors in motivation or reaction.

Meanwhile, it's time you turned at least part of your attention to the dramatic scene as a useful tool for building conflict.

CHAPTER 4

Conflict and How to Build It

A story is a chain of scenes and sequels.

How do you build a story?
With scene.
With sequel.
Two basic units. That's all. Master their construction and use and you've won half the battle. At least.
To that end, you need to learn five things:

1. How to plan a scene.
2. How to plan a sequel.
3. How to write a scene.
4. How to write a sequel.
5. How to mesh the two together.

❋ ❋ ❋

A scene is a unit of conflict lived through by character and reader.
The big moments in your story are scenes. Or, to put it the other way around, if you want some incident or bit to loom large to your reader, cast it in scene form.
A sequel is a unit of transition that links two scenes.
How do you handle them? Let's start with . . .

The scene in skeleton

To repeat: A scene is a unit of conflict, of struggle, lived through by character and reader. It's a blow-by-blow account of somebody's time-unified effort to attain an immediate goal despite face-to-face opposition.

What are the functions of scene?

a. To provide interest.
b. To move your story forward.

How does a scene provide interest?

It pits your focal character against opposition. In so doing, it raises a question to intrigue your reader: Will this character win or won't he?

Exhibit A: Round X of a prize fight. Will Our Boy knock out the villain—or vice versa?

How does a scene move your story forward?

It changes your character's situation; and while change doesn't always constitute progress, progress always involves change.

Again, consider the prize fight: A hero knocked out is in a far different situation than he was at the beginning of the round.

Same if he knocks out the villain.

What unifies the scene, holds it together?

Time. You *live through* a scene, and there are no breaks in the flow of life. Once the bell rings, there's no surcease for the fighter. Until the bell rings again, he has to stand and take his lumps—moment by moment, blow by blow.

Scene structure is as simple as *a-b-c:*

a. Goal.
b. Conflict.
c. Disaster.

Just to see how this works, let's build a scene or two or three. Take our boxer. His goal is to knock out his opponent.

His opponent has a goal too: to knock *him* out.

Warily, they circle . . . feinting, punching, counterpunching. Conflict.

Now Our Boy lands a solid blow. His adversary lurches—staggers—goes down.

Our man steps back. Triumphantly, he sweeps the arena with his glance.

Only then, incredibly, in that tiny moment of distraction, the other fighter comes up from the canvas. He throws a wild hay-maker.

It connects. Our man falls.

Desperately, he tries to rally. But his muscles have turned to water. Numbly, he hears the referee count: ". . . eight . . . nine . . . ten!"

A knockout.

Disaster.

Goal . . . conflict . . . disaster. All the parts are there. It's a scene.

Let's try it again, with something not quite so neatly struc-tured.

Start with a character, any character—John Jones, say.

We zero in on John as he sits down beside cute Suzy Smith at the campus malt shop.

Why's John there? What does he want?

Enter *goal:* Ever and always, in scene, John *must* want some-thing.

In case classification systems intrigue you, "something" always falls into one of three categories:

(1) *Possession of* something . . . a girl, a job, a jewel; you name it.
(2) *Relief from* something . . . blackmail, domination, fear.
(3) *Revenge for* something . . . a slight, a loss, betrayal.

Here, this time, we'll be arbitrary: John wants Suzy.

But what does he propose to do about it?

Axiom: A goal is not a goal until it's specific and concrete and immediate enough for you to take some sort of action toward achieving it. The essence of goal choice is decision to act. *Your character's* decision.

Ideally, this decision should focus on a target so explicit that you might photograph your hero performing the act to which he aspires. If you can't, the goal isn't yet specific and concrete enough. "To win love," as a goal, is weak. "To get Letitia into bed"? Stronger!

Maybe John's goal at the malt shop is to persuade Suzy to go to the prom with him tomorrow night. There, helped along by a pale moon, soft music and spiked punch, he hopes to convince her that she should marry him.

Enter *conflict*.

Conflict is another name for opposition: a man trying to walk through a locked door. It's irresistible force meeting immovable object . . . two entities striving to attain mutually incompatible goals. For one to win, the other must lose.

Readers like conflict. It creates and heightens tensions in them, as we'll see later. Thus, it enables them to vent repressed feelings of aggression and hostility vicariously, without damage to themselves or others.

Back to John and Suzy: He wants her to go to the prom.

To that end, he gets together with her.

Conflict presupposes meeting. A fighter can't fight if his opponent doesn't show.

Then, he states his case.

Your reader needs to know what your hero proposes to attempt. Or at least that he proposes to attempt *something*. For if no attempt is made, how can there be struggle?

If Suzy is as eager for the date as John is, in turn, you have no conflict; no reader-intriguing, interest-provoking question of who wins and who loses; no scene.

So we make Suzy hesitate. It seems she's already tentatively agreed to go to the prom with George Garvey, the school's star halfback.

This means that John's going to have to fight if he's to get his way, achieve his goal.

If he takes no for an answer easily, we can assume one of two things:

(1) He didn't really want the date very much after all; or,
(2) He lacks the strength of character to fight for what he wants . . . hence is weak and ineffectual and why should anyone—least of all your reader—give a damn what happens to him?

But let's assume that John *is* strong, and *does* want the date and Suzy. So he fights, via anything from blandishments to persuasion to blackmail.

Finally Suzy agrees. O.K.?

No.

Why not?

Because we've made it too easy for John. The conflict is too limited, the scene too soon played out.

Maybe the two of them can debate at greater length?

No. The endless rehashing of a single issue soon grows dreary.

Is there a remedy?

Yes: Bring in additional external difficulties related to the situation. Offer new developments: more hindrances, more obstacles, more complications.

In a word, make it *harder* for your character to win his goal. Treat him rough. Throw roadblocks at him.

How can you do this?

Emphasize the strength of the opposition. Build up the forces that block John.

This is another way of saying, let John receive new and unanticipated information that makes his situation worse.

This information may be received verbally, or it may come visually, or via any of his other senses. Information is still information, even though you acquire it by opening a door and discovering your bride's stark, mutilated corpse; or by catching a scent of violets and thus learning that your husband still has contact with his mistress; or by noting the bitterness of your drink and realizing that Uncle Alph is trying to poison you again.

Like maybe, here, John successfully brushes off Suzy's date with George. Whereupon she brings up another matter:

"What about Cecile?"

John shifts uncomfortably. "Please, Suzy. You know that's all over."

"George doesn't think so."

It's a new tack, but John rallies to it: Who, he wants to know, is Suzy going to believe: him, or George?

Suzy shakes her head ruefully. "I'm sorry, John. But it isn't a question of *me* believing."

"What do you mean?"

"Just what I said. It isn't me; it's father."

"Your father! What about him?"

"He believes George."

Again, a twist: new information received; a new complication, new trouble.

"He's forbidden me to date you," Suzy confesses.

"What's that got to do with it? You're a big girl now!"

"Not that big."

More groping on John's part. More fumbling for an angle. "Suppose I can get him to change his mind?" he asks at last.

That would indeed solve the problem, Suzy agrees. And so it's settled: If John can persuade her father to O.K. the date, she'll go with John to the prom.

Do you see how much more meat this scene now holds, even telescoped as here? Thanks to new developments, new complications, action and interest continually rise. John, stimulated by the seeming progress of the opposition, puts forth renewed effort. And this in turn intensifies reader excitement over which side ultimately will win or lose.

Finally, as we've seen, he persuades Suzy. But even this victory has consequences projected into the future, for it commits him to changing her father's attitude . . . a chore which, viewed objectively, may prove to take a bit of doing.

For the moment, however, everything is sprigged with roses.

Enter *disaster*.

What is disaster?

Disaster is a hook.

What's a hook?

A hook is a device for catching, holding, sustaining, or pulling anything—in this case, a reader.

To this end, disaster (as we use the term) offers a logical yet unanticipated development that throws your focal character for a loss. It puts him behind the eight-ball but completely—"Sudden and extraordinary misfortune; a calamity," in the words of Mr. Webster.

Such a development upsets your reader as well as your hero. Instantly, it raises a new question to hold him fast on the tenterhooks of suspense: What oh what will the focal character do now?

Disaster comes in the form of *new information received*—like the unanticipated arrival of George Garvey at the malt shop, to illustrate the principle in terms of our example.

George is outraged to discover that John is attempting to beat his time. He swears that if Our Boy ever again so much as looks at Suzy, there'll be mayhem.

To emphasize his point, he throws John bodily from the shop. Time out for a few objections:

> (1) "But suppose my hero doesn't have a goal when the scene starts?"

Goals are of two kinds: goals of achievement, and goals of resistance. The first is explicit, as in our examples; the second, implicit.

Let's illustrate: This time, pretend that John already has his date with Suzy scheduled. She's agreed to it delightedly.

Enter George. He announces that he's taking over, and that he'll rend John limb from limb if there's any further talk of dating Suzy.

Observe: Though John had no goal when this action started, now, abruptly, he acquires one: to resist George.

In other words, the goal of achievement is George's; that of John, counterpoint.

So, John resists. George promptly turns to violence. The malt shop's proprietor threatens to call the police. Panicked, Suzy tells John to forget the prom.

John refuses. Whereupon—disaster. For George throws him out, precisely as in the original version.

> (2) "I want to write about life, not artificial, contrived conflicts."

Pardon me, but you *don't* want to write about life; not if you'd eschew conflict.

For again, what *is* conflict?

It's opposition. It's two forces striving to achieve mutually incompatible goals.

To describe conflicts as artificial or contrived is merely to damn yourself for your own ineptitude in the handling of them.

There's conflict in birth, and in life, and in death; in an ax murder and, equally, in the softly whispered words of a seduction. Conflict is in the plight of the refugee who seeks a path across a hostile border, and in that of the stepmother who strives to break through the sullen silence of her husband's children. It engulfs the old man thrust from his job by retirement rules, and the public-health nurse who tries to bring solace to the parents of a malformed child. Wherever you find him, man stands in conflict with other men, with nature, and with himself. He can clash with a mountain, an animal, a robot, a dollar, a germ, a neurosis, a theory. A touching scene can be built around the stubbornness of a drinking glass opposed to a child too retarded to feed himself, or a grain of sand wearing at a pump valve.

True, man against man, human opponents, are most easily handled while you're learning. But that only makes the challenge of less obvious struggles all the more intriguing.

You want to write about life? By all means.

But don't confuse life with mere word photography. It's not a cruise through the alimentary canal with gun and camera, nor the sterile, egocentric thought-spirals of the immobilized neurotic brooding over his plight.

Life *is* conflict. If you deny it, the scene indeed isn't for you. But neither is commercial fiction.

(3) "But must a scene always end in disaster?"

It must raise an intriguing question for the future—a question designed to keep your reader reading.

To that end, no better device has ever been conceived than the confrontation of your focal character with disaster. That's the reason the old movie serials always ended with a cliff-hanger—Pearl White tied to the railroad tracks and the five-fifteen roaring round the curve.

Once you've gained sufficient skill, however, you *can* make the disaster potential and not actual. Thus, George might not throw John out, literally. Maybe he just hints darkly at trouble to come, all the more menacing because it remains not quite specific.

Similarly, you can reverse the disaster, as it were. Instead of ending your scene on a down-beat note, with the focal character sucked into a bottomless whirlpool of trouble, you play the other side of the record and set him up to ride for a fall.

For example, you might let him launch some diabolically clever scheme to do in his foes.

This gives you some devastating question "hooks" to pull along
your audience: Are things *really* going to work out this well, this
easily, for Hero? Will Villain fall for such a stunt? Or, has he
some trick up his sleeve with which to turn the tables?

(I must add that though this "reversed disaster" system sounds
fine in the abstract, it's harder to make work than appears at
first glance.

For one thing, it takes the initiative away from your focal character and gives it to the opposition. This forces your hero to wait
more or less passively to see how said opposition is going to
react. And that's a dangerous situation, always, where you the
writer are concerned.)

In any event, you do have a choice as to how to end a scene.
So take whatever path you prefer, so long as you conclude with
your story pointed into the future: some issue raised that will
keep your reader turning pages, ever on the edge of his chair
as he wonders just what's going to happen now!

> (4) "The scenes you build are rude and crude—not at all
> the kind of thing I want to write."

Please, please, friend! Never confuse example with principle,
or demonstration with device. All the illustrations in this book are
painted in bright colors and splashed on with a barn brush. Subtlety too often defeats itself if you try to use it to make a point.

But that doesn't mean you can't apply principle in a subtle
manner. There, the issue is always *you:* the way you see your
world; the kind of story you want to tell.

Thus, your particular scene may involve neither fighting nor
young love. The pattern works just as effectively when you use
it to develop the plight of a fat, aging recluse as he tries to cir-
cumvent efforts to evict him. And you can write it on any level,
including stark understatement, or pathos, or drab tones of gray
and beige.

> (5) "Scene format as you describe it is rigid; mechanical."

May I plead guilty to oversimplification?
What I offer here is merely a beginning. It's a basic approach;
a springboard to help launch you into fiction.

Once you've mastered the elements of the form, experience and study of published copy will teach you how to vary it in terms of your own taste and judgment.

Remember just one thing: As a tool, the scene is designed to make the most of conflict. To that end, it organizes conflict elements. It telescopes them. It intensifies them.

Without such a tool, even your best material may come forth diffuse and devoid of impact.

(6) "But surely not everything in story is scene?"

True enough. What's left is sequel. —But more of that later.

        ❖ ❖ ❖

Where is scene planning most likely to break down?

Some thousands of student manuscripts convince me that key errors are relatively few in number:

(1) Orientation is muddled.

Your reader's got to know where he stands. That means he needs a character to serve as compass.

Therefore, even if your *story's* focal character isn't on stage in a given scene, that *scene* still must have a focal character.

Pick this character by whatever standard you choose; but *do* pick him! Then, hold him in the spotlight. See that motivating stimuli motivate and stimulate *him*. Make *him* react to them.

Whereupon, your reader can use him as a yardstick with which to measure and evaluate what happens.

(2) The focal character's goal is weak and/or diffuse.

That is, it's not sufficiently specific, concrete, and explicit.

The remedy?

(*a*) Keep the goal a short-range proposition.

Make it something that the focal character can logically strive to achieve in a relatively limited, time-unified, face-to-face encounter.

(*b*) Be ruthless in forcing yourself to reduce said goal to a single, photographable act.

A goal, remember, is the target your character shoots for in order to unify a particular scene. Therefore, keep it dominant —the center of attention, like the duck at which you aim as the flock passes overhead.

Other targets may present themselves to your character in the course of a scene; granted. —Here's a girl to flirt with him. There, a chance to pick up a sorely-needed dollar.

Temporarily, such may attract him. But you *must* hold them to a subordinate level or your scene will veer off like a car in a skid.

(3) The character himself is weak.

"Why doesn't he quit?" is the key phrase here. If enough is at stake for him, he'll fight!

(4) The scene lacks urgency.

What is urgency?
Time pressure.
That means, there must be some reason for John to act to attain his goal *right now*. Always, force him to take *immediate* action. If he can postpone his efforts without loss; if he can date Suzy as well next week or next month or next year, then urgency will vanish.

On the other hand, suppose that John learns that the day after the prom Suzy leaves on a European tour. It's a graduation present from her Aunt Hephzibah. George, a favored suitor, will accompany the party. John envisions a jet-speed romance between the two, complete with marriage at the nearest American consulate.

Result: time pressure on John to line up Suzy *now*. —Plus a feeling of urgency that won't stop, for your reader.

(5) The opposition is diffuse.

A swarm of anopheles mosquitoes can very well prove more dangerous than a Bengal tiger. But the big cat offers unified and obvious menace, and that's why a good many more people come down with malaria than are eaten by tigers.

It's also the reason why *unified* opposition is more useful in building reader interest than is fragmented opposition. Small, annoying oppositions wear out your focal character rather than overwhelming him. Like guerrilla fighters, they hack away at him without giving him a chance to join battle.

But heroism ordinarily lies in striking back. Your character needs some one central figure he can defeat and thus resolve his problem.

This is where a villain comes in handy. Broad social forces may, in the last analysis, be at the root of your hero's troubles. But it helps if you bring them to life in the person of one individual, if only so that John has someone to punch in the nose at the climax!

(6) The opposition is weak.

The strength of your villain is the strength of your story.

Writers who lack confidence in their focal characters sometimes try to solve the problem by making villains weak. Result: weak scenes. Remedy: stronger villains. Under stress, your hero may prove doughtier than you think!

(7) The scene is fragmentary or trivial.

Another name for this headache is *lack of adequate external development*. The fact that someone spills a drink on your hero's freshly-pressed pants doesn't offer meat enough to build a scene, unless further complications ensue.

(8) The scene is monotonous.

Same problem; same solution.

The key symptom here is a tendency on the part of your characters to go over and over the same ground, haggling and rehashing the same issues endlessly.

What to do about it?

(*a*) Throw in more external development.

Especially, throw in more unanticipated twists. If the wife insists on calling the telephone number she found in her husband's wallet, and which he insists he knows nothing about, let one of the wife's old flames answer. Then the happy couple at least will have something fresh to argue over!

(*b*) Give the characters themselves more diversity.

Extra facets and modifying traits will keep them from growing so dull and predictable.

(9) The disaster isn't disastrous enough.

Again, don't be afraid to give your hero trouble. The future should always hinge on each scene's outcome—that is, its disaster. It should have potentially disastrous consequences for your character.

If it lacks such, who cares about it?

(10) The disaster isn't indigenous to the scene.

A disaster should be unanticipated yet logical. That means, it should grow out of your materials. Every writer uses Acts of God now and then, in order to get his hero deeper into trouble. But as a general rule, it's wise to maintain some sort of relationship between your key story people and a scene's disaster.

Thus, rival George Garvey provides John's disaster in our sample scene. A belligerently drunken bum might have caused trouble just as well. But he'd have had little relationship to the story beyond mere complication; and readers draw more satisfaction from *motivated* action.

* * *

Does all this sound ever so complicated to you? It isn't; not really. Once you get the knack of manipulating your goal-conflict-disaster pattern deftly, you can lay out a scene on a three-by-five card and still have plenty of room left over to set down . . .

The sequel in skeleton

A sequel is a unit of transition that links two scenes, like the coupler between two railroad cars. It sets forth your focal character's reaction to the scene just completed, and provides him with motivation for the scene next to come.

What are the functions of sequel?

a. To translate disaster into goal.
b. To telescope reality.
c. To control tempo.

How does sequel translate disaster into goal?

It provides a bridge that gives your character—and your reader—a plausible reason for striking out in a particular direction that will bring Character into further conflict.

Exhibit A: The prize fight.

Recovering from his k.o., Hero faces the future. He's been licked. So, should he now retire from boxing . . . seek a rematch . . . attack his opponent again—this time, outside the ring? His possible courses of action are virtually infinite.

Yet only when he reaches a decision as to which road to take can your story logically proceed.

Why?

Because each road sets up a different goal. A decision to retire establishes one objective for our boxer: to find a job. Let him seek a rematch, and he's faced with a different problem: to persuade various powers that be that he's not a has-been. And so on.

Enter *sequel:* the decision-making area; the bridge from one scene to another.

A scene, remember, is a unit of conflict. Your reader reads it because he likes to live through a struggle with your character . . . battle opposition . . . find an answer to the implied question of who wins and who loses.

But sooner or later, every battle ends: on a hook, a question, a disaster.

Eagerly, then, your reader reads on. He seeks that happy moment when your story-forces once again come into conflict.

Here, you must be very, very wary. For conflict for conflict's sake isn't enough.

Why not?

Because it's meaningless.

That is, it bears no clear-cut cause-effect relationship to what's gone before. It's not the result of, or reaction to, preceding struggles. When a stranger "just happens" to slug your character in a barroom brawl, it's conflict without cause within the limits of your story. As such, it's also an evasion of the long-range issues.

This your reader won't accept. He demands that your character's efforts have meaning. They must be the consequence of prior development and the product of intelligence and direction. So, unless you've planted proper motivation, he'll resent it if your boxer, for no apparent reason, slugs a cop or stomps the arena doorman. Nor will he be satisfied, for that matter, if a gang of young hoodlums chooses this particular moment to pelt your vanquished warrior with rotten eggs, not even knowing/who he is.

In other words, your reader must have *logic* as well as interest . . . *plausibility* in addition to excitement.

Without such, the very tension Reader seeks is likely to be lost. Fiction is built on a suspension of disbelief. If your story people behave irrationally or without cause, normal discernment rises to shatter the illusion you're trying to create. Your reader insists that there be a *reason* for each new battle; that conflict be *motivated;* that it *make sense* for your character to strive toward a particular new goal.

This is where sequel comes in. Implicitly and/or explicitly, it reveals how your focal character chooses his new course of action. It reassures your reader that this is a sensible person, worthy of acceptance.

To that end, sequel traces Character's chain of logic; his pattern of rationalization.

Thus, sequel is *aftermath*—the state of affairs and state of mind that shapes your character's behavior *after* disaster has knocked him down.

How does sequel telescope reality?

Making a decision may take time.

It may demand movement.

Often, it calls for introduction of new material . . . undramatic material, even . . . to help your character decide.

Again, consider our boxer. Hours or days or weeks may pass before he can make up his mind as to precisely what he wants to do about his lost fight.

Presented in detail, such a time lapse will bog down your story.

Finally, Character decides to meet his opponent in Minneapolis: a transition in space. Yet the trip itself is unimportant. It's a mere means to the end of a return match.

Travel with Character mile by mile, and again your story will bog down.

Before Character can fight, he must attend to a host of undramatic details. There'll be meals to eat, nights to sleep, people to meet . . . plus endless hours of routine training.

Written in scene-type detail, all this will bring your yarn to a grinding halt.

You face a problem of proportion. Summary is essential.

Summary is what you get when you abstract or abridge. It's that part of a story in which the writer *says* that things are happening, or that they have happened. It's *telling*, not showing; or, at best, a combination of the two.

Summary telescopes reality. And this telescoping is sequel's second function.

How does sequel control tempo?

It lets you allocate space and emphasis to get the effect you want.

A story is a series of peaks and valleys; big moments and small.

It's *not* just a continuing climax.

To that end, you work for mood . . . select detail . . . capture the flavor of life. Through elaboration or excision, you thrust the peaks high, cut the valleys deep . . . hammer home the climactic moments without losing contact with the incidental.

Thus, where our boxer is concerned, we must give the big fight its full due as climax and milk it of every ounce of impact.

At the same time, however, in brief space, we must somehow convey the sense of time passing, and capture the grind and dreariness of the training routine.

In fact, we must *contrast* the peak of emotional intensity of the fight itself with the dragging hours that go before. It's essential to speed up here, slow down there . . . in brief, control the tempo.

* * *

What unifies sequel and holds it together?

Topic.

What is topic?

The subject of a discourse or any section of it.

What's the subject of sequel?

It's your character's reaction to his plight. It's preoccupation with the problem the preceding scene posed.

It says, in effect, "I've been defeated, humiliated, overwhelmed by a disaster. What do I do now?"

With that preoccupation riding him, Character works out an answer. Then he pinpoints it in a decision to attack a new goal.

Thus, sequel has a 1-2-3 structure:

(1) Reaction.
(2) Dilemma.
(3) Decision.

How does this work?

To demonstrate, let's build a sequel to follow the scene that starred our fighter.

The scene climaxed in a knockout—for Character, disaster.

Where does that leave our man? What's his state of affairs and state of mind?

His manager will have a role in this: "Sorry, kid; you've had it. Don't call me; I'll call you."

His girl too, maybe: "Sure, I love you, honey. But marry a punch-drunk pug—what's there in that for anybody?"

State of affairs often is revealed in the reaction of others to your character's disaster.

How about state of mind?

What would you expect? What's happened is enough to rouse fears in anyone: Is he really no good? Has he, indeed, had it?

Together, state of affairs and state of mind constitute the aftermath of disaster.

Out of it all, a question rises: What's Character to do now? Should he accept defeat? Find a new girl? Get a job hustling packing-cases in a warehouse?

Character broods about it numbly while the trainer strips off the gloves and cuts away the bandages. He goes on brooding while he showers and dresses. What happens doesn't matter, save insofar as it lends reality to the moment. The disaster is all that counts; the disaster, and your character's preoccupation with it.

Later, he walks the streets. There's a steak that somehow turns to ashes in his mouth, and drinks that burn but don't brighten.

That night he tosses, sleepless, on a lumpy mattress in a cheap hotel room.

This black despair—it may go on for days or weeks, or it may be over in a moment.

Or, perhaps, the thing he feels isn't despair, but fury, or relief, or grim determination. But whatever it is, it's reaction: *your character's reaction* to his very real, very personal disaster.

Then that too fades, pushed back at least a trifle by the need to face the future.

What should he do? That's the question.

It's also Character's *dilemma:* a situation involving choice between equally unsatisfactory alternatives.

Deftly or clumsily, blithely or bitterly, our man works out an answer. *Decision* emerges: He'll try to set up a rematch in Minneapolis.

It's a new goal. Our character's efforts to attain it will give rise to further conflict; another scene to catch and hold a reader.

Logically, plausibly, sequel has brought it into being.

Now let's try the pattern again . . . this time on our other scene, the one that featured John and George and Suzy.

Scene climax: disaster.

What's John's *reaction* to it?

Humiliation, of course. How would *you* like to be thrown out of the malt shop, right before the very eyes of the girl you're trying to impress?

So, John feels humiliation. Plus rage. Plus frustration. Plus half-a-dozen other mixed, unnamable emotions that add up almost to apoplexy.

Sensible enough, right? Understandable? Acceptable?

But what can he do about it? George is big and brawny and in star-halfback condition.

Besides, in her panic, Suzy has already backed down on going to the prom.

Enter *dilemma*.

So, John goes off to lick his wounded ego and to brood: Should he appeal to Suzy's father? To Suzy herself? To Aunt Hephzibah?

Ridiculous thoughts, all of them. Even John can see it. Yet he's got to do something—not only because he wants Suzy himself, but because he's convinced that George is interested in her for purely mercenary reasons.

Notice what this does for your reader:

First-off, he gets a chance to suffer and worry with and about John.

Second, he considers the possibilities that he himself might come up with. Seeing the weakness in each, he realizes that John can't take those roads.

Third, he sees there's a reason John can't quit.

In other words, here in the sequel we've introduced additional elements to logic and plausibility to hook your reader tighter to the story.

Perhaps we even add an *incident* or two, in which John asks friends for advice, to no avail.

(An incident is a sort of abortive scene, in which your character attempts to reach a goal. But he meets with no resistance, no conflict. When a boy seeks to kiss a girl who's equally eager to kiss him, you have an incident.)

Or maybe there are *happenings* along the way, in which John meets acquaintances. But because he's preoccupied with his problem, he fails to respond to their greetings.

(A happening brings people together. But it's non-dramatic, because no goal or conflict is involved.)

Both these sub-units are legitimate enough. In fact, they're desirable, insofar as they add touches of realism to your work. But since they lack conflict, they don't hold enough real interest to sustain attention for long.

So here stands John, balanced precariously on the horns of his dilemma. By now the whole situation seems so impossible to him that he begins to wonder if he was a fool to give up Cecile for Suzy in the first place.

Cecile—!

Suppose he were to take Cecile to the prom instead of Suzy! While she bears him no love, at this point, she still might be persuaded if he could put forth the right incentive. Mercenary little minx that she is, she might even agree to make a play for George; and if George responded, Suzy's eyes would indeed be opened!

It's a long shot, obviously . . . the kind of deal that very well might backfire. But under the circumstances, it's worth a try.

First step: Sell Cecile!

It is *decision* . . . a new goal for John to strive toward. And count on it, conflict will inevitably follow.

At least, it will if we make proper use of our scene pattern!

Reaction . . . dilemma . . . decision. All the parts are there. It's a sequel.

* * *

Sequel and scene: the search for a goal . . . then the struggle to attain it. These are fiction's two basic units.

To lay out a story, repeat the pattern to fill the desired length: scene . . . sequel . . . scene . . . sequel . . . scene . . . sequel. . . .

Can you begin with sequel?

Yes, of course. —More about this, though, when we get to the problems of the beginning.

These are basic tools. They work. Practice using them every chance you get. Goals, conflicts, disasters, reactions, dilemmas, decisions—you meet them a hundred times a day, in fragmentary form, whenever you come in contact with other people.

So, take advantage of those fragments. Build forward and/or backward from them, elaborating from chance remarks or observed details into complete scenes, complete sequels; even combinations.

My late colleague Professor Walter S. Campbell used to say that he began to sell as soon as he mastered scene format.

One of my former students echoes the sentiment. He's just seen his thirteenth book published.

So, is that all there is to fiction? Just learning to plan scenes and sequels?

Well, not quite. It also helps if you can *write* them!

Writing the scene

Whether you're aware of it or not, you've already acquired most of the technical tricks you need to write a scene. You picked them up in Chapter 3.

What are they?

- *a.* Orientation.
- *b.* Motivating stimulus.
- *c.* Character reaction.
- *d.* Pattern of emotion.
- *e.* —And all the other implications and side issues Chapter 3 set forth.

A scene is a struggle, a unit of conflict, remember. So you put it together like the fight in which our boxer was knocked out: The bell rings. Focal character and opponent come out of their corners, each determined to attain his private goal. And from there on, it's just a matter of motivation and reaction: for every move, a countermove; for every punch, a counterpunch . . . until one or the other goes down or the bell again rings.

The big thing to bear in mind is that a scene is unified by time. There aren't any breaks or lapses in it, any more than there are in living.

Consequently, you write in a series of interlocked M-R units, as continuous as water gushing from a faucet. Each motivating stimulus evokes an appropriate reaction from the focal character. Each character reaction triggers—or at least is followed by —a pertinent motivating stimulus. Unit hooks to unit in a fast-linking chain. State of affairs intermeshes with state of mind. Goal is established. Your character's efforts to attain it plunge him into conflict. He fights through a seesaw pattern of furtherance and hindrance, gain and loss, until—just when he thinks he's won—disaster suddenly overwhelms him.

If you do your job well, your reader lives through the battle with your story people.

And believe it or not, that's all there is to it! —Though the specific points that follow may also prove helpful, by steering you away from common pitfalls.

Herewith, three do's:

(1) *Do* establish time, place, circumstance, and viewpoint at the very start of each and every scene.

Confusion infuriates your reader. To avoid it, keep him properly informed.

Especially is this necessary where changes in situation are concerned: "The sky to the east was gray and the street lights had gone out before Greer left the apartment." "The Three Brothers was a squat adobe building, huddled in a wild crook of the hills half a mile beyond the town." "It was too dark to see the man who shook him awake." "The Murderer never knew quite when it was he made that final, awful, inevitable decision to kill."

(2) *Do* demonstrate quickly that some character has a scene goal.

The first half-page of a scene should make it clear that somebody has a goal.

To this end, let that somebody show purpose—preferably, urgent purpose. Make him *act* as if he had a goal . . . as if he were out to do something specific and important right now: "He clung to the shadows, studying the place for the space of a cigarette." "She came in the night, long after he'd given her up." "The lawyer called at nine-forty. He said he represented Daniel O'Connor, and that in the interests of justice, culture, and peace on earth, it was vital that he see me right away."

Ideally, make your character's goal clear-cut and explicit from the beginning: "Very coolly, very carefully, he raised the rifle and drew a bead on the back of Sortino's neck: one dead dictator, coming up." "Cox said, 'I want some facts, Heffner. All the facts about what happened on Calisto.'" "One thing was certain: Charlene was going to leave this house. Tonight. He'd see to that for sure." But if you have trouble pinning the goal down that tightly right at the start, the *impression* of purpose alone will carry the ball for a while.

Remember, too, that like everything else in fiction, a goal is better shown than told. The things your character does, a demonstration, will come through stronger than mere words.

Why make such a big thing of introducing goal so quickly?

(*a*) Interest rides with purpose.

The sooner you introduce the idea that somebody's traveling toward a given destination, the sooner your reader will become intrigued with wondering what will come of the journey.

(*b*) Goal often represents only the *start* of scene.

In other words, goal is primarily a springboard to plunge your character into conflict. Once he's caught up in such, the situation will change on him, likely as not. So the more quickly you establish goal, the more quickly you can move on to the meat of action and unanticipated development that your reader loves.

Thus, maybe your hero wants to punch the villain in the nose, or to obtain an answer to one pointed question. But bug-eyed monsters are waiting for him in the cellar, or the heroine has disappeared, or the houseboat on the Styx has sunk. By the time the disaster is reached, in fact, no one even remembers the initial goal. Yet that goal is still infinitely important, for without it the scene itself would have had no excuse for coming into being.

Must the goal always be that of your focal character?

Not necessarily. Perhaps his role, in this particular instance, is less to achieve than to resist. But try to avoid having him merely *acted upon* too much of the time. In most scenes, he should be the aggressor—active, dynamic, driving forward.

So much for scene goals. Whether they come forth on the printed page as implicit or explicit, all must be ever so sharp in your own thinking. Each should be epitomized into some single act so pertinent and urgent that a character could believably aspire to perform it—and so concrete and specific that you the writer could snap a picture of that performance!

(3) *Do* build to a curtain line.

Some scenes have punch and some don't.

The ones that do have been written so that the disaster comes suddenly and in unanticipated form—a shock, focused needle-sharp in a curtain line: "'Congratulations, Mr. Goss,' the alien said. 'With you, your race comes to an end.'" "But dead Wang's fingers still clung to a tuft of Clare Kennedy's shimmering auburn hair." "He shoved the white-hot iron between Will Evans' toes."

Now I grant you that this sort of thing can easily be overdone. Also that there are indeed a host of other factors that go to create punch. But when all the critical smirks have faded, and all the intellectual laughter has died down, ordinary readers will still be reading—avidly, enthusiastically—stories that cap off their scenes with curtain lines.

And now, three don'ts:

(1) *Don't* write too small.

There are those who'll tell you a scene can't be developed satisfactorily in less than four pages—a thousand words.

They just might be right, too.

Why?

(a) Because scenes constitute the most important portions of your story, and it takes space to impress your reader with the importance of anything.

(b) Because most of us *need* space, if we're to build to any kind of emotional peak.

(c) Because—in brief, fragmentary scenes—you're hard put to offer enough of the kind of color, characterization, conflict, complication, maneuvering, punch-and-counterpunch, and unanticipated development that it takes to hold reader interest.

Four pages, then?

No, let's not make it anything arbitrary or resembling a rule. But on the other hand, let's not try to put across a climax in a paragraph either! A John Collier can get away with it. The rest of us don't dare to write too small.

(2) *Don't* go into flashback.

Flashback is somebody remembering in the present what happened in the past. It brings your story, your present action, to a dead halt for the duration.

Now there's a place for this kind of thing, upon occasion. But that place is *not* within a scene.

Why not?

(a) It's essentially unrealistic.

Most of us, when we're in conflict, are far too involved with keeping our heads above water to indulge in any great amount of reverie.

(*b*) It strains reader patience badly.

When you write a story, you try to sweep your reader along with you on a rising wave of tension. Particularly is this true in those units of struggle we call scenes.

Go into flashback, and tension tends to drop to zero.

Why?

Because you've halted forward movement and present action, and your reader knows that what's already past just can't be changed.

Then, when you return to the present, you have to start building excitement again from scratch.

Are these grounds enough to warrant your keeping past history out of your scenes?

For my money, yes—especially since flashbacks fit more neatly into sequel anyhow.

(3) *Don't* accidentally summarize.

Actually, you do summarize even in scene, of course. The fact that your heroine absent-mindedly picks her nose in an embrace doesn't necessarily demand mention, nor is its exclusion missed.

On the other hand, there are certain slips that sneak into everyone's copy, at one time or another. They're dangerous. They jar readers. They crack or shatter story illusion.

No one can ever hope to make a complete list of such, of course. But here are a few samples of the kind of thing to watch out for:

(*a*) "He told her that—"

This is indirect discourse—a paraphrasing and summarizing of the actual words spoken. Run from it! What you want is speech— the genuine article, down to the last slur and contraction.

(*b*) "He hunted for the elevator without success."

That's what you tell me, anyhow. But I'd rather *see* what happened:

Definitely hurrying now, he loped down the corridor to the left.

Still no elevator. Not even a fire stairs . . .

. . . and so on. Step by step and blow by blow. After all, that's how your character lived it.

(c) "Time passed."

Then skip to where things start to happen.

(d) "They had a couple of drinks."

Why not

"Beer here," grunted Paul.
Laird considered for a moment. "Make mine rye and water," he said finally.

The thing to bear in mind is that nothing ever really comes alive in summary. Life is lived moment by moment, in Technicolor detail. To capture it on paper, you have to break behavior down into precise and pertinent fragments of motivation and response.

* * *

And that's enough instruction. If not too much. Once you understand the fundamentals, the way to learn to write scenes is to write scenes.

While you're practicing, though, you might like to consider a few thoughts on . . .

Writing the sequel

When you sit down to write a sequel, you're faced with problems in three major areas:

a. Compression.
b. Transition.
c. Credibility.

Consider your focal character. Time: post-disaster. He's lost his girl. His job's no more. The friend he trusted has betrayed him.

Now, he tries to decide what to do; how to readjust to his changed circumstances.

To that end, he must pace the floor and walk the streets and face the disdain of a dozen different people.

How do you squeeze it all into a paragraph or a page?

Similarly, a week may pass between the time he's struck down and the time he starts toward a new goal. In that week, he may travel from Milwaukee to Madagascar; from bruises to blooming health; from black gloom to wild elation.

How do you make the jump from time to time and place to place and state to state and mood to mood?

Disaster tends to paralyze a man. Beaten down, he finds it hard to rally. Yet only a few lines after the blow descends, story requirements demand that he charge into the fray anew, undaunted.

How do you make it believable?

You already know the answer to all three of these questions. Where time unifies the scene, *topic* unifies the sequel. In the process, it also gives you the essential tool you need to handle compression, transition, and credibility properly.

How does topic do this?

To be preoccupied with a topic is actually to be preoccupied with a particular set of feelings. If your girl runs out on you, in all likelihood you feel hurt and angry. If your boss fires you, you feel angry and panicky. If your friend betrays you, you feel grieved and confused.

Or, perhaps, your own feelings are different. That doesn't matter.

What does is that until you decide what to do about the situation, your feelings can't help but be the thing uppermost in your mind.

Therefore, in writing sequel, you act on the assumption that feeling is the common denominator that unites all other elements.

Then, you move from one such element to another across what might be termed an emotional bridge . . . subordinating facts; emphasizing feeling.

Take *compression*, for example. You skip or summarize the emotionally non-significant or non-pertinent, as pointed out in *The Problem of Proportion* in Chapter 3. If what's needed is a picture of Lisa, and the process of portraiture isn't itself devastatingly important, we very well might end up with some such abridgment as "Now the sketch took form. In a few deft lines, Lisa stood re-created there on paper."

Since few details can be included, when you're trying to keep wordage down, the selection of those you use becomes a matter of major concern. Frequently, the bit that serves you best is the *symbolic* fragment—the tear blinked back, the buffalo skull bleaching on the prairie, the bedbug crawling along a pillow. A whole frame of mind may be summed up in a mockingbird's song; a way of life in the fact that the plumbing has been stolen out of a vacant house.

The trick is to find the single feature that captures the essence of what you want to say. You need the lone item which, brought into close-up, speaks volumes about your character's state of mind.

Link enough such details into an impressionistic montage and there's virtually no limit as to how much ground you can make a sentence cover:

> Fog and smog and soot-streaked snow. Steaming summer nights in New Orleans; the parched miles going across Wyoming. He knew them all, in the months that followed; knew them, and ignored them, because there was no room in him for anything but hate.

Transition offers much the same situation. You need to bridge time or space or mood or circumstance or what have you.

To that end, you spotlight your focal character's dominant feeling: Is it depression? Rage? Passion? Fear?

Emphasize that feeling immediately *before* the lapse in time or space or action or whatever begins . . . and then again immediately *after* said lapse ends.

In other words, set up your material so that the chosen feeling is the element the "before" and "after" situations have in common.

Let's say, for instance, that the feeling is guilt. Our technical problem, in turn, is that we need to jump from Friday night in New York City to Monday morning in Tulsa.

> Sleep came quickly, easily, to his surprise.
> Only then he wished it hadn't, because it brought strange, dark, half-nightmares with it . . . weird dreams in which Irene somehow always stood beside him, mute, dark eyes accusing.
> The sense of guilt those images engendered still nagged at him when he deplaned in Tulsa Monday morning. . . .

Because feeling is the dominant factor in your story, it's also the most favored bridge. But you can, upon occasion, use well-nigh anything as a device—weather, for instance:

"I hate it when it drizzles on and on this way," she sighed. "I hope it clears before we leave."

But the rain was still coming down when Sid's car swung into the drive. . . .

Credibility? It's the element you need most when you set about translating disaster into goal.

To achieve it:

(1) Set your focal character against a backdrop of realistic detail.

Though he be dropped down on Arcturus, a hero needs to eat sometimes, and sleep, and perhaps even bathe.

All about him, too, life drifts along. People chat and haggle, love and laze, laugh, grumble, gamble.

For the sake of credibility, your reader needs to find these elements of the familiar in your story. High adventure is fine, but too much of it all at once smacks of the comic book, and it's nice occasionally to have relief from tension.

Such lulls are developed best in sequel: the transition between dramatic scenes.

(2) Push your focal character in the right direction.

You want your hero, defeated, to go after a job out of town. But if he leaves the moment the villain triumphs, your reader will sneer. So, you follow up the initial disaster by having Our Boy's boss fire him. His landlady tells him she's got to have his room for someone else. The P.T.A. protests that he's a bad influence on the young.

Now, if your character takes off the way you want him to—though vowing to return, of course—Reader will class it as understandable behavior.

Why?

Because you gave him proper motivation in the sequel.

(3) Let your reader see the focal character's chain of logic.

This is the reaction side of the motivation coin set up in (2), above. In large measure, it means simply that you give your character a chance to think things through. Because he's between scenes, he isn't under immediate attack; isn't locked in conflict. So, what with more time and solitude, it's plausible that he should here think as well as act. We might even drop into flashback with him . . . appraise those experiences in his past which influence his attitudes where the present and future are concerned.

* * *

Again, in sequel as in scene, you learn to write by writing. Get busy!

Integrating scene and sequel

Up to this point, we've treated scene and sequel almost as if they were separate entities. Actually, of course, they must complement each other . . . link together smoothly into that unified, cohesive whole that's known as story.

Are there any problems involved in thus melding the two together? What points should you bear in mind as you combine them?

Herewith, a few observations on the subject which it might pay you to consider:

a. You control story pacing by the way you proportion scene to sequel.

As a general rule, big scenes equal big interest.

Long sequels, in turn, tend to indicate strong plausibility.

So, in writing, you must decide which element is most important to you at each given point. Thud-and-blunder melodrama may jump from death threat to fist-fight to rape to ambush, virtually without sequel. It's all conflict; no transition.

Some of the more precious literary pieces, on the other hand, offer endless discussion of the protagonist's psychic turmoil as he tries to decide whether he should order ice cream tonight, or sherbet. The only hint of strife is a warming of his cheeks as he observes the waiter's raised eyebrow.

All of which gives us a few practical hints:

(1) If your story tends to drag or grow boring, strengthen and enlarge the scenes. Build up the conflict.

(2) If an air of improbability pervades your masterpiece, lengthen your sequels. Follow your character step by step, in detail, as he moves logically from disaster to decision.

Proportioning thus becomes a matter of individual taste. While extremes that amount to "all scene" or "all sequel" exist, most of us prefer to take the middle ground and strike some sort of balance.

b. Scenes dominate story development.

Any story, diagrammed, resembles a mountain range—a succession of peaks and valleys. You spotlight the peaks, the big dramatic moments, by presenting them as scenes.

(1) How big you build a scene depends to a considerable degree on its placement in the story.

An opening scene that features the fall of the Roman Empire may rock your reader back on his heels. But what do you do for an encore? Too large a dose of vitamins at any given point always carries with it the hazard that everything which follows will seem anticlimactic.

Consequently, it's good sense to arrange your scenes, your peaks, in order of ascending importance and/or intensity.

(2) You can control scene placement, to some degree, by manipulating sequel.

Partly, this means that you can expand or contract sequel so that scenes fall farther apart or closer together.

Partly, it means that a sequel frequently includes material which could just as well or better be developed as a scene. For example, here's an incident in which your hero stops to get gas. To build it into a scene, all you need to do is inject conflict: Maybe your guy irritates the attendant, who in turn releases his hostility by somehow "accidentally" immobilizing (disaster!) the car.

Partly, finally, it means that small scenes may be reduced to sequel. Instead of making Character have to pressure Doctor Jones in order to get in to see Marie at the hospital, you let the nurse on the ward admit him as a matter of routine.

c. Flexibility is all-important.

Each story offers different problems. A mechanical approach won't solve them. You *must* stand ready to adapt your methods to your materials.

Thus, officially, a sequel involves reaction, dilemma, and decision.

Yet if a man is drowning, do you need to state explicitly that he decides to try to keep his head above the surface? Or is it enough that he fights his way up from the depths . . . breaks water . . . flails, gasps, struggles?

It's that way, often, in sequel. If your character does something in a manner that indicates he's picked a goal, we assume it represents a decision, accept it, and let the rules go by the board.

In the same way, at first glance scene often seems to flow directly into sequel. Yet experience soon will teach you that often you build impact if you allow a time-break, great or small, after the scene-disaster's curtain line . . . as if your focal character were numbed by shock, perhaps.

Here, for instance, a hero gets the wrong answer:

"I've tried to tell you, Ed," she said. "I'm not going with you."

It was one of those moments—the kind that last and last and last. Then, when he finally found his voice, he discovered that he didn't have anything to say.

Pivoting, he strode down the walk, back to his car.

* * *

If you can write scene and sequel, you can write stories.

But you'll write them easier and better if you also understand the strategy of fiction: a most intriguing subject, in its way, and the topic of the chapter just ahead.

CHAPTER 5

Fiction Strategy

A story is a double-barreled attack upon your readers.

You want to write successful stories.

To that end, it will be a help if you first understand two things:

1. Why your reader reads.
2. The source of story satisfaction.

* * *

How do you define story?

You don't.

Why not?

Because it's impossible to arrive at any useful, meaningful, all-inclusive definition. Each person who reads and/or writes is different. Each defines story to fit his own tastes, his own prejudices. Tennyson's *Lady of the Lake* and Henry Miller's *Tropic of Capricorn* both have been termed stories. Same for assorted sketches, vignettes, anecdotes, word photography, chronicles, plays, folk tales, and what have you. The piece which Reader A likes and labels good is, to Reader B, distasteful and bad. "Strong" and "weak" mean different things to different people. So do "trite" and "fresh," "profound" and "shallow," "obscure" and "rich with hidden meanings."

Definition tries to reduce a host of objects or events or experiences to their lowest common denominator. It sucks out their life for the sake of a post-mortem on dead flesh and bare bones. Individual differences go by the board.

Such an approach is of little value to a writer. To bring a story into being, you need to think of it not as a *thing*, but as something you *do* to a specific reader—a motivation; a stimulus you thrust at him.

Your goal, in turn, is to elicit a particular reaction from this reader. You want to make him feel a certain way . . . suck him into a whirlpool of emotion.

To do this . . . to make your reader feel the way you want him to feel . . . is your story's whole and total *function*.

Now this can prove a tricky business. It demands skill. There are techniques to be learned, just as in figure skating or baking angel-food cake or playing the piano.

The aggregate of all these tricks and tools, these devices you use to help your story fulfill its function properly, may be said to constitute *process*.

Learn to work in terms of function and of process, and you're on the shortest, straightest road to success as a fiction writer.

The function of a story is to create a particular reaction in a given reader. Therefore, this might be a good point at which to consider audience briefly.

You use one kind of saw to cut wood, another to shape metal, a third to slice marble.

The same principle applies to readers. Don't try to be all things to all men. Universality of appeal is a myth. *Superman* and Marcel Proust seldom strike sparks in the same audience. So, accept difference, in literary preferences as in women's hairdos. Quit wasting your time pretending that it doesn't exist, or that there's some esoteric way around it.

Does this mean that you should consciously slant your story to a certain reader?

Yes. But not to *any* reader. The one you want is the one who shares your tastes and interests. For you, too, are individual. You can't change yourself at will to suit a given public. You must accept yourself the way you are. Then, seek out an audience that sees the world the same way you do.

Can you be sure such an audience exists?

You can. Individual you are indeed; and different. But not *that* different, for you're human also.

And then?

Master story dynamics.

How do you go about that?

You start with one simple statement: A story is the record of how somebody deals with danger.

Isn't that definition?

Of course. But it's more rule-of-thumb and statement of what happens than it is an all-inclusive formulation. I'll admit in advance that it won't satisfy every critic, every reader.

It applies more often than not, though, on a practical level. And it's flexible. Once you get hold of how to use it, you'll find you can adapt it to almost any taste, or type of story.

Even more important, it's the best possible place to start if you want to learn. . . .

Why your reader reads

Your reader reads fiction because it creates a pleasurable state of tension in him, line by line and page by page.

But don't analysts say that the thing that makes a story good is structure?

They're only half right. For as the late Raymond Chandler once observed, "The ideal mystery [is] one you would read if the end was missing."

Why would anyone read such a mystery?

Because it holds your attention as it unfolds. The climax is important, true; but not to the exclusion of that which goes before. Though the over-all pattern of a story may be ever so sound, the reader won't ever know it if he tosses the book or magazine aside in the middle of first page or first chapter.

This is the reason why a writer's approach to his story must be double-barreled. His reader must be captured and held by what's offered him *at this moment:* not the whole; not the ultimate pattern, but the present experience. Immediate and continuing involvement is what counts. Reader attention must be seized *right now.*

What seizes attention?

Tension. All attention is based on it.

Tension, to reiterate a few points made in Chapter 3, is a physiological phenomenon: **"tension** . . . Act of stretching, or tensing; state or degree of being strained to stiffness. Hence: **a** Mental strain; intensity of striving. **b** Nervous anxiety, with attendant muscular tenseness." (*Webster's Collegiate Dictionary,* Fifth Edition.)

When your muscles contract, you have tension.

Some tension is voluntary. More is involuntary.

The thing that creates involuntary tension, most often, is fear.

That is, you experience an unpleasant emotional reaction at the prospect that something will or won't happen: Your wife will say unkind things if you lose your job. Your friends will laugh at you if you freeze up in the middle of your high-school speech. You'll feel intensely alone and unhappy if your mother dies. Objectively, the issue may be ever so slight. No mad murderer threatening you with an ax is needed. It's *your feeling* alone that counts. For when you feel fear, it makes your muscles tighten up, and plunges you into a state of tension, mild or extreme or in between.

What creates fear?

Danger.

What is danger?

Change. When any given situation is altered, the result is a different situation. This new state of affairs may demand adjustment on your part. Such adjustment may be beyond your capacity, and thus may endanger your survival or happiness. Anything endangering survival or happiness creates fear.

Two factors are involved in this process:

a. Perception.
b. Experience.

Perception means merely that you must be aware a change is taking place.

Experience warns you that this particular change may expose you to injury, loss, pain, or other evil.

Must both exist, in order for you to experience fear and its concomitant, tension?

Yes. It's like the stories the newspapers carry every once in a while about a child caught blithely playing with a cobra, or the like. The child *perceives* the snake, but he lacks the *experience* to know that it is dangerous. Hence, the child feels no fear, no tension.

Or, *experience* tells you that guns are dangerous. But if you don't *perceive* that one is pointed at your head, your degree of tension remains unaltered.

But suppose both perception and experience exist?

Consider a party. You're introduced to several new people.

This is change. New elements have been brought into your sphere of awareness. But if the situation doesn't go any further, your tension increase will be relatively limited.

Suppose, however, that one of the strangers is a tall, dark, handsome man.

Now, enter experience: Your wife is a woman particularly susceptible to such men.

At once, your tension level rises. For whether you acknowledge it or not, fear has entered your life. Specifically, you're afraid that she'll involve herself in an affair with this particular man.

Or again: One of the strangers is a man you intensely desire to impress, in order to win a much-needed promotion. Result: a marked rise in your inner tension. It's based on your fear that somehow you'll fail to create as favorable an image as you wish to.

Or again: One of the girls makes a flip, somewhat slighting remark about your taste in ties. Embarrassment—fear that your taste is indeed inadequate—sends tension soaring in you, out of all proportion to the motivation you've received.

How does all this apply to story?

"We go to the theatre to worry," remarks the late Kenneth Macgowan in his *A Primer of Playwriting*. "Whether we see a tragedy, a serious drama, or a comedy, we enjoy it fully only if we are made to worry about the outcome of individual scenes and of the play as a whole."

That's why a story must deal with danger. No danger, no worry.

Why should we want to worry?

Because tension is vital to the survival of any species. It represents awareness, alertness, preparedness for action. It's readiness for fight or flight; the automatic reaction of each and every organism in the face of peril. Prod a tiger; he attacks. Prod a rabbit; he runs. Both leap from springboards of instinctive tension.

Take away that ability to react to threat with tension, and a hostile world overwhelms the victim.

Because tension has this survival value, mankind as a species has learned to enjoy it, in controlled amounts. So, to varying degrees, and in accordance with our individual tastes and metabolisms, we involve ourselves in situations which create tension in us. We play handball. We hunt big game. We get in fights. We seduce our neighbors' wives.

And, we read. Especially fiction.

Why fiction?

Experienced directly, tension-inducing situations can prove dangerous. *Physically* dangerous . . . dangerous on the level of reality. A handball game may rupture an aging heart. The hunted animal may turn hunter. A killing blow may end the fight. The neighbor may resort to firearms or a messy lawsuit.

So?

So, for most of us, tension achieved secondhand proves less hazardous and therefore more satisfactory than actual experience. That's why we go to football games and prize fights . . . listen by radio to astronauts' reports . . . gossip and follow disasters on TV newscasts and peruse the true-crime magazines and the confessions. We're ever avid in our search for other people's troubles. Sharing their peril gives us a kick.

Fiction, in turn, creates an especially vivid vicarious tension for us. It brings a character face to face with danger, so that he feels, or should feel, fear.

And then?

Fear is contagious. When you live through a properly written story with a character, his experiences and tensions become yours.

Your job as a writer is to control and manipulate this tension. To that end, and using your central character as a vehicle, you create it, intensify it, focus it needle-sharp, and then release it.

Through the character, your reader empathizes matching emotions, matching tensions.

A plot is merely your plan of action for thus manipulating tension. And the simplest formula is still that set down by old H. Bedford-Jones, king of the pulps, more than thirty years ago: "Get your hero in danger—and keep him in danger!"

In essence, the habitual reader is a tension addict. Tension is what he hopes to buy when he tosses down his quarter or half-dollar at the corner newsstand.

This is the reason that he spends his time and money on your story. This is why he reads.

The source of story satisfaction

What, specifically, is the source of story satisfaction?

A most intriguing question—even though you have to approach it just a bit obliquely in order to get a properly comprehensive answer.

Let's go:

A story is the record of how somebody deals with danger.

But in a story, danger isn't just danger in the abstract. It's a definite and immediate menace to a particular person.

Specifically, it's a threat to your focal character.

It's this fact which gives your story its form.

Exhibit A: Your focal character, blithely going about his business.

Enter danger.

Reacting, your focal character fights this peril until, eventually, he wins or loses.

The duration of the danger defines the limits of your story. Roughly speaking, we can say that the story begins when the situation plunges Character into jeopardy. It ends when he emerges from the shadow of said hazard.

Plot-wise, the *beginning* of your story *creates* tension.

The *middle* builds up and *intensifies* it.

The *end*, in turn, breaks down into two segments: *climax*, and *resolution.*

In *climax*, the tension you've created is *focused sharply.*

And, finally, *resolution* sees the tension *released,* in character and in reader.

Which brings us back to our original question: What, specifically, is the source of story satisfaction?

Answer: *Release* of tension.

All through the beginning and middle and climax of your story, the excitement of danger keeps your reader tense and eager, line by line and page by page.

But excitement doesn't constitute satisfaction. Maintain tension too long, or carry it too far, and it becomes as unpleasant as extended tickling. You begin to ache for it to end. You want to let go, give up . . . relax and rest awhile.

To trigger such release is the whole and total function of your story's resolution. It *pays off* your reader . . . rewards him with a sense of satisfaction and fulfillment for the strain of undergoing tension.

In other words, *the way your story turns out* is your reader's key source of satisfaction. A story is a fight. Danger is the focal character's opponent. So, Friend Reader wants to know what happens to your imperiled hero . . . who wins the battle, and how. Leave him hanging in suspense about it, and you throw him into the state of frustration of an avid ball fan dragged bodily from the park in the ninth inning, with the score tied, the bases loaded, and the world series hanging in the balance.

If the end of a story is "right," your reader's tension is released. He sinks back satisfied, relaxed, fulfilled.

If it isn't, he's left raw-nerved and jittery; on edge. At best, he feels let down and disappointed.

To make a story end "right," ask yourself one simple question: How does your hero defeat his danger?

The answer is always the same: *He demonstrates that he deserves to win.*

* * *

So much for the broad outlines. Now, let's look at the factors involved in a bit more detail.

Release of tension, it was noted above, is what gives your reader satisfaction.

So, what releases tension?

Fear creates tension. Dissipation of fear releases it. If you're afraid the boss plans to fire you, a raise or a promotion may improve your outlook. If you're dubious about your chances with a girl and she smiles at the right moment, that smile may change your mind. If the issue is ulcers, a few X rays might calm your nerves.

Do all dissipations of fear give the same degree of release; the same satisfaction?

No. Fear is a complex thing, and a matter of degree. You never can eliminate it completely. The promotion may create doubts in you as to your adequacy to the new job. The girl's encouragement may make you wonder, later, whether she encourages others also. The X rays can set you searching for another ailment to account for the pains you feel.

It's the same in story. Not all dissipations of fear give your reader the thing he seeks.

What does he seek?

He seeks security.

What constitutes security?

Safety. Freedom from danger or fear of danger.

What gives this sense of security to your reader?

The feeling that he controls his own destiny; that he's not a pawn of blind fate or a helpless victim of chance or a hostile universe.

It's the same for all of us, in life as in fiction. Infinitely small, pitifully weak, we face a world that's both frightening and overwhelming. So, a dozen times a day—a hundred; a thousand—we question our own adequacy: Can we really cut it in our pressure-laden private situation? Do we actually stand a chance to win happiness?

Constantly, we need encouragement and reassurance. We yearn for some small demonstration that it's worth our while to go on fighting.

If happenstance alone is what decides the issue, we know we're licked before we start. Luck's just not sure enough to tie to, and we've got experiences to prove it.

What we want, instead, is a setup where what *we* do has a bearing on outcome. We need to feel as if how a man behaves, his personal performance, helps to decide the way he fares in this life. We like the idea of individual worth and individual reward.

In practical terms, this means that a character's fear shouldn't be cleared away by accident or coincidence. Happy circumstance shouldn't solve his problems. Your reader gains no ultimate story satisfaction from a resolution in which lightning strikes the villain, or the convenient death of an Australian uncle ends the hero's financial crisis. He wants an outcome in which man *masters* fate. It's one of his deepest emotional needs.

To create this sense of control, this feeling of security, you must relate your story material to reality in such a manner as to help give life meaning to your readers, by reaffirming their wishful thinking and emotion-based convictions.

To that end, in each story you write, you establish a cause-effect relationship between your focal character's behavior and his fate; his deeds and his rewards.

Here's how:

a. You pit your character against danger.
b. You let him demonstrate whether he deserves to win or lose.
c. You fit the story's outcome to his behavior, in terms of poetic justice.

Thus, the beginning of a story hypothesizes:

(1) A state of affairs, present or projected, that symbolizes happiness to your hero.
(2) A danger that threatens his chances of achieving or maintaining that state of affairs.

It's helpful, at this point, to cast these two elements into the form of a *story question:* "Will Joe win Ellen despite the crippling of his arm?" "Will the Things from Space wipe out the human race and Our Hero with it?" "Can Suzy prevent her too-loving mother from spoiling the children?"

The *answer* to this question constitutes the resolution of your story, and grows out of your hero's demonstration of whether he deserves to win or lose.

How do you arrange for your hero to demonstrate this, in terms that make for reader satisfaction?

You focus his fight with danger down to a moral issue. At the climax, he acts on this issue; chooses which of two conflicting roads to take . . . which of two antithetical courses of action to pursue.

In what sense is the climactic issue moral?

One road's right; the other, wrong.

What constitutes "right"?

Unselfishness. Adherence to principle despite the temptation of self-interest.

And "wrong"?

Selfishness. Abandonment of conviction for the sake of personal advantage.

What's the deciding factor in your character's choice between these roads?

Emotion. His own subjective feelings. The kind of person he intrinsically is.

Isn't selfishness often more logical than unselfishness? Mightn't it be more sensible, more intelligent, for him to follow the wrong road?

Of course. But our object here is to test your character's character, not his intelligence; his instinctive reactions, not his logic.

Does this mean your hero should be unintelligent?

On the contrary. Further, he should use to the full every ounce of brain-power he possesses.

But moments come to all of us when thinking-through isn't enough. If a thick-headed clerk gives you too much change, you can accept it; or, you can call his attention to the error and give the money back. Crumpling someone's fender in a darkened parking lot, you can leave a note; or, you can merely drive away. Welcomed too well far from home by the wife of a good friend, you can take advantage of the opportunity; or, you can bow out.

When such times come, we must act—spontaneously, instinctively, on the basis of the things we believe, the way we feel, the kind of men we are. Principle and character are the issues.

How does all this bear on your reader? How does it help him to achieve the sense of security he seeks?

Because your reader lives through the story with the focal character, he shares the testing of that character. Instinctively, he knows that he himself isn't necessarily strong enough or intelligent enough or lucky enough always to be able to defeat danger. But no matter how weak or dull or ill-omened he may be, he tells himself that he *can* act on principle . . . do the thing he knows emotionally to be right, even though such a course seems destined to lead to sure disaster.

So?

So, you then resolve the story problem. If the character does right, you give him victory. You let him defeat his private danger.

In brief, you reward your character for his display of virtue.

Whereupon, fear dissipates. Tension ebbs. The character relaxes, safe and satisfied and happy . . . and, with him, your reader.

Even granting the validity of all this . . . isn't it a childish pattern, ill-suited to mature readers?

That depends on you: your skill as a writer. The pattern can be presented childishly, of a certain. Thousands of times it's been done crudely, on a comic-book level.

But it's also the configuration in *Oedipus* and *Crime and Punishment;* in *Of Human Bondage* and the Holy Bible. Skill and subtlety are the only issues.

But doesn't a writer falsify reality when he uses such a pattern? Isn't it pure hypocrisy to pretend that a cause-effect relationship exists between deed and reward, even in the confines of a story?

The answer here falls into two parts:

(1) To prove satisfying to a given reader, a story must necessarily reaffirm that reader's own philosophy of life.
(2) Historically, sociologically, and philosophically, a strong case can be made for the cause-effect pattern as it exists in life as well as fiction.

Where Point 1 is concerned, most American readers believe in the pattern here outlined; the cause-effect relationship set forth. It therefore is the most effective approach to a mass audience.

On the other hand, it obviously will offer no satisfaction whatever to the writer who wants to present a different philosophy of life.

All that means is that said writer should work out a pattern more in keeping with his beliefs and write his stories to it. It's done every day: witness some of the material occasionally published as novels or in magazines.

However, because any book has limitations as to length, I've chosen here to pass such by, in order to focus more fully on the form dominant in commercial fiction: the approach taken by most selling writers.

Point 2 warrants further immediate consideration. For most of us have an unfortunate habit of ignoring the doughnut in favor of the hole; of becoming so enamored of the exception as to overlook the rule.

A story shouldn't do so.

Actually, in this life, exceptions notwithstanding, most of us get about what we deserve.

This isn't any accident. All society is based on the principle of mutual aid. Precisely *because* he's so helpless and alone, man limits his selfishness, his pursuit of and preoccupation with self-interest, in order to enjoy the benefits to be gained from living at peace with his fellows. "Free enterprise" is held in check by fraud laws. Speed limits and stop signs restrict freedom of movement. Safety regulations control conditions of work. Police protection reduces the need for arming of the individual.

Nor are our controls merely external. Honesty, truthfulness, kindness, integrity, chastity, piety, courage, dignity, humility, sensitivity, honor—these are more than just words. They're inner standards, restrictions on self-interest and self-indulgence. People live by them.

Often, there's disagreement on just how far such limits—internal or external—should extend. The rules vary from time to time and place to place and culture to culture; and individual circumstances alter cases. But most men, most of the time, abide by them.

When they don't, the result is anarchy.

Because man acts on principle, sacrifices self-interest to the larger cause of his own standards, ordinarily he benefits.

The main reason, of course, is that our fellow men continually sit in judgment on us. Courage, moral or physical, attracts attention. The fact of known honesty opens avenues before us. Opportunity knocks on the door of the man devoted to duty. Kindness and hard work and loyalty are noted.

Contrariwise, the schemer, the sharp operator, the malcontent and the philanderer soon are labeled and appropriately dealt with.

Rewards of the spirit loom even larger than rewards of the letter. Though public ignominy may crucify the conscientious objector, he still can stand tall and proud if he's doing what he believes is right. Court-martialed, a Billy Mitchell remains a better man than his accusers, and he knows it.

What about the exceptions—those individuals who refuse to play by the rules?

(a) Relatively speaking, they're isolated and few in number.

The day they grow so numerous as to dominate the picture, the rules change—witness America's repeal of Prohibition. Or, the society itself collapses, as in the case of the Roman Empire.

(b) They do get caught.

Cheat in school, your ignorance later loses you a job. Cheat on the traffic laws, a tank truck becomes your funeral pyre. Cheat in a crap game, a perceptive soul with a switchblade perforates more than your ego.

(c) They live with guilt.

Hypertension and insomnia and ulcers are constant occupational hazards for them. Often they make psychotherapists wealthy. But even if they escape such, conscience still travels with them in most cases, and their triumphs all taste of bitter ashes.

In essence, life and fiction alike assume that ruthless self-interest takes the short view of any issue. The man without principle is in effect blood brother to the alcoholic whose perspective on life has narrowed to the problem of how to get just one more bottle, or the armed bandit so preoccupied with the seventy dollars in a cash register that he never stops to figure out what his hourly wage will be if he pays for the caper with a five-year prison sentence.

The implicit truth of all this is the bedrock upon which our society is erected. Fiction merely epitomizes it . . . telescopes and condenses the broad picture into capsule form so that it may more easily be digested by the average reader. As Raymond Chandler once observed in commenting on the fantastic aspects of the hard-boiled mystery, "Such things happened, but not so rapidly, nor to so close-knit a group of people, nor within so narrow a frame of logic. This was inevitable because the demand was for constant action; if you stopped to think you were lost."

✿   ✿   ✿

A good story provides your reader with Pleasurable Tension plus Ultimate Satisfaction. These are the fundamentals. This is what constitutes the double-barreled attack.

The carrying out of that attack, however, demands a bit more detail: detail about the most effective tricks for developing the beginning of your story, and also its middle and its end.

For a look at such, turn to the next chapter.

CHAPTER 6

Beginning, Middle, End

A story is movement through the eternal now, from past to future.

All stories are "about" the same thing: desire versus danger. Each concerns a focal character's attempt to attain or retain something in the face of trouble.

To translate this general principle into a specific piece of fiction, you need a grasp of five broad subjects:

1. How to line up story elements.
2. How to get a story started.
3. How to develop middle segments.
4. How to build a climax.
5. How to resolve story issues.

The first step in this direction is to get the basic outlines of your story clear in your own mind. A certain amount of organization is essential. Lack of direction and form can send you off into a trackless maze of false starts and blind alleys.

To avoid such confusion, there are worse tricks than to lay out your material in a *starting line-up*.

How to line up story elements

Five key elements go into every solid commercial story. The line-up arranges them in dynamic form, so that you can check their strength or weakness.

These are the five elements:

a. Character.

Without a focal character, you have no story. He brings it into being when, affected by and reacting to external events, he fights back against the danger that threatens him.

b. Situation.

No focal character exists in a vacuum. He operates against a backdrop of trouble that forces him to act. That backdrop, that external state of affairs, is your story situation.

c. Objective.

A focal character who has nothing he wants to attain or retain can't be endangered, and so has no place in any story. Whether he succeeds or fails is immaterial. He still must strive.

d. Opponent.

Dig a ditch, and you find that even the earth resists you. But obstacles personified in an opponent—who not only resists but fights back—make for more exciting reading.

e. Disaster.

Every story needs to build to a climax. So, you threaten your focal character with Something Unutterably Awful which he must face close to the end, just before you let him off the hook.

—And *do* try to make each item as specific and concrete as possible!

Next, these five elements are cast into two sentences.

—No more than two, either. Here we want black versus white, forces in conflict. The starker and sharper, the better. Extra words only blur the issue. Every writer needs the self-discipline of forcing himself to slash away verbiage and get down to essentials. Slickness and subtlety can come later.

So, we need two sentences, and two only.

Sentence 1 is a statement. It establishes character, situation, and objective.

Sentence 2 is a question. It nails down opponent and disaster.

How you put together this *olla-podrida* is unimportant. The big thing is to force yourself to do so! Any effective story *must* incorporate the materials of conflict if it's to prove effective. If you don't go through this ritual, or one similar, over and over again you'll kid yourself into thinking you have a story where none actually exists.

So, now, let's try out the pattern.

On a science-fiction story, for example:

Situation:	When humans suddenly begin to grow to twelve-foot height,	*Sentence 1*
Character:	John Storm	(Statement)
Objective:	tries to find out why.	
	But can he defeat	
Opponent:	the traitors in high places	
Disaster:	who want to kill him in order to make the change appear to be the result of an extraterrestrial plot?	*Sentence 2* (Question)

The issue in a story always is "Will this focal character defeat his opponent, overcome his private danger, and win happiness?" Your reader gets maximum tension release from the resolution if Sentence 2, the story question, is so framed that it can be answered with a clear-cut "yes" or "no."

A broader or less rigid approach ("How can Sam win Esmerelda back from Jacob?" "Why did old Mansford fire the swamp?") takes emphasis off the basic conflict and moves it over to a puzzle element. Such a curiosity angle is valuable as a component of your story—a twist, a complication, a sub-plot. But avoid it as a dominant, over-all story question. Though intellectually intriguing, perhaps, in most instances it proves less suspenseful to a mass audience than does the simpler, more obvious, "Will he win or won't he?" pattern.

This is because your reader reads first and foremost for *emotional* stimulation. He has no great desire to think. A story that hinges on analysis or logic—no matter how elementary—holds little appeal for him. He prefers to keep the cerebral factor subordinate. As a sub-plot or the like, it's there, pleasantly present if he happens to feel in the mood for it. But it's not so important that he can't skim over it without damaging the story's total impact if he wants, tonight, to read just for what he describes as "relaxation."

Use of the starting line-up approach in no wise limits your range. Here, for example, it's applied to a confession yarn:

Situation:	Lonely, frustrated, and tired of living in a home where she's treated as an unpaid servant,	*Sentence 1*
Character:	widowed Irene Boone	(Statement)
Objective:	wants to marry widower Frank Dawes.	
	Will she lose this chance for happiness because her selfish, sanctimonious	*Sentence 2* (Question)
Opponent:	daughter, Connie,	
Disaster:	accuses her of immorality?	

Or, here's the kind of story that might be developed on almost any level, from the lower-bracket men's magazines to a literary novel:

Situation:	Sick of the conformity and hypocrisy that go with his high-paid job, and with a modest life income assured,	
Character:	Dale Boulton	*Sentence 1*
Objective:	decides to retire ten years early, to go live on a shanty-boat and poke through crumbling river ghost-towns, in fulfillment of a boyhood dream.	(Statement)
	Can he make the break successfully, when	
Opponent:	his hostile wife, Sandra, fights him all the way and,	*Sentence 2* (Question)
Disaster:	finally, threatens to have him declared incompetent?	

And there you have the starting lineup . . . as useful a tool as you'll ever find.

One warning: This sort of device is an aid only. A semi-mechanical procedure, its purpose is to help keep you reminded of the dynamic elements in your story. And that's all.

Like any mechanical or semi-mechanical approach, it's anything but foolproof. In no sense will it substitute for thinking. Unless you adapt it to your own temperament—your own ideas and tastes and readers—it very well may do you far more harm than good.

Nor is it the only such way to go about things. Lester Dent's old Master Fiction Plot has served a similar function for many and many a writer. Others prefer the "Three O" system—Objective, Obstacle, Outcome. "Who wants to do what, and why can't he?" is a pattern-pregnant question that's started hundreds of Hollywood scripts down the road.

Whatever approach you take, you yourself remain the most vital factor. The fresh idea, the unique twist, the sudden insight into character, the enthusiasm that captures and excites your reader's imagination—these are yours and yours alone.

*　*　*

The concept of beginning, middle, and end spring from life itself: You're born, you live, you die.

At six, you enter school. For twelve long years you wrestle with friends and enemies and teachers and subjects. Then, you're graduated.

You take a job. You work it hard. You move on again to something better or worse.

You go to the races. There's a start and a run and a finish. A football game or a bullfight see conflict open and seesaw and close.

The sun rises. The daylight hours pass by. The sun sets.

These things you know. As corollaries, you know also that for the individual human being, whatever happens (1) has duration, and (2) is in a continuing state of flux, a process of development and change. Time forms a framework that puts limits on both your tragedies and your triumphs. Each situation coalesces, shapes and is shaped, dissipates.

So, though Advanced Thinkers proclaim the cosmos to be self-renewing and unending, you pay them little heed. You've too many immediate pressures to deal with, day by day.

Further, we like it that way. Both adventure and security go with delimitation. Show me the long view of my fate—or that of the human race, or Earth, for that matter—and likely I'll hang myself in the nearest corner. The immediate is better. There's hope and excitement in the prospect of a new town, a new job, a new girl. Release comes with completion, closure, the end of a day or a problem. The visitor who breaks in on the climax of your favorite TV show strikes sparks of irritation in you. The legend of the Wandering Jew is a frightening thing.

Within time's framework, for each of us, feeling reigns supreme. It doesn't matter how much you talk about objectivity or perspective. As a feeling unit, you still have to sweat out your mortal span minute by minute and hour by hour and day by day —every moment, with none skipped; and each one brings its own reaction. Does automation claim your job? Economists' reassurances have a hollow ring to this noon's empty belly. When your girl marries someone else, you feel the hurt *right now*, and what difference does it make to you that next year you'll find someone else less fickle? The man in grief is closer kin to the child whose balloon has burst than he is to theologian or philosopher.

Fiction may not too awkwardly be defined as life on paper. It, too, flies the flag of feeling and takes the short-term point of view. It, too, ranges through a world in which the moment is what counts, and life and the events that make up life have a beginning and a middle and an end.

"I want a story to have form," W. Somerset Maugham has said, "and I don't see how you can give it that unless you can bring it to a conclusion that leaves no legitimate room for questioning. But even if you could bring yourself to leave the reader up in the air, you don't want to leave yourself up in the air with him."

How do you bring yourself and your reader back to the ground? Well, let's start from . . .

How to get a story under way

The function of your story's beginning is to let your reader know there's going to be a fight . . . and that it's the *kind* of fight that will interest him.

To that end, beginning spotlights three things: desire, danger, decision. Someone wants to attain or retain something. Something else threatens his chances of so doing. He decides to fight the threat.

The thing Character wants, the danger that threatens fulfillment of this desire, and the decision he makes, determine what specific readers will enjoy the story. One likes sex and violence, another tenderness and love, another the competitive striving for success, another intellectual stimulation. Relatively few college professors are Tarzan fans—and even fewer sharecroppers succumb to *Finnegans Wake*. The trick, for the writer, is merely to pinpoint audience taste . . . then to refrain from attempting to inflict his copy on the wrong people.

The problems of beginning break down into six categories:

  a. Where to open.
  b. How to open.
  c. What to put in.
  d. What to leave out.
  e. How to introduce needed information.
  f. When to close.

Let's take these one at a time:

  a. Where to open.

You can start a story in any way and at any point and, regrettably, I've read the manuscripts that prove it. But that doesn't mean that some beginnings aren't better (read: "more effective") than others.

Thus, you can open on a landscape or a fist fight, a still life or weather talk, or a close-up of a character or an object. Or on any of a thousand other angles.

Confession editors sometimes say, "Start on the day that's different." A Hollywood axiom recommends, "Start with an arrival." Pulp writers used to advocate starting with a fight. A general rule, across the board, has been that you should start with trouble.

So, where *should* you start?

Which immediately brings up another question: What do you *need*, to start a story?

You need change.

"Start on the day that's different"? Something made it that way—a *change* from someone's accustomed routine; what had been.

"Start with an arrival"? An arrival is injection of a new element into a situation; therefore, a change.

"Start with a fight"? Some deviation from the *status quo* caused that fight to explode at this particular time and place.

"Start with trouble"? Trouble is only a name for what happens when new developments can't be fitted into an existing pattern.

So, change is the thing you need to start a story.

Next question: How do you build the beginning of a story around change?

You need four things:

(1) An existing situation.
(2) A change in that situation.
(3) An affected character.
(4) Consequences.

These four items are listed here only as *ingredients* of the beginning, you understand; necessary elements; components. No order of presentation is implied.

Now, what's there to say about each one?

By the *existing situation*, we mean the state of affairs in which your focal character functions.

In a suburban home on a quiet weekday morning, that state of affairs may be placid. On a battlefield, it may be violent. At a high-level business conference, every word may crackle with tension. Along a shady creek-bank, the mood may be one of peace and relaxation.

But whatever the situation, your focal character accepts it. It follows an anticipated routine.

Enter *change*.

Change is some new element or relationship injected into the existing state of affairs. Something happens that makes the original situation different. Perhaps the temperature drops, or the sun comes up, or a stranger enters, or a girl says yes.

In the quiet household, change may be a leaky pipe or a visiting neighbor or a backfiring truck that wakes the baby. On the battlefield, it may be a machine gun that jams, or a sniper's bullet that kills the squad leader, or an enemy rush that cuts off a unit.

—Not that changes necessarily appear to be disastrous. Good news—new information received on anything from health to weather—may upset a situation every bit as much as bad.

So: Change impinges on an existing situation.

And someone is affected by it.

This *affected character* is one whose state of mind is somehow altered by the modification in state of affairs.

This, of course, presupposes that the character has a state of mind to alter. That is, he can't be a blank when you introduce him. His behavior must reveal already-existing attitudes, principles, prejudices, direction.

So, faced with a change in his state of affairs, this character reacts in characteristic fashion.

Nor does it matter whether his actions are warranted, objectively, by the facts of what has happened. How he interprets those facts—how he *feels* about them, subjectively—is what counts. For if you rob a grocery store tonight, and tomorrow morning a squad car pulls up in front of your rooming house, you very well may jump to and act on the conclusion that you're about to be arrested—even though, in actuality, the officers have stopped merely to investigate a smoking trash pile.

In the same way, loss of one friend may spell loneliness to a man, even though he moves through a crowd of others. Many a woman sees tragedy and old age in the first slight creeping of her skin. Named West Coast manager, an executive quits because he thinks he rated a home-office job.

Situation, change, character. Three essential ingredients down; one more to go.

Consequences.

That one can spell the difference between success and failure when you start a story.

Situation: A bright, brisk winter day.
Change: Wind—icy, biting, out of the north.
Character: A pedestrian.

Sweeping down, wind stings pedestrian. He shivers . . . turns up his collar . . . hugs his coat tighter about him . . . hurries on home.

And that's all.

Same way, a girl runs a red light. A cop stops her. The girl smiles. The cop tears up the ticket. The girl drives off.

No aftermath. By tomorrow the incident is forgotten.

An old woman lives for her son's rare visits. He comes. She berates him for his neglect. He ignores her and goes away again.

The state of affairs is back where it began.

To start a story, a change must prove the trigger for continuing consequences.

That is, it must set off a chain reaction. Responding to change, your character must do something that brings unanticipated results. He must light a fire he can't put out.

Thus, regardless of your story's original situation, or the initial change, sooner or later—and preferably sooner—the affected character must find himself in an intolerable state of affairs.

What's intolerable?

Anything is intolerable which endangers a person's chances of attaining or retaining something subjectively important to him.

Or, to put it even more simply, it's anything he finds too upsetting to ignore.

If you like to walk, and arthritis begins to stiffen up your feet, it's a painful annoyance.

If your livelihood depends on walking—that's intolerable. Win or lose, you'll fight against it any way you can.

A wife contemptuous of you is an affront to your pride.

One who backs her contempt with demands for a divorce and property settlement that will leave you penniless is intolerable.

The lazy, insolent, disobedient child may be frustrating and infuriating. The one who sets fires every chance he gets forces you to do something about him.

Existing situation plus change plus affected character plus consequences equal desire plus danger.

Desire plus danger plus decision opens any story.

Decision is a factor we'll take up later. For now, just remember that the stronger your character's desire and the stronger the danger that threatens it, the stronger your opening.

If the intolerable element can be personified—given life in an active opponent—that's even better.

* * *

So much for the ingredients you mix into your story's beginning.

And that brings us back to the place we started: Where do you open?

Each story constitutes a new and unique problem. No one ever knows for sure just which spot is the best from which to start. Given identical material, no two writers would begin at precisely the same point.

But in general—?

There's an old rule-of-thumb that you should open just before the trouble starts . . . or just as the trouble starts . . . or just after the trouble's started.

Let's modify that a bit . . . substituting *change* for *trouble*.

Change is what creates your story. So, start as close to change as possible.

More specifically, start *just before* the change impinges . . . *just as* it takes place . . . or *just after*.

Thus, if a tornado is what precipitates your story, you might open with generalized concern about the weather this particular morning . . . or with the tornado sweeping down . . . or with your focal character bleakly surveying the shattered wreckage of his farmstead.

If a beautiful blonde is to be slain, we could begin with her alive and in characteristic action . . . or reeling back with a shriek before the killer's onslaught . . . or lying in alley or park or boudoir, stiff and stark and dead.

—And just in case I make "change" and "trouble" seem too close to synonymous in the examples above, note that the pattern works just as well on two miners striking it rich: Opening

1 shows them on the verge of giving up . . . Opening 2 lets sand swirl from one's pan to reveal a dozen nuggets . . . Opening 3 finds the miners by their fire that night, gloating over their triumph.

Which of these approaches is best for your particular story?

That's your decision, and no one else can make it for you. However, certain points are worth consideration:

    (1) Open too far ahead of your initial change, and you may bore your reader.

This doesn't mean that you can't zero in first on existing situation. But today's readers tend to be impatient. You either hook them fast or not at all. Film people say that in Europe you can start a picture with half-a-dozen cloud shots, just to set the right mood. But in the United States, your audience begins to shift in its collective seat on shot 2, and shot 3 had better have a bomber hurtling through the overcast unless you want to play to an empty house.

Similarly, in fiction, a beginning that opens with a half-page description of the old family manor will probably kill you dead, dead, dead.

    (2) Open on the change itself, and your reader may feel he's hanging suspended in a vacuum.

To evaluate any phenomenon, you need perspective. A change that comes out of nowhere, unrelated to any background or existing situation, may lose most of its impact. The blow struck by a thug in a barroom brawl has different implications—and touches a different reader interest level—than the punch thrown by a preacher.

    (3) Open after the change has taken place, and you may find yourself forced to sandwich in a lumpy mass of explanation later.

"I dropped to one knee and fired twice," wrote Carroll John Daly, beginning one of his Race Williams stories in *Black Mask* many years ago. Although this is the very first line, obviously the change in state of affairs that precipitates the yarn has already taken place, offstage, and Williams is reacting to it.

This kind of fast take-off is fine, if you're as deft at it as Daly was. But many a new writer, tackling it, has difficulty incorporating a smooth explanation of precisely how the whole business started.

So there you are. Every opening has its problems, and you yourself must choose between them.

And if you choose wrong?

Well, so what? You won't be the first or the last man to learn the hard way, from his own mistakes!

b. How to open.

In terms of actual presentation, a good first paragraph is one that persuades your reader to read the second.

To this end, you should write Paragraph 1 in such a manner that it piques your reader's curiosity.

To rouse curiosity in anyone, raise a question in his mind. Specifically, make him wonder, "Hey, what's this leading up to?"

How do you do this?

You present your material in terms which indicate that you *are* leading up to something.

This demands that you state and/or imply:

(1) Uniqueness.
(2) The unanticipated.
(3) Deviation from routine.
(4) A change about to take place.
(5) Inordinate attention to the commonplace.

Classification of approaches in this manner is as an aid to clarity only. In practice, the degree of overlap between categories is great, and there's no point to trying to keep them separate.

(1) Uniqueness.

To be unique is to be without a like or equal.

To call attention to uniqueness is to make your reader wonder what you're leading up to.

The job can be done obviously: "She was the only artificial woman in the world."

Or, subtly: "He couldn't sleep that night." (*That* is the key word. It implies that most nights he *can* sleep . . . but something different about this one prevents him from so doing.)

Or, on a variety of levels in between: "It was a different sort of a town." "The contrast between the two girls was what he noticed." "'It's this week or never,' Susan said."

(2) The unanticipated.

If the beautiful blonde turns out to have multifaceted insectile eyes, or the book on Grandma's parlor table is illustrated with luridly pornographic pictures, or the hero starts out the story by proclaiming himself a damned fool—it's unanticipated. Intrigued, readers read on, to find out what's behind it all.

(3) Deviation from routine.

Instead of getting off the elevator at her usual floor this morning, Eunice rides two stops higher, then walks back down.

Mr. Hersey approaches the front door of his home . . . gets out his key . . . pauses . . . walks back down the steps . . . goes around the house to the back door and enters there.

Mrs. Grimes, professional sourpuss, sails gaily down the corridor, radiating sweetness and light upon everyone she meets.

Again, readers wonder why.

(4) A change about to take place.

If a man's lawyer calls and asks him to drop by, your reader assumes that something's in the wind.

Same when a boy winks at a girl in a bar, under the very eyes of her burly escort.

Or if somebody hears the hoofbeats of a galloping horse, coming closer and closer down the road.

(5) Inordinate attention to the commonplace.

Describe a doorknob in tremendous, painstaking detail, and a reader will figure there must be a reason for giving it such unusual attention. He'll read on to find out what that reason is.

A grandmother's gnarled hands, the shabbiness of a run-down house, a little girl peering out from behind her bubble gum—portray them with special care and they'll hook readers.

* * *

Needless to say, these aren't the only ways to begin. Start with a still life. Describe it skillfully enough and your reader, knowing that it can't stay still forever, will assume a change must be impending. Mirror routine activity, and he'll conclude that something will happen soon to break the routine. Show purposeful activity, and he'll be prepared for it to create or collide with opposition.

In the same way, you can begin on either motivating stimulus or character reaction; on the search for a goal or on the struggle to attain it. You can start with the big picture and move to the small, in the manner of the motion picture's familiar long-shot, medium-shot, close-up pattern. Or, you can reverse the process . . . begin with the close-up, the significant detail, and then pull back to view the broader frame of reference that is the detail's setting.

As a matter of fact, you have a certain amount of leeway in your first paragraph and on your first page.

Why?

Because your reader wants so badly to be entertained. Therefore, he *assumes* that sooner or later what he reads will relate to something satisfying and exciting—desire, danger, a character fighting for fulfillment and future happiness.

The place where story openings go wrong is when a writer rides this reader assumption too hard.

That is, Writer takes it for granted that Reader will suffer drabness and ineptitude indefinitely. So, he plods through his first page or two or three, laying groundwork and that's all. He doesn't work for interest. The vivid noun, the active verb, the colorful phrase, the intriguing detail, the clever twist, the deft contrast—these aren't for him.

Above all, he doesn't plan his presentation to make his reader curious as to what those first few crucial lines are leading up to.

And that's literary suicide.

It's not enough, in an opening, just to set the stage or to introduce the characters or to have something happening. What hooks your reader isn't the present, but the future. He wants to be reassured that something worth reading about is *going* to happen—and he wants that reassurance *now*.

So, give him what he wants. Show him that your story deals with something special—something outside the framework of routine and day-to-day anticipations.

Show him now. Right from the start. The next line, the next paragraph, the next page may be too late!

c. What to put in.

To begin a story, you must create a story world.

You start with your reader's mind a blank. Then, a step at a time, you lift him away from reality and transport him into the imaginary land you have conceived.

To travel thus into the story world, your reader instinctively asks three questions:

(1) Where am I?
(2) What's up?
(3) Whose skin am I in?

Your job in beginning your story is to provide answers to these questions. —Though not necessarily in any particular order.

How do you present this information to your reader most effectively?

You pinpoint the significant.

What's significant?

That incident or detail is significant which epitomizes and/or symbolizes and/or captures the essence of whatever aspect of the story world you're attempting to communicate. Describe a girl as a "dizzy blonde," and you tag her far beyond mere appearance. Fairly or unfairly, her hair symbolizes her as a particular type of woman. In calling attention to it, you give it weight as a detail which holds significance, and your reader will so use it in evaluating her.

In the same way, a "Charles Addams sort of house," for many, conjures up a mood of the macabre. It epitomizes feeling in the image of a gloomy, decaying, mansard-roofed Victorian mansion.

Connotations of sensitivity and taste seldom are implied when you refer to a man as "bull-necked." A Modigliani print on the wall establishes one tone for a room; a needlepoint sampler, another. If cockroaches are crawling over greasy, egg-smeared dishes in the sink, a still different note is struck.

This process of symbolization by significant detail isn't unique to fiction. You find it every day in routine living also, whenever you use a picture that already hangs in someone's mind as a sign or reference point to help label an unfamiliar object. A handy adaptation of the principle of association, it draws upon comparison, similarity, contrast, analogy, and the like. It forms the basis for the stereotyping which, while frequently unjust and/or unwarranted, is also ever so convenient.

What if no obviously symbolic detail is immediately at hand? Create one.

That is, spotlight some phenomenon—anything at all. Then, let a character react to it. The interpretation he places on it, the conclusions he draws from it, will at once endow it with "significance," where your reader is concerned.

Thus, bring a rain spot on the ceiling into focus as a significant detail, and it may in all seriousness be viewed as symbolic of (a) recent bad weather, (b) a leaky roof, (c) a poverty-stricken family's pride, (d) a proud family's deterioration, (e) a chink in the villain's armor, (f) the heroine's vulnerability, (g) a stain on honor, (h) aristocracy's feet of clay, (i) proof that trouble is a common denominator which touches rich and poor alike; and so on, to and past infinity.

In other words, you blow up any fragment in any situation to a close-up so big it fills the screen. Then, you have someone state or imply that it's important to and indicative of a particular frame of reference. Whereupon—count on it—your readers will go along.

And if you think this is a ridiculous exaggeration, pause for a few minutes this evening to glance over your favorite manual of Freudian dream interpretation.

Extend this same process of creating significance by association and conditioning to a sort of running gag, an emotional doorbell, and it gives you a handy device for establishing and re-establishing mood with minimum wordage.

Thus, let your hero note and feel as blithe, at one point, as the mockingbird's song he overhears. Your public then will be delighted when, later, you use a sour note from the bird's midnight serenade to reflect Hero's conviction that life is doing him

dirt. Does the heroine shut him out? The bird's song now sounds
sad. Does the villain fall in the horse trough? The bird lets go
with a cadenza similar to a razzberry. And so on.

Carried far enough and used with sufficient skill, this reiteration of emotionalized detail becomes what's sometimes called a
gimmick—one of the most useful devices for resolving your story.
But more of that later. Right now, let's consider briefly how best
to help your reader answer the first of his three questions about
the story world.

(1) Where am I?

Your reader needs to know your story's locale: It won't do to
have him think he's on the seacoast when he's really in the
slums. Does the action take place in a barroom, a ballroom, a
bedroom, a barn? Is it midday, midnight, dusk, or dawn? He
must know!

You need to convey this information to him early—the sooner,
the better. Otherwise, he may make false assumptions that
throw him for a loss later.

But no matter how important this information may be, you
don't dare indulge in long-winded explanations or descriptions.
Such take up too much space and bore your readers.

So, what do you do?

You use the significant detail, of course. Which is to say, you
pluck a symbolic fragment or two or three from the setting. By
describing them in such terms as to provide an implicit or explicit interpretation, you give your reader the impression you
want him to have. Are the grounds neat? Then say that the
flower beds appear to have been aligned with a micrometer and
the grass mown both ways before a trimming with manicure
scissors. It will draw a sharper picture than several paragraphs
of more generalized detail. Sawdust on the floor of a bar says
more about it than any cataloguing of the bottles on the shelf.
Squalor can occupy pages of description, or you may just observe that the shanty's walls had cracks so wide you could throw
a cat through them.

There's more to establishing locale than this, of course. But
it's a start, and the fine points will wait a few pages, till we
can take time out to discuss the technique of exposition.

For now, let's move on to Question Number 2:

(2) What's up?

As pointed out above, your beginning must establish time and place; a locale.

It also must set forth a situation—an existing state of affairs; the way things stand as your story starts.

Situation breaks down into two components:

(a) What's going on?
(b) Who's involved?

Let's begin with . . .

(a) What's going on?

One of the hardest things a writer has to learn is that "What's going on?" means precisely that—"What's happening *right now?*" —*Not*, "What *has* gone on?" or "What's the background and/or past history of the present action?"

How do you thus communicate present action?

You *show* what happens.

You show it *as* it happens, moment by moment, in strict chronological order.

The sense of this at once becomes apparent if you stop to realize that the present is the only thing you *can* show. The past is already gone. Your only link to it is memory. The future waits in the wings, not yet on stage. It may be set forth only as conjecture or imaginings.

Here's a sentence:

"The ancient wagon had been wallowing heavily across the prairie all day now."

O.K.?

No. "Had been" instantly tells us that we're dealing with past action. And while the past certainly has a place in many stories, that place isn't in the beginning.

How better to handle it?

"Sagging under its load, the ancient wagon wallowed heavily across the prairie."

Present action. A word picture of the here-and-now.

If there's sound, let's hear it:

". . . rattling and creaking and groaning."

Is odor a factor?

"The air, despite the dust, held also a paradoxical steaminess of wilting vegetation."

Heat?

"Even the tough, low-growing buffalo grass seemed to shrink from the blazing rays of the morning sun, high now and climbing higher."

How about a change in the situation?

"Ahead, far in the distance, smoke rose—a slender, wispy plume."

What happens when we put all these together?

Sagging under its load, the ancient wagon wallowed heavily across the prairie, rattling and creaking and groaning. The air, despite the dust, held also a paradoxical steaminess of wilting vegetation. Even the tough, low-growing buffalo grass seemed to shrink from the blazing rays of the morning sun, high now and climbing higher.

Ahead, far in the distance, smoke rose—a slender, wispy plume.

And so it goes. With manipulation of language and selection of detail, you capture a state of affairs on paper. No matter what fragment you need to introduce, you call it to your reader's attention as an immediate stimulus, a present action.

Won't you ever deviate?

Of course you will, a thousand times. But when you do go into past or future at the beginning of a story, it should be a matter of conscious and intentional technique, designed to create a predetermined effect and to solve a specific, clearly thought out problem. It should *not* represent mere clumsiness and lack of insight.

Most of the time, you'll get best results if you make it a habit to stick with the here-and-now approach.

❋ ❋ ❋

Beyond "What's going on?" lie other implicit questions: "What *should* be going on?" "What else do you need to establish a proper story world?"

Answer: Conflict. Desire plus danger.

How do you establish conflict?

You face somebody with opposition.

—At which point, 999 would-be writers cry out, "But how can you establish conflict without telling past history? How can you have a fight without a background?"

Our answer here goes back to our original point: Show what happens as it happens, moment by moment, in strict chronological order. You don't have to know what's gone before in order to see somebody slug somebody else. Explanations can come later. All you need is a man or woman with a goal—a he or a she or an it going someplace.

Then, bump this being into opposition, and you're in business.

Obviously, such a clash should have some bearing on or relationship to the central issue of your story. But all that takes is a bit of planning. The important thing is to find a striking, self-explanatory scene, so that you can establish the element of struggle and, through it, hook your readers early.

In this connection, what's sometimes termed a *bone of contention* or *weenie* may help you to demonstrate that something's at issue, even though for the moment your reader doesn't understand how come.

Thus:

> The paper clip lay on the desk between them. It was an old clip—discolored, somewhat bent, with a couple of small rust spots visible upon it.
>
> Idly, Olivas reached for it.
>
> In a voice dangerously gentle, Sheehan said, "Touch it, you son of a bitch, and I'll cut your throat."
>
> Olivas' hand stopped.

You see? Itself unimportant, perhaps, the paper clip is a symbol of the relationship between these men. Their reaction to it and to each other bring a host of elements into focus—the state of mind of each; their caliber and potential; all sorts of things.

So, whether the paper clip itself is intrinsically of worth or consequence or not—and it quite possibly may be—it serves here primarily as a bone of contention between these two. Objectifying an issue, it creates conflict in a striking, self-explanatory scene. And your story gets under way.

(*b*) Who's involved?

Ever and always, your story deals with people. The beginning is the place where you introduce them to your reader.

To introduce any given character effectively, you must first of all bring him on *in character*.

That is, the character must behave like the kind of person he is. Otherwise, how can your reader know what to expect of him? That's why, in a less sophisticated period, the villain so often kicked a dog in Chapter 1, or the hero saved a child from a bully.

Today, we smile at such obviousness. But the principle is still sound, when used with even a modicum of taste and judgment.

To bring a character on in character demands three things:

/1/ The character must have character.

To say that someone "has character" means that you know where he stands. He's for or against something. He exhibits desire, direction.

The same idea applies to your story people. A successful character is more than just warm meat. He's a living, breathing human being, with all the drives and ambitions and attitudes and prejudices of such. A drab nonentity who blends into the woodwork simply isn't strong enough.

To interest your reader in a character, therefore; to make him care about someone, pro or con, you must give him some definite something to which to react. The character must exhibit traits designed to arouse emotion. He must be for or against things, in word or deed, about which your reader too feels strongly. You may not like a man who drinks too much, or beats his wife, or picks his teeth in public. But at least he gives you cause for your attitude.

So, too, do you judge the man who gambles his life on his faith that he can climb a dangerous mountain . . . or who refuses to lie despite his employer's threats . . . or who stays with his wife—or a woman not his wife—in the face of community scorn and condemnation.

/2/ The first time he appears, the character must perform some act that characterizes him.

Character can't be demonstrated save in action. What others say about you may be merely reputation. Your own self-description can range from delusion to plain-out lie. But when you act—ah, then the cards are down and we see the stuff you're really made of!

For this reason, you as a writer should devise incidents that will force your story people to reveal early—or at least hint at—their true natures, *in action*. Each must display, and thus establish, that aspect of himself which is of top importance to the story. Is your man a thief? Show him stealing. A scholar? Let him abandon the party for the library. Ambitious? Have him maneuver a chance to impress someone who can help him.

Note, please, how this implies that one trait, one aspect of personality, stands dominant in each character.

Play it precisely that way. Human patterns are infinitely complex, granted. But a story focuses on a crisis in someone's life. Under crisis conditions, a single trait frequently *does* dominate. If you don't think so, try sometime to persuade a teen-age girl to break away from the behavior patterns of her group, or a fat-and-fiftyish male to stick with a diet.

Thus, while each of us possesses a host of attitudes and traits, not all get equal emphasis at a given moment. Today, passion may drive me to the exclusion of all else. Tomorrow, it may turn to disgust; or, under the pressure of a change of circumstance, be moderated or overshadowed by a desire for security or fame or intellectual achievement.

For the duration of your story, then, let one trait stay dominant in each character. Keep Tom honest, Dick cruel, Harry stupid.

—Which is not to say that you shouldn't modify the picture upon occasion. Perhaps Tom is greedy as well as upright. Cruel Dick, on the side, is a doting father. And though Harry can't count past ten with his shoes on, he's a wizard where motors are concerned.

Such divergences, such contrasts, such apparent contradictions—in large part, a story's sense of reality springs from them.

But *do* keep one trait in the spotlight. For the moment your reader grows confused because emphasis is too evenly divided —(Is Tom primarily honest or primarily greedy?)—you've lost him.

/3/ The characterizing act must be both pertinent and characteristic.

This simply means that you should match characterizing act to role. If your story demands a man whose dominant trait is courage, with all other aspects of personality ignored, then for heaven's sake don't show him at the start behaving in a manner that places prime emphasis on how kindly he is.

In the same way, and for the same reason, try not to present a character in a characterizing act that's non-typical of him. Don't bring on a sourpuss in one of his rare moments of congeniality, for example. Your reader will, justifiably, resent it, when he later discovers that the guy ordinarily goes round biting babies.

*　*　*

So much for dynamics. On the "how-to" side of introducing characters, there are three main points to remember:

/1/ Introduce characters realistically.

That is, give an impression of the person first—"a cute little chick with red hair," "a shambling, slab-like man," "a shadowy little woman in a big feathered hat that would always be remembered long after she herself was forgotten."

Why handle it this way?

Because that's the way most of us see people. We pay no heed to details until person and/or detail become important to us.

Apply the same idea when you write.

Your handiest tool in capturing a first impression is our old friend the significant detail. Center your description on whatever sticks out like a sore thumb, the way a cartoonist does when he caricatures a prominent person. The big ears, the buck teeth, the potbelly, the turned-up nose—these are the handy tags to tie to. Further, failure to note such at the start will breed all sorts of trouble for you later, when your reader discovers that the girl he assumed was pretty and petite actually is tall, sallow, and overweight.

Many characters—the minor ones—will need no more than the most obvious, abbreviated kind of label. The others you can build as you go, salting in more detail and description as it's required.

On the other hand, there *is* one situation that warrants more than impressionistic detail to begin with. That's when another character is for some reason eager to appraise the person to be introduced. Exhibit A: Mama, as she glimpses Sonny's bride-to-be for the first time. But even here, a little restraint ordinarily is desirable.

/2/ Bring your characters on in action.

The day when readers would hold still for a long-winded, static description of a character, complete with family tree, is long gone. Now, they want him alive, breathing, doing something—preferably, something interesting.

So, figure out some business for your boy or girl, as if you were a theatrical director blocking out a play. And prepare your reader for each impending entrance, whether by a knock at the door or a sudden awareness of the scent of lilacs or the sound of running feet. Do *not* just let someone pop out of nowhere. A menace, especially, loses half its punch for Friend Reader if he's not aware that something unpleasant is about to happen.

/3/ Don't bring on too many people at once.

Here I have no choice but to contradict flatly all the hallowed advice you've read about the need to introduce all your characters in a hurry. True, it's good to get them on stage early. But it's even more to the point that no one will remember or give a hoot about them if they're presented as a mere jumble of names and/or faces. A vivid entrance that hooks your reader's interest is infinitely more vital.

(3) Whose skin am I in?

To begin a story, traditionally, you must first establish time, place, circumstance, and viewpoint.

Time, place, and circumstance we've already dealt with. Now, what about viewpoint?

Viewpoint is the spot from which you see a story. It's the position and perspective you occupy in order best to savor a fictional experience.

Ordinarily, that vantage point is inside somebody's skin.

That is, your reader will live through your story as some specific character experiences it. He'll see and hear and smell and taste and touch and think and feel precisely what that person sees and hears and smells and what have you.

And he'll see, etc., nothing which that character doesn't. No looking through walls. No second-guessing motives. No sneaking around inside somebody else's brain.

Maybe this puts Friend Reader inside the focal character, the center of attention. Or perhaps he'll be another major participant in the action.

Or, he may be a minor player—an observer, a bystander, a sideliner.

Or, he may be the author, or even (though not so commonly these days) God.

Or, if your story's long enough, you conceivably will introduce several different viewpoints—major, minor, author-objective, or what have you.

How do you establish viewpoint at the beginning of your story?

The trick is simple: As early as possible, you let your reader know that he's looking at the story world through a particular person's eyes . . . living the story, as it were, inside that person's skin.

Like this:

Smiling greasily, Quintus Kerr spread his cards on the table. "Three aces, Mr. Devereaux," he observed.

Mr. Devereaux eyed the cards bleakly. Why was it, he wondered, that he so often seemed to run afoul of cutthroats and connivers?

Here, viewpoint—specifically, Mr. Devereaux's viewpoint—is established the moment we introduce that word *wondered*. The only way you can know that someone is wondering—or thinking, or feeling, or aching, or what have you—is to be inside his skin, living and experiencing with him. It's an effective device, and one that does the job in a hurry.

But suppose we played it a different way:

> Smiling greasily, Quintus Kerr spread his cards on the table. "Three aces, Mr. Devereaux," he observed.
> Mr. Devereaux's eyes flicked to the pasteboards. His lips seemed to draw a trifle thinner. "I see them."
> "Well, then . . ." Beaming now, Kerr reached for the pot.

Here, we see externals only . . . what's done, what's said. And precisely *because* nothing's revealed which would place us inside either character's mind or skin, your reader realizes that you're making like some sort of literary motion-picture camera equipped for sound. Viewpoint: author-objective.

Author-objective it will stay, too, until you move into the heart or brain of some particular person. —Or, you can write the entire story on an objective level, if that appeals to your taste.

Thus it goes. One way or another, viewpoint is established. Your reader, in his turn, makes appropriate assumptions as to where he stands . . . considers the events that transpire in properly objective or subjective fashion.

In the process he also becomes aware, to a greater or lesser degree, of each character's traits and attitudes and state of mind. But that's a subject that calls for greater detail later.

Meanwhile, it's enough that your reader's found a skin to be in!

* * *

Where am I? What's up? Whose skin am I in? Those are the questions your reader asks when he begins a story.

In answering him, bear in mind two do's and two don'ts:

(*a*) *Do* prepare your reader for what's ahead.

The habit of planting and pointing is one of the easiest yet most effective ways to strengthen your story.

(*b*) *Don't* give bum steers.

A wrong assumption infuriates your reader. Help him to guess right by careful planting.

(c) *Do* establish in action.

This is just another way of saying, "Don't tell it; show it!" Wherever possible, translate information into people doing things.

(d) *Don't* get too eager.

Try to crowd in too much too fast, and you're on a sure short cut to disaster.

d. What to leave out.

The thing to leave out of the beginning of your story is past history.

Why?

Because your reader's interest centers on the future, not the past. He wants to know what *will happen* as desire struggles against danger; not what *did happen* that led to the present conflict. Fans pay a lot more for prize-fight tickets than they do for reminiscence.

The reason for this is as ridiculously simple as it is often overlooked: *Nothing can change the past.* It's over; done. So, what suspense can it possibly hold?

Your story's beginning thus should stick to present action . . . what's happening right now.

What's happening, in turn, should center on desire colliding head-on with danger . . . the conflict of irresistible force with immovable object, as it were.

How about the background of this conflict? Must it forever be forgotten?

On the contrary. Background can add insight to present problems . . . provide motivation for future action. Quite possibly it's of major importance to your story. You need merely to be careful as to where and how you bring it in.

Ways to present it? Try these:

(1) Flashback.

Flashback is someone remembering in the present what happened in the past.

There's one key point to remember where flashback is concerned: Don't open with it!

In the early stages of a story, you see, interest often is a fragile and tenuous thing. Though your reader is in search of entertainment, he's by no means sure that he'll find precisely what he wants in your particular story.

Bore him with flashback, past history, even briefly, and likely as not he'll turn to someone else's yarn.

Once his interest is aroused, however, it's entirely possible that he'll ache to acquire the self-same data he'd have spurned a page or two or three before.

So, do try to open on a striking, self-explanatory scene. Hold the flashback for later, after the end of the beginning (a subject with which we'll deal shortly), when the story question is established and Reader firmly hooked. If a girl's going to slap a boy's face, and he in his turn then will knock her down, let me *see* the bit first, *before* you explain the background of their quarrel. Believe me, the delay will make me an infinitely better listener!

(2) Discussion of past action.

Such discussion is flashback verbalized. Don't put it at the beginning either.

Also, and no matter where in your story you present it, don't let it drag out and become a bore.

To avoid such, use these three tricks:

(a) Figure out a way to show the event itself, instead of having people talk about it.

(b) Reduce the *content* of the comments, by consolidating two or three events into one, limiting the number of points to be made, and the like.

(c) Reduce the *length* of the comments, by making the speakers talk with normal succinctness, instead of with that phony fulsome quality that marks speech for the convenience of the author. —More about this, too, later, when we get to the technique of exposition.

(3) Summary of past action.

This amounts to flashback in the author's words.

Two solutions:

(*a*) Translate history into action.
(*b*) Quit thinking your reader needs to know as much background to read your story as you need to know to write it.

* * *

Is there anything else you shouldn't put into your opening? Yes: too much.

For example, too many characters, too detailed a setting, too involved a setting situation—the list could go on forever.

Clutter and confusion are mortal enemies of good fiction. The thing to strive for is the clean, sharp, simple line.

To that end, you need to devote some attention to . . .

e. Techniques of exposition.

What is exposition?

Exposition is whatever your reader needs to know about what happened in the past, in order better to appreciate what's going to happen in the future.

Your worst foe here is a literary plague called author convenience.

Author convenience is what makes a writer have a character say, "Father, is your sister Lucille, whose husband Gregory died last August and left her penniless, coming to visit us?"

Is this a normal question for anyone to ask his father?

Of course it isn't. But a less-than-inspired writer could think of no more intelligent way to get the facts of past action before his reader.

This is the same writer who insists on telling us how the heroine's twin sister was born with a horn-shaped birthmark because a bull chased their mother across the pasture while she was *enceinte*.

He also has the villain's accomplice explain the villain's proposed plot against the hero to the villain. Nor is it any problem for Hero to acquire this same data, since the villain's mistress is happy to volunteer it to him.

Further discussion reveals that the killer is a dangerous man with a knife. And Author, in ever-so-convenient asides, remarks that a minor character is a diabetic, and that the hero is still very much emotionally involved with the villain's sister.

Need I say more? This obviously is *not* the right way to present background information!

To write successful exposition, motivate your reader to *want* to know the past.

That means: Make the past important to him.

Which is to say, make the facts to be presented important to your story—and to the people in your story.

Then, set said facts forth in a manner that allows your characters to appear as normal, intelligent human beings, and not cretins.

Techniques which may help you to achieve this worthy end include the following:

(1) Cut to the bone the amount of information you give your reader.

Is all the data as to what caused that horn-shaped birthmark really necessary?

(2) Break up the essential content.

Instead of shoving a half-page of past history at me in a lump, like soggy, dripping laundry, maybe you could plant the pasture in one spot, as part of the setting; the bull in another, as a continuing menace; sister's birthmark in a third, with a sex-tinted situation to carry it, and so on.

(3) Make someone need the information.

You motivate reader attention when you set someone in search of *needed* information. But your reader recognizes that the villain already knows the details of his own plot, so any scene that involves his accomplice telling him about it automatically rings as phony as a lead nickel.

(4) Make that "someone" have to fight to learn what he needs to know.

If I want you to Tell All and you don't want to, conflict and story interest are in the making.

On the other hand, if the villain's mistress starts to volunteer information, Hero and Reader likely will head for the nearest exit . . . much the way you do when Auntie decides the time has come to share all the details of her latest operation with you.

(5) Tie information to action.

Tell me a given man is dangerous with a knife, and I may or not believe you. Let me see him carve somebody up, and my hair stands on end with no resort at all to conscious logic.

I may even grow willing to listen to a few lurid details about the guy's past history!

(6) Motivate some character to pay attention to anything you want your reader to notice.

You establish a character's diabetes—a vital plot issue, perhaps—more vividly if you let him give himself a shot of insulin in another character's presence. Whereupon, Character Number 2 is appropriately motivated to ask if your diabetic is on heroin, and an explanation of the facts becomes in order.

(7) Present your data subjectively, in most instances.

If the hero is emotionally involved with anyone, your reader rates the *inside* dope. Let him experience the pain or passion or yearning in viewpoint . . . not hear about it through the writer, secondhand.

(8) Above all, let no one talk about anything he wouldn't normally discuss.

There's a thing in this world called reticence. It prevents some women from discussing the clinical details of their sex lives; some men from talking about their dreams or failures; some children and adolescents from opening up to adults; some older people from dwelling too much verbally on death.

All of us feel a certain reticence, at one time or another, to some degree or another, on some subject or another.

Consider reticence, next time, when in the name of exposition you're tempted to endow a character with an unduly loose lip.

Intelligence also must be considered. Just because you need a particular fragment of data doesn't mean that you can legitimately wring inane observations from an otherwise sharp character and have your readers accept it.

❊   ❊   ❊

In fact, intelligence is an element you might very well apply to the whole cotton-pickin' business of techniques of exposition.

f. The end of the beginning.

Desire plus danger give you a beginning for any story.

But what determines where the beginning of your story ends?

This is anything but an academic question. A beginning that drags on too long inevitably costs you readers.

Not to mention sales.

Yet that drag, that fumbling, is totally unnecessary. One simple rule eliminates it.

So, again: What determines where the beginning of your story ends?

Decision.

As early as possible, make your focal character commit himself. Let him decide to fight the danger that threatens his desire, instead of stalling or backing off or running from it.

The moment he so decides, by word or deed, your beginning is over. Your story has begun.

Why?

A story is the record of how somebody deals with danger.

Until your focal character makes up his mind to fight the danger, rather than to run from it, you have no story.

The thing that hooks your reader, in the opening, is *curiosity*.

The thing that holds him the rest of the way, straight through to the final paragraph, is *suspense*.

Curiosity is the element, on page one, that makes your reader wonder: What's this leading up to?

So, what *is* it leading up to?

The fact that there's going to be a fight.

What's the fight about?

It concerns your character's efforts to achieve a goal—to attain or retain something in the face of danger.

Enter the story question: Will your focal character win, or won't he?

Enter suspense also.

Suspense is reaction. It's a feeling your story develops in a reader. You compound it of hope plus fear—the fear that something will or won't happen.

To have suspense, you must have uncertainty of outcome.

That's where your story question comes in. As noted earlier, it's always the same: Will St. George succeed in slaying the dragon—or won't he?

Will Sam beat Ed's time with Suzy—or won't he?

Will Joe convince Mr. Rice he's the man for the job—or won't he?

Will the sergeant make it through the enemy lines—or won't he?

Will Ellen get her husband off the bottle—or won't she?

The key ingredient each time is doubt; uncertainty of outcome.

That doubt, that uncertainty, is what ties your reader to your story.

In other words, you open your story with curiosity-arousing devices, designed to establish (1) that your focal character has a goal, and (2) that this goal is somehow threatened.

After which, suspense takes over: Does your focal character win or lose; achieve his goal or miss it?

The issue is the moment of commitment. True suspense comes only when you establish the story question. And the story question moves into focus only when your character, desiring, looks danger full in the face and then takes up the challenge that the situation offers.

Implicitly or explicitly, he must say, "I'll fight!" before your story can begin.

As soon as he says it, the beginning automatically ends, and we move into the story proper . . . the body of the central conflict.

This is the moment when your reader adds suspense-involvement to mere interest. Until now, there's always been the chance that Sam will let Ed have Suzy without a struggle; that Joe will shuffle dully away to a job on the section gang when Mr. Rice turns him down; that the sergeant will surrender; that Ellen, despairing, will join her husband in alcohol's embrace.

With commitment, however, your focal character takes his stand beside the feudist who cries, "I'll die before I'll run!" Talk's done. Hesitation's over. Now, his decision's made. And whether that decision is intelligent or foolish, he has no choice, in your reader's eyes, but to fish or cut bait.

Whereupon, instinctively, said reader grips book or magazine a little tighter and frames his private version of the story question: "Will this guy win—or won't he?"

* * *

I can't overemphasize how important this matter of commitment is. An amazing number of potentially good stories bog down just because the central character refuses to come to grips with the issues. Consequently, Character himself seems passive, the beginning gives an effect of dragging on forever, and the reader is denied all possibility of the vital "Will-he-or-won't-he?" involvement that glues him to the story.

So: *Do* let your hero decide to fight!

Closely related to this is the matter of peripheral versus main-line action in beginning a story . . . starting with an immediately intriguing side issue instead of attacking the central problem.

It should be obvious by now, I trust, that you have wide latitude in selecting the curiosity-bait to hook your reader. But if you choose a side issue on which to open, you need to bear in mind that you *must* establish a clear and perceptible relationship between this peripheral material and your main story issue. Starting with an introductory scene in which your focal character dallies with a seductive blonde will only prove infuriating to your reader, if said blonde plays no vital role in the body of your story.

In the same way, your hero's decision to commit himself *must* center squarely on the core of the story, rather than something extraneous.

Thus, in order to get a mystery off the ground fast, you might begin with the murder of your focal character's sister. He promptly commits himself to avenge her.

Later, however, it develops that his wife is suspect, and the rest of the story centers on his efforts to clear her.

Result: a confused, diffuse, unsatisfactory story. If the vengeance motif is to dominate, then it should dominate all the way. If wife-clearing is the issue, then set up your situation so your hero commits himself to it at the start, leaving vengeance subordinated or eliminated.

Finally, bear in mind that suspense is compounded of hope as well as fear.

In other words, your reader must care what happens. Otherwise he won't worry; and worry is the big product that a writer sells.

You can't care if the character himself shows no signs of caring. Feeling, remember, is largely a matter of shared reaction.

Neither can you care about something obviously trivial and unimportant.

What's most important—for all of us?

Happiness.

Whatever your character desires and/or whatever endangers that desire must, potentially, affect his future happiness. The transient or inconsequential just aren't good enough. They don't provide sufficient motivation to make him commit himself to fight.

* * *

And that's more than enough about desire and danger and decision. More than enough about the beginning of your story, too. It's time we moved on . . . on into consideration of solutions to the problems you encounter as you write the middle scenes.

How to develop middle segments

"A middle," says Aristotle, "is that which follows something, as some other thing follows it."

You already know how to write the middle segment of your story. You mastered the essential techniques when, in Chapter 4, you learned to manipulate search and struggle, sequel and scene.

The middle consists of a series of sequels and scenes linked together; nothing more. Your focal character searches till he finds a goal that suits him . . . then struggles to attain it. When further difficulties assail him, the process is repeated.

Beginning starts a fight between desire and danger. End

brings a knockout punch to resolve the conflict, one way or the other.

Middle lies between the two. It's the body of your story . . . that portion which details the ebb and flow of battle. Starting with establishment of the story question, it carries your focal character forward to that climactic moment of decision which marks the beginning of your story's end.

How do you develop the middle?

Life, it has been said, facetiously and otherwise, is a series of adjustments.

So is a story.

Change is what forces you to adjust.

Some changes wreak more havoc than do others. Some adjustments are easier to make than others.

In all probability, I'll regroup easily if the problem is merely that, for today, okra has been crossed off the café menu.

Accepting the fact that my wife is dead may take considerably more doing.

Conviction for a murder I didn't commit could very well push me past the breaking point.

In each case, faced with a change, you try to figure out what to do next. That is, you search for a goal—a substitute for okra . . . activities to help fill the lonely hours a loved one's departure leaves . . . revenge for the perjury that put you behind bars.

Then, once you've decided, you do your best to follow the course you've chosen. You strive to reach your destination.

Again, change intervenes. Again, you adjust via search and striving.

This routine is repeated as many times as space will allow.

And there you have the pattern and dynamics of the middle. There's no point to belaboring them further.

There are, however, a few specific rules-of-thumb that may help you . . . a don't, four do's, and a don't, chosen to pinpoint some of the errors that trap too many writers:

   a. Don't stand still.

The difference between the end of your story and its begin-

ning lies in the amount of information reader and hero have at
their disposal.

Thus, a love story might open as a girl first becomes aware
that a particular boy exists.

Sixteen—or 316—pages later, she pledges herself to be his.

Between page one and page sixteen, or what have you, Girl
acquires certain data. In consequence of certain events and
drives and conflicts, she learns various things about Boy: the
kind of person he is; how he reacts; how she herself reacts to his
reactions.

Pleased with what she finds, she behaves in a manner appropriate to love-story resolution in that particular market.

This lengthy process of story development represents change
for Girl—change from one state of affairs to another, and from
one state of mind to another.

Which is as it should be. Change in a story must take place
well-nigh continuously.

Why?

Because each change moves your story closer to its conclusion.
If it doesn't, it's the wrong change.

No story unit—not even a paragraph—ought to begin and end
with the state of affairs and state of mind of each person involved exactly the same. Even the falling of a leaf should, implicitly or explicitly, bring into focus the subtle variation of feeling tone that it engenders. Always, there must be some new
fragment of fact or thought implied or stated; some fresh development, some growth of insight, some hint of fluctuation in
relationship. Maybe Girl finds her rival's earring in Boy's pocket.
Maybe Boy notes irritably that Girl wears too much lipstick.
Maybe there's sullenness in a glance, or tenderness, or precisely
the right or wrong words spoken. Maybe the sun's just warm
enough, or a rainstorm strands Boy and Girl in the mountains.
But whatever the time or place or circumstance—count on it,
something happens. One way or another, great or small, a change
takes place to help or hinder.

Why must this be so?

Partly, because your story needs to drive ahead, straight toward its conclusion.

Even more so, because your reader needs these facts, these

insights, in order properly to share your focal character's experience.

Most of all, because without such change your story grows static, and hence boring.

When that happens, your reader quits reading. And that's a luxury you can't afford.

A static scene or story may even bore you, its author. When that happens, it becomes hard to write.

Why?

Because the only thing any writer really has to write about is change. When there isn't any change worth noting, your unconscious instinctively recognizes it and goes on strike. —After all, how long can anyone sit staring fixedly at a still life?

In fact, whenever a given yarn bogs down, it might be worth your while to ask yourself three questions:

(1) Where's this scene and story going?

It *does* have a goal, doesn't it?

(2) What change will help it get there?

In what respect might this situation be different? Could day be night? Could apartment be office? Could Character A be present or absent? Could the money be found instead of lost?

(3) How will each character react to such a change?

Will it please him? Upset him? Force him to change his plans or attitudes?

*   *   *

Remember: The difference between the end of your story and its beginning lies in the fact that reader and hero have gained information in the course of events recounted.

Information is the fruit of change.

So, incorporate appropriate change into every unit.

b. Do maintain unity.

You the writer need some sort of yardstick to help you decide what to put into your story and what to leave out.

Where middle is concerned, this yardstick is the story question . . . the issue, whether desire will defeat danger: Will your focal character attain his goal, or won't he?

Back to Aristotle: ". . . a thing whose presence or absence makes no visible difference is not an organic part of the whole."

Anything that helps or hinders your focal character's efforts should go into your story. Anything that doesn't, shouldn't.

That sounds simple enough, doesn't it? So where do the problems arise?

They grow out of the fact that, in order to achieve his story goal, your character must first attain a whole series of scene goals.

Thus, Montmorency's objective in your story may be to win election as state senator. But to do this he must, en route, gain support of key people in precinct, county, and state organizations . . . raise campaign funds . . . overcome his wife's fears and the antagonism of his employer . . . defeat a host of other would-be candidates for the office, at all levels.

Short of a novel, you obviously can't cover all this ground. But you *will* develop certain selected bits—the ones which you consider most important—as scenes.

Now the situation set forth in each scene must be sufficiently different from the rest that your reader's interest is held firm. To go over and over the same ground isn't unity; it's disaster.

Precisely at this point, trouble gallops across the horizon. For as you lay out individual scenes, repeatedly you'll find yourself tempted to write in characters and locales and actions that pop out of nowhere to intrigue you. Like, here's this gorgeous gal—or this glamorous ski resort—or this wild wisecrack—or this wonderful ironic thing where the honeymooners' plane crashes right there on the runway—

The only difficulty is, these items have little or no bearing on your focal character's goal and efforts, and the story question.

When that's the case—leave it out! No matter how superficially appealing an incident may be, forget it unless it ties tight to the story question. Or, if it's so overwhelming that you can't leave it alone—then pace the floor till you find a way to forge some sort of bond between it and the crucial issues.

As a corollary to the above, certain scenes *must* be included, even though you have no yen to write them. Again, it's because they have a vital bearing on the story question. If your hero's whole future depends upon his freeing himself from a given girl, and then you play the bit offstage, covering with his casual remark that he "got rid of her, all right," your reader's thwarted anticipations very well may flame into open anger.

So there's the heart of this particular *do:* Include whatever influences the outcome of the story question. Leave out those things that don't.

Not to do so will destroy the unity of your story.

   c. Do build to a climax.

In practical terms, "build to a climax" means "increase pressure on your focal character."

Which is to say, "increase tension and excitement for your reader."

To that end, see to it that the changes you introduce constitute complications.

What is a complication?

A complication is a new development that makes your focal character's situation worse.

What makes your character's situation worse?

Anything that endangers his chances of attaining his story goal.

The way this works out, ordinarily, is that your focal character picks an immediate goal which, he believes, will move him a step closer to his story goal. Then, he takes action to attain that immediate goal.

These efforts bring him up against opposition. Conflict follows, complete with assorted strainings and strivings and maneuverings.

Finally, the fight comes to a climax. And then—

Disaster.

What I'm describing is, obviously, a scene.

It's also a complication.

Why?

Because your focal character hasn't just failed to win. Rather, his efforts have thrown him farther than ever behind the eight-ball. The new external development we label as disaster pulls the rug out from under him totally. In effect, he now must adjust to a whole new situation . . . one worse than the one he confronted at the scene's beginning.

Thus, determined to keep mysterious prowlers away from his home, your hero supplements the six-foot chain-link fence with a particularly savage dog.

This upsets his wife. Her idea is to move.

While they're still arguing the point, there's an animal scream of anguish outside. Hero rushes into the yard.

There's the dog—chopped in half with a machete.

Note how this affects your hero's situation. Before, he stood infuriated and adamant. Now, he sees living—pardon me, dead —proof that neither fence nor dog can protect him and his family from their hidden foe.

Further, said foe assumes new dimensions of the hideous. If this menace can somehow get inside the fence and kill a dog and then vanish—well, how can anyone be safe, and how far may foe go?

Or, here's a girl eager to impress—and thus arouse personal interest on the part of—her handsome junior-executive boss. To this end, she demonstrates super-efficiency and gives all sorts of little extra services.

Whereupon, fat old senior-executive lecher orders her transferred to *his* office—and she knows that if she refuses to accept the assignment, she'll have to leave the company and so lose all contact with her chosen guy.

Or, widowed mother tries to tie teen-age son to her with the traditional silver cord . . . talks him out of taking a job in another town because, she claims, she so desperately needs the financial help that comes of his living at home.

At which point, he signs to go to Saudi Arabia with an oil company, so that he can provide her with more cash.

Do you see how this system works? All you have to do is string together a series of such episodes, *each ending with your focal character in hotter water than before*. Result: a continuing rise in tension, until eventually you reach the climactic peak you seek.

Herewith, a few useful tools to help you in your efforts thus to create complications, intensify tension, and build to a climax:

(1) Build with scenes.

A character in a scene is a character in conflict, and conflict breeds tension.

(2) Don't confuse delay with complication.

A boy waits for a girl. She doesn't show up. Finally, phoning, he learns that she thought he was going to drop by her home to get her. Though disgruntled, he drives on over for her, and they start on their date nearly two hours late.

A detective seeks to locate a missing witness. The man has moved. After considerable legwork, the detective at last finds him.

Fishing, a fat, middle-aged farm wife snags her hook . . . falls in the creek as she attempts to free it. By the time she gets herself and her tackle ashore, she's in somewhat less than a gay mood. It takes her the better part of an hour to dry her clothes and drop her baited hook back in the water.

Now such incidents are common and useful in fiction. But don't call them complications.

Why not?

Because they merely delay the action. They don't make the character's situation worse. Consequently, they don't increase your reader's tension.

A rule-of-thumb of complication might very well be, "Out of the frying pan, into the fire."

In other words, if your character doesn't get burned, you don't have a complication.

Can such bits be developed into complications?

Of course. If Boy, waiting for Girl, were picked up as a robbery suspect, or fell in with a gold-digging floozy, or lost a chance for a promotion because he and Girl didn't make it to the boss's party, the situation would be dynamic instead of static.

That is, the delay would have plunged him into trouble . . . created new problems for him to cope with . . . shaped and influenced his future.

And that's complication.

Same way if a dangerous criminal had been freed because the detective couldn't find the witness in time for the trial.

Result: The detective is placed on suspension. A complication.

Or suppose a gossipy neighbor had spread a rumor that the farm wife was having an affair, because he glimpsed her naked on the creek bank while she was drying her clothes. Isn't her plight then made more difficult?

Which isn't to say that delay, *as* delay, can't be most useful. But delay in and of itself is a subordinate element, not at all on a level with or fit to substitute for complication.

(3) Tie your characters to your story.

It's hard to build tension if your reader is continually wondering why the central character doesn't ride out of the story to greener pastures. After all, how much sense does it make for the marshal to stand and be shot at, or the heroine to accept her jealous lover's violence and abuse, or the teacher to go on teaching despite poor pay, pupil disdain, and community ingratitude?

For this reason, you need to train yourself, at every juncture, to chant one ritualistic question: "Why doesn't he quit?"

No answer is acceptable that doesn't offer a mighty solid reason for your guy's continued presence.

Reasons for a character's not quitting fall into two categories: physical situation, and emotional involvement. A high proportion of story people have both.

Physical situation may range from the financial (your hero will lose his shirt unless he fights out the story issue) to the geographic (Joe's got to come in out of the desert and face the baddies who hold the spring or he'll die of thirst).

Emotional involvement covers everything from a mother's refusal to abandon her child to a soldier's stubborn pride in his dedication to duty.

How do you acquire such situations and involvements for your story?

You devise them.

Which is to say, you use the brains and imagination God gave you to think them up.

(4) Balance your forces.

Put a high-school football team on the field against the Green Bay Packers, and it's no contest.

Same for a little old lady in a wheelchair, confronted with a two-hundred-pound homicidal maniac.

Or a convent girl delivered into the hands of a professional pimp.

To build to a climax, you need well-matched opponents. Neither side should have such markedly superior strength as to make the outcome a foregone conclusion.

This is *not* to say that you can't do wonders with David and Goliath. When you're tempted to try it, however, remember one thing: David had a sling. That was his ace in the hole, the derringer up his sleeve.

Assailed by overwhelming odds, your character, too, needs an equalizer—some trick, some angle, some trait of character that gives him at least a remote fighting chance.

Maybe the high-school team has a science-fiction-type kid quarterback who can control passes by mental radio. Maybe the little old lady is a retired psychology professor who considers the maniac a challenge. Maybe the convent girl holds such sublime and innocent faith in the goodness of all men that she shakes even the pimp.

And so it goes. Both forces in your story, hero and villain alike, must have the strength or cleverness or perseverance or what have you that's needed to make their struggle a fight in fact as well as name. They must be foemen worthy of each other's steel.

(5) Have enough at stake.

If I have $1.12 total in my pocket and a holdup man sticks a gun in my ribs, it won't be too surprising if I don't put up a fight.

But will I surrender as easily if the sum is $9000 and it represents my aged parents' life savings?

Or, if I'm messenger for a hoodlum and know he'll fit me with a concrete overcoat if I lose the money?

Or, if I have a prized reputation as tough and dangerous that will be forever shattered if I let this cheap thug clean me?

The more I have at stake, the greater will be the pressure on me to fight.

The greater that pressure, the higher the tension, and the stronger the chances of building to a powerful climax.

Nor is your focal character the only one you need to think of in

these terms. Give *each* person in your story something at stake—
so much that he fights desperately. For any man among us struggles harder if he knows his foe will kill him if he can.

(6) Force continuing adjustments.

Both hero and villain must continue to play dynamic roles
throughout your story. Neither should become static. Each must
adjust as the story progresses. Whenever one makes a move, it
should evoke a countermove by the other, in a clear-cut, motivation-reaction pattern. And whenever one side seems to be making progress, it should be a signal for the other to put forth renewed effort.

(7) Keep the action rising.

Always arrange your scenes—or groups of scenes—in an as-
cending order of intensity.
Why?
Because the main line of your story's development must continually increase your reader's tension. Try merely to hold it at
the same level, and Friend Reader will feel as if it's falling off.
Whereupon, his interest in your story will sag.
It will help, here, if you think of your story as a series of peaks
and valleys.
The valleys we'll take up later, when we talk about balancing
your story. At this point, we're dealing only with the peaks.
The peaks are your scene climaxes. In general, each should
carry your reader to a higher level of tension than the one before.
That is, each should increase your reader's foreboding of potential disaster. It should make him devastatingly aware that your
focal character may not attain his goal.
In a long story—a novelette; a novel—scenes may be grouped
into larger units. Then, some scenes will be preparation, groundwork, build-up, foothills.
The true peaks, in such cases, will be the climaxes of the
major story segments. They'll tower like mountains, each higher
than the one which precedes it.
How do you manage this?
A good idea is to decide in advance which moments in your
story are the big ones. That is, which blows struck against your

hero are the most devastating? Which scene disasters shatter him the worst?

Then, separate those big moments, and plan an appropriate build-up for each one. The bigger the moment, the bigger the build-up.

Here an eye for story values can prove a crucial thing. The flamboyant, the spectacular, the cosmic mean less than nothing. Always, always, you *must* measure in terms of the effect the event has in relation to your focal character's feelings and the story question. A steak dinner may be more important than a death, a quick-drawn breath more exciting than the sack of Rome.

In the same way, crowding two climaxes too close together will drain the punch from both. And if the issue is too few climaxes versus too many, choose too few every time. Build-up can give the few importance. Too many automatically come out as melo-dramatic drivel. A girl may have one affair, or two, or even three, and still rate as a best-seller heroine. Push her into a dozen, and she's judged a tramp.

(8) Box in your hero.

To box in our hero, restrict his freedom of choice where movement and/or course of action are concerned.

Ordinarily, the first phase of a story gives the focal character a fair amount of leeway. Like the queen in a chess game, he can move in almost any direction he desires.

Then, threatened, he commits himself to fight for what he wants.

That decision blocks off a number of avenues previously open to him. Unless he's willing to betray himself or others, he can no longer run, or ignore the situation. He must center his attention on one area of activity until his problem is solved.

In the same way, each scene narrows his radius of action . . . cuts down on the choices he can make. Trapped in a maze of dangers and decisions, contradictions and dilemmas, he attempts one course after another, only to discover that each in its turn is a dead end. The friend he relies on betrays him. The weapon he seeks is missing. The time he needs runs out. The assumptions he makes are wrong.

All of which increases tension . . . builds the sense of rising action in your story.

Step by step, then, your central character is forced into a bottleneck, a funnel. Less and less frequently are there a variety of directions in which he still can turn.

Finally, he reaches a point at which he's restricted to a choice between two specific, concrete, alternative courses of action.

But that's a subject we'll take up later. For when your hero reaches it, he's also reached the beginning of the end.

For now, the important thing to remember is that, in the middle stages of your story, you must be sure that this narrowing takes place. Your job is to spot holes and plug them; to foresee escape routes and block them; to cut off your hero from all apparent hope.

If you don't, your reader's going to see those holes, and scream because your hero doesn't duck out through one.

And idiot heroes seldom please.

(9) Drop a corpse through the roof.

I've saved this point for last because, though obvious, it's so often overlooked.

Which is tragic, since it very often can make the difference between a pedestrian story, and one with verve and sparkle.

The "corpse" referred to above is the unanticipated.

More specifically, the disastrously unanticipated . . . and the unanticipatedly disastrous.

Injection of the unanticipated is a major function of disaster in your scene pattern. So, keep your disasters disastrous! Throw in the least likely development, the startling twist! Don't be afraid to shock or hurt your hero. He—and your readers—will thrive on such abuse. For nothing helps more to build exciting climaxes.

If this sounds like a plea for blood and thunder, please remember that you, as a writer, are supposed to have sufficient taste and intelligence and judgment to adapt such suggestions as this to your own chosen field. —Though how much difference there is between the unanticipated as exemplified in the rawest pulps and that found in more "literary" circles is open to question, in view of some of the writings of such figures as William Faulkner, Tennessee Williams and Calder Willingham.

And just in case you wonder precisely to what ultimates this matter of the unanticipated can be carried, I give you, in conclusion, an editorial communiqué I once received from my old friend Howard Browne, who now make fabulous sums of money in Hollywood, but who at the time was riding herd on a chain of pulp magazines.

Herewith, Mr. Browne:

> I've got an assignment for you, keed. I want 25,000 words a month—one story—that is ACTION! The type of yarn, for instance, where a group of people are marooned in, say, a hilltop castle, with a violent storm raging and all the bridges out and the electric power gone and the roof threatening to cave in and corpses falling down the stairs and hanging in the attic and boards creaking under somebody's weight in the dark ("Can that be the killer?") and flashes of lightning illuminating the face of the murderer only the sonofabitch is wearing a mask that makes him look even more horrible, and finally the girl has been given into the safekeeping of the only person who is absolutely not the killer—only he turns out to be the killer, but he has taken the girl where no one can get to save her and you damn well know he is raping her while everybody stands around helpless. Do these stories in the style Burroughs used to use; you know, take one set of characters and carry them along for a chapter, putting them at the end of the chapter in such a position that nothing can save them; then take another set of characters, rescue them from their dilemma, carry them to a hell of a problem at the end of the chapter, then switch back to the first set of characters, rescue *them* from their deadly peril, carry them along to the end of the chapter where, once again, *they* are seemingly doomed; then rescue the second set of characters . . . and so on. Don't give the reader a chance to breathe; keep him on the edge of his goddam chair all the way through. To hell with clues and smart dialogue and characterization; don't worry about corn. GIVE ME PACE AND BANG BANG! Make me breathless, bud!

What more can anyone say? What more could anyone want to?

d. Do strive for balance.

Hike up a mountain sometime. You'll find, very shortly, that some slopes are steeper than others; some trails more devious or difficult. Here, you'll move slowly . . . there, swiftly. And up ahead you'll want to stop and rest and catch your breath.

A story is like that mountain. You don't present it all in the same manner or at the same pace. A pulse of tension runs through it—here, strong and vibrant; there, more relaxed.

Thus, the main line of the action—the development from climax to climax—continually rises. Your focal character stands in ever greater danger. So, the peak of each major story segment, whether scene or group of scenes, is higher—more tense; more exciting—than the one before.

But if you attempt to maintain this same high level of excitement *between* the peaks, your reader soon becomes exhausted. Overstimulated, continually under experiential and emotional bombardment, he loses his sense of proportion and, quite possibly, quits reading out of sheer fatigue.

So, you give him a chance to rest a bit along the way. Between peaks, you let him relax.

You do this in the moments that follow each disaster.

That is, you slow the pace, reduce the tension, in those portions of your story that are termed sequel: reaction to disaster, readjustment to changed situation, search for new goal or approach, groundwork and build-up, preliminary feints and thrusts and conflicts.

In other words, you balance your peaks, your climaxes, with valleys.

How?

The first step is to devise ways to build your big moments, your climaxes, to the desired heights.

Here are five of the many tools that help you do this:

(1) Group as much significant action as possible into each scene.

Too often, a writer is tempted to set forth his story in a loosely connected series of simple, trivial scenes.

A simple scene may show your focal character try to persuade his girl's mother to tell him why Sophronia has ditched him. Failing to get satisfaction from her, he tackles Sophie's father . . . then her brother.

String the three scenes together, and odds are that you rack up more length than tension.

On the other hand, if your focal character starts on Mama . . . whereupon Papa charges in and orders Mama to keep quiet and Character to leave the house . . . and Character tries to pressure Papa into talking . . . only just then Brother enters and assaults Character—well, you may find you've built to quite a peak.

All of which is not to say that the simple, uncomplicated scene doesn't have a place. But for climax purposes, you'll get more mileage from units in which you arrange and compress your material in a manner designed to achieve maximum effect.

(2) Make the situation demand action.

A buzzing fly is an annoyance. A buzzing rattlesnake encourages you to do something about him.

In general, the more dangerous a situation, the more important it looms in your character's eyes, and the more inclined he is to take action.

Action begets reaction and conflict, and the better are your chances, out of it, to build a big scene.

The inconsequential, in contrast, lacks red blood and vitamins. It's unlikely to provide a basis for any major climax.

(3) Increase time pressure.

If the above-mentioned rattlesnake sounds off as you cross your yard at dusk, you'll probably put off hunting him till morning. If he's in the same room with you, you feel a degree of impulse to do something right now.

Which is why urgency helps, ever and always, when it's time to build a climax.

(4) Foreshadow your story's climax.

Your reader takes it for granted that a story's climax will center on an explosive showdown between desire and danger.

Therefore, as your story progresses, the tension engendered by each new crisis grows.

Especially is this so if you keep building up the strength of the opposition and a sense of potential ultimate disaster. It's as if each step your character takes forward brings him closer to impending doom. He's like a man trying to break down a door in order to save a loved one, knowing even as he does so that a berserk gorilla is waiting for him on the other side.

(5) Pace your presentation, mechanically, to increase your reader's sense of tension.

Tension does things to people. Under its pressure, perceptions and reactions heighten. You move faster. You respond quicker. Time stretches out. There's a jerky, staccato, exaggerated quality to everything you say and do.

These are elements you can capture in your copy. Your reader, reading, catches the excitement of the moment by the very way you write, the words you use.

What kind of words?

Short words. Harsh words. Pointed words. Slashing words.

What kind of writing?

Terse writing. Action writing. Short sentences. Short paragraphs. The tunnel vision that shuts out everything except the moment and the danger. The prolongation of crisis that stretches time like a rubber band.

How do you learn to write such copy?

You hunt down the moments that thrill you in the other man's story.

Then, you copy them, word for word and line for line . . . study them in typescript . . . experiment with word substitutions and with sentence changes until you uncover the way he turns his tricks.

After which, with his tools buried deep in your unconscious, you're ready to go on again and write more effective climaxes of your own.

❋   ❋   ❋

So much for peaks.

Now, in the period immediately following each climax, each disaster, you *reduce* tension.

These five techniques will prove useful to this end:

(1) Pace your presentation to reduce tension.

How? By reversing everything said in (5), above.

That is, lengthen sentences a little, perhaps. Paragraphs, too.

Consider euphony when you choose words. Work more for flow; less for the staccato and the punch.

Again, the other man's copy is your best guidebook. And the reason I recommend no models to you is because your taste is your own, and private . . . a subjective thing; so what seems good and/or well done to me might very well prove completely wrong where you're concerned.

One warning, though: Please don't go to extremes. Because I talk about short words and short sentences to create a sense of tension doesn't mean that anyone, ever, should forget the need to balance short with long. And to confuse polysyllabics and convoluted sentence structure with tension reduction is even worse.

Again, it helps to have horse sense if you want to be a writer!

(2) Make decision the issue.

The situation that demands action, it was pointed out above, is a useful tool in building tension and climax.

To relax tension, in turn, focus less on such immediate striving . . . more on search.

Thus, when I lose my girl or my job or my status, I have to draw back and regroup . . . rally my inner resources and try to figure out what to do now; which way to go. Do I hunt another girl or job or point of prestige, or do I slash my wrists or join the army?

In other words, I must make some decisions.

How I go about making them will depend on my own personality and background; my emotional patterns. Maybe I walk the streets. Maybe I get drunk. Maybe I try to find a priest to tell my troubles to.

Be that as it may. In all cases, passage of time will be involved: time to react, time to think, time to work things out. Eventually, I'll choose a new goal to strive for, a new course of action to pursue. But in the interim between the moment when Dame Fortune knocks me down and the one when I finally get back up to fight again, seconds and minutes and hours and days—or maybe even weeks or months—will tick by.

In your copy, you use that time lapse to reduce tension . . . give your reader a chance to rest from his excitement. And it's probably your most useful tool in this regard, since you can telescope it or expand it to fit your needs.

(3) Decrease urgency, time pressure.

How?

Let the disaster put your character in a situation in which he can take no action until tomorrow or next week or what have you. Maybe the man he needs to contact is out of town, or the lodge is snowbound, or there's nothing to be done at the legislature till the bill comes out of committee.

(4) Develop non-tension factors.

A story is the record of how somebody deals with danger.

But no matter how threatening the situation, between moments of crisis life goes on. You eat. You sleep. You shop, change a tire, make polite conversation, take in a movie.

Ignore such routine, trivial though it may seem, and your story takes on a somehow shadowy, unsubstantial air. Include it, inserted between climaxes, and you increase the feeling that you're dealing with actual people, real events.

In the process, you also give your reader a chance to catch his breath.

In the same way, side issues come up in the lives of all of us. There's a boy you like, and so you take time out from your own concerns to help him find a job. A stuffed shirt irritates you; you pause a moment to deflate him. You've promised to spend a weekend with friends in Dallas. Even though it holds no satisfaction for you, you feel obliged to keep the date.

Similarly, your reader knows the people in your story only to the degree that you develop them on paper. Yet their reactions are important. He needs to understand them as people and not puppets. That calls for exploration of attitudes, philosophies. Is this man's morality that of the Honest Brakeman, so called because he never stole a boxcar? Does this woman's outspoken belief in equality, in practice, make Christians just a bit more equal than Jews, or vice versa? Is sympathy an emotion a character feels for alcoholics, but not for the girls in the home for unwed mothers?

The moments that you take to give such dimension to your people also help you to slow pace a fraction, as needed.

A setting can be as flat as a canvas backdrop. Or you can add details that make it come to life.

And the best place to insert them is in the lull that follows disaster . . . in the pause between climaxes, where emphasis is more strongly on decision than on the striving and urgency and danger out of which you build your story peaks.

(5) Change viewpoint.

When you change viewpoint, tension drops.

Why?

Because instantly, your reader is faced with a totally new and different situation. He must adjust not only to a change in time and place and circumstance; he must also get inside somebody else's skin.

That somebody sees the story issues through private eyes. His background and attitudes and problems aren't the same as those of the character your reader was living and experiencing with before. Hero, heroine, villain, bystander—each has his separate outlook.

That new outlook, those unique attitudes, must be made clear to your reader each time you change viewpoint.

Which takes time, and space. Friend Reader can't just do a flip and automatically be somebody new. He has to readjust; learn his new role.

Result: tension reduction . . . an opportunity to pause and rest awhile.

*   *   *

From valley you build to peak . . . then drop back down again and start anew. And thus do you create a sense of balance and of pacing in your story.

e. Do snip off the threads.

The middle of your story is a time of building.

It's also a time of tapering off.

If a story is of any length, a number of issues are likely to develop as adjuncts to the story question.

Thus, the central character seeks to clear himself of a murder charge. One of the factors that helps to increase pressure on him is the reaction of family and of friends. Not to mention associates and enemies and casual acquaintances.

Specific friends. Specific members of his family. Specific associates and enemies and acquaintances.

Take his girl's father. Upset by certain past history of the hero, he swears that such a man never will be allowed to marry his daughter.

An opportunist associate, in turn, snags Hero's job.

And a tough cop, angered over an embarrassing incident, stands determined to force Hero to leave town, no matter how the case comes out.

Now all these angles are necessary, if the story is to build to a proper peak. But if they ride clear through past the climax to the moment of resolution, they'll be difficult to wind up in any reasonable wordage. Consequently, the end of the story will dribble off unsatisfyingly in a series of anticlimaxes.

To avoid this, the wise writer cuts things down to size *before* the climax, by snipping off subordinate threads as middle begins to merge with end.

Thus, Hero perhaps discovers that Girl's father was, in his day, a bit of a dog himself. The old man feels guilty about it. That's why he's so rabid over any hint that Hero has been less than perfect.

When Hero faces him with these facts, Father sees the error of his ways and flips over to Hero's side. It's a thread snipped off, and it's out of the way *before* the climax.

Similarly, Hero may decide he doesn't want the job, or he may come up with a better offer, or receive recompense from his contrite employer. The cop, in his anger, may attempt to frame Hero, be caught at it, and himself be forced to leave town.

In each case, elimination of minor issues simplifies and shortens resolution. Even more important, it clears the stage for the climax, so that the reader can devote his full and undivided attention to the big "Will-he-or-won't-he?" issue posed by the story question.

  f. Don't rehash.

You know how it sounds when a phonograph needle gets stuck, and the same strain of music repeats endlessly.

Middle-area copy too often follows the same route. The story stops moving forward . . . bogs down on reiteration of one theme.

When you write a story, in effect you present a sequence like the alphabet: A-B-C-D-E-F-G-H-I-J-K-L, and so on.

It should *not* read, A-B-C-D-D-D-E-F. One D—or F, or H, or X—is enough. You need to establish the necessary information and move on. To have your character go through the same routine undeviatingly, again and again, is sure to bring boredom. Same for reiterated threats, all essentially the same, mouthed by the villain.

What's the cure for repetitiousness?

Change. The unanticipated. New elements and twists continually injected. A story that doesn't stand still—one with soundly structured sequels and scenes, searchings and strivings.

Given such, everything else will work out.

* * *

Let's end this section on the same note we struck at the beginning: The middle consists of a series of scenes and sequels linked together.

If you frame each solidly; if you incorporate all component elements; if you force yourself to keep each individual fragment fresh, then your story will move and build and hold your reader, in fit preparation for what's to follow: that climactic moment of decision that marks, in good fiction, the beginning of the end.

* * *

How do you bring a story to an end?

(1) You set up a situation in which your focal character has a choice between two specific, concrete, alternative courses of action.

(2) You force Character to choose between these two courses.

(3) You make him translate this choice into an irrevocable climactic act.

(4) You reward or punish Character for this act, in accordance with poetic justice.

(5) You tie up any loose ends.

(6) You focus fulfillment into a punch line.

Why follow such a pattern?

It provides your reader with story satisfaction, through release of tension.

How does it trigger such release?

Two basic issues are involved:

  1. What does your character deserve?
  2. What does he get?

These two factors, in turn, correlate with the two subdivisions of your story's end: climax, and resolution.

Climax gives final, conclusive proof of what your focal character *deserves*.

Resolution sets forth what he *gets*.

Thus, tension builds on the conflict between desire and danger that you establish at the beginning of your story. Experiencing with the focal character, your reader yearns to see said character attain his goal. But so powerful is the opposition that he fears, simultaneously, that his man won't make it.

Now, enter the deciding factor: What does the focal character deserve?

How to build a climax

It's in his ability to perceive principle and separate it from self-interest that man is distinguished from the animal.

This isn't to be considered validation of any specific principle, you understand. Principles may be right or they may be wrong; and certainly they change as man moves through time, space, and circumstance. But in judging behavior by ethical standard rather than mere expediency, we establish an absolute by which to test character and to orient ourselves meaningfully to life. Only in terms of principle can we demonstrate the triumph of free will over determinism . . . of cause-effect pattern over blind fate . . . of spirit over external reality. It's principle and principle alone that gives meaning to the whole concept of control of circumstance.

Principle also provides the basis of climax. In adherence to or abandonment of principle, your focal character proves ultimately and beyond all doubt what he deserves.

Climax itself merely dramatizes this adherence or abandonment. In the process, it demonstrates the relationship between cause and effect in parable form, so clearly that no one can miss it. If the character acts on conscience, despite the pressure of self-interest, he attains his goal. If he doesn't, his efforts fail. It's as simple as that.

All of which serves to reaffirm your reader's philosophy of life, with its built-in assumption that self-sacrifice for the sake of a larger issue is worthy of reward. His fears and tensions are released. He relaxes into that happy state that comes with fulfillment and satisfaction.

As a corollary to the above, a narrative that concerns action unrelated to principle can never be more than chronicle; can never rise to the status of story. Sans principle, behavior can't be evaluated and consequently ceases to be fit subject for fiction.

"A storyteller is passionately interested in human beings and their endless conflicts with their fates," observes screenwriter Dudley Nichols, "and he is filled with desire to make some intelligible arrangement out of the chaos of life, just as the chairmaker desires to make some useful and beautiful arrangement out of wood." And Professor Franklin Fearing adds, "It is this intelligible arrangement that the reader seeks, whatever his level of sophistication and regardless of whether he is able to be articulate about it."

Fiction thus is basically a tool to give life meaning. It does this, as we've seen, by establishing a cause-effect relationship between the focal character's behavior and his fate; his deeds and his rewards. So a story without pattern is a contradiction of terms.

The trouble with the "slice of life" approach is that it most often is formless and so lacks the power of resolution. As a sociological document, a case study that draws attention to a problem, it may prove excellent. But it's not a story. When the end of a film about a retardate sees the mentally deficient focal character walk off down the street into a future no different from his past, it resolves nothing. Consequently, it leaves the viewer in a state of frustration; unreleased tension. And as dramatist Howard Lindsay has remarked, "The play that ends in mere frustration for the people in whom the audience is emotionally interested will not satisfy them, for frustration is one of the most unhappy experiences in our lives."

Now, back to climax, and to the first three steps listed preliminary to the beginning of this section:

(1) You set up a situation in which your focal character has a choice between two specific, concrete, alternative courses of action.

In good fiction, a climactic moment of decision marks the beginning of the end.

So, how do you set up such a moment?

A story, remember, is the record of how somebody deals with danger.

It begins when desire bumps into opposition, and your focal character commits himself to fight for what he wants.

This gives you a story question: Will Joe attain his goal? Will he overcome the forces that oppose him, or won't he?

Result: Conflict. Suspense. Tension.

The middle of your story develops, builds up, and intensifies these elements. Conflict grows sharper. Suspense mounts. Tension rises higher.

There's a limit to tension, however. Sooner or later, at the end of the story, it must be released.

The moment of decision provides the trigger mechanism to discharge it.

Up to this point, your focal character's courage and intelligence and strength have carried him.

But you and I know that there are moments when courage isn't enough, and neither is intelligence, or strength.

When such moments come, there's only one recourse left for us.

Feeling.

That is, we act on emotion; impulse. We don't think. We respond spontaneously, on a visceral, well-nigh instinctive level, without regard for rules or logic or for hazard. We throw ourselves between the child and the speeding car. We step from the ranks to back a friend. We speak out for truth when silence would serve self-interest better.

Or, if such are our emotional patterns, we break and run in

panic. We harden our hearts to pity or tenderness or ardor. We snatch the cash and say to hell with conscience.

Feeling reflects something deeper and more profound than strength, or intelligence, or even courage. It comes from the heart and guts, not the head. It speaks for the man or woman you really are; the secret self; the naked I.

It's this secret self that climax tests.

Why?

Because you can fool the world, and sometimes you can even fool yourself. But you can't fool your own feelings. They tell the truth about you, every time, without regard for rationalizations or excuses.

That's why climax is so vital. Only as we see a man in crisis, when under stress he acts on feeling, can we gain the final, conclusive proof we need to determine whether or not he deserves to attain the goal he seeks.

Your reader likes that. If he himself were to be judged, he hopes it would be on such a basis. He knows that externals can deceive. He recognizes his deficiencies in strength and intelligence and status. Over and over again, reality has forced him to acknowledge flaw and weakness.

But his feelings, his impulses—those are different! He lives in a world of good intentions. He sees himself as, at heart, a man of principle and honor. That's his inner reality.

In an ultimate test, he feels that he would prove it.

So you test your focal character by the same standard.

To that end, you strip away all pretense from him. You make him reveal himself as he really is.

How?

You offer him an easy way to reach his goal.

Thus, Ichabod has sweated blood for sixteen pages now, in his pursuit of fair Griselda. It's time to bring the business to an end.

So, you build a climax scene. In it Ichabod discovers that his rival, Roderick, was driver of the hit-run car that crippled Griselda's brother.

Roderick promptly agrees to let Our Hero have the lady—providing that Ichabod will remain diplomatically silent about Roderick's guilt.

It's a fair enough deal, isn't it? What Griselda doesn't know won't hurt her, and wealthy Roderick will even go so far as to endow Brother for life.

Besides, Brother was only a drunken bum to start with. Ichabod detested the very sight of him.

As an alternative, if Ichabod refuses to play ball, Roderick will accuse him of the crime, plus blackmail. True, Griselda may not be convinced. But enough doubt will be raised in her mind that things will never be the same between her and Ichabod again.

So, Ichabod now has an easy way to reach his goal: All he needs to do is keep quiet.

He also has a disastrous alternative: to speak, and lose Griselda. In fact, with all Roderick's wealth and power arrayed against him, he might very well end up convicted of hit-run himself.

Two specific, concrete, alternative courses of action. They constitute a fork in the road for Ichabod . . . a test situation to bring final, conclusive evidence as to whether or not he's worthy of reward.

If he accepts Roderick's offer, he gets Griselda and, in her, fulfillment of all his dreams.

If he refuses, the payoff is black oblivion. On all counts.

Not much of a choice, is it? Intelligence, logic, and self-interest stand shoulder to shoulder on the side of buying Roderick's scheme.

Against it—well, what is there? Square-type puritan prejudices against conspiring to help a criminal evade the penalty for his crime? Silly scruples over marrying a girl under false pretenses? Qualms of conscience involving words like *right* and *honesty* and *love* and *justice*?

Abstractions all. They count for nothing.

That is, unless principle means more to you than victory.

And that's the way you set up the situation for a climax scene . . . an easy path to goal on the one hand, a disastrous alternative on the other, and your focal character standing at the fork in the road.

* * *

What are the most common weaknesses, in climax?

(*a*) The focal character isn't properly boxed in.

In other words, the perceptive reader (and an amazingly high proportion of readers *are* perceptive) instantly spots loopholes in a climax situation: "Why doesn't Suzy just *tell* John that her dad's gone broke?" "Isn't Brent bright enough to realize that his aunt was senile when she made him promise to stay on in that old house?" "What keeps Link from calling the police?"

Result: a spoiled climax.

Remedy: a writer who thinks his story through, then plugs all loopholes and boxes in his focal character *before* the climax.

(*b*) No barrier of principle blocks the easy way.

All her life my mother's hated whisky worse than snakes. Now she lies dying, and I'm too broke to give her proper care. To make matters worse, my fiancée returns my ring. A man who can't look after his dying mother has no business taking a wife, she says.

Enter the town bootlegger. He offers to loan me the cash I need, on my tacit agreement to let him set up a secret still in the swamp on Mother's farm.

Should I take the money? It's an easy way out.

But there's also a matter of principle involved; a moral issue. For in sanctioning the still I'll be betraying everything that Mother believes in.

Of such materials are solid climax situations built.

Suppose, however, that it's an old friend, and not the bootlegger, who offers me the money. What then?

Even to ask the question is to see the climax fade away.

Why?

Because the function of climax is to test character, and without principle at stake there can be no test. The friend's money has no strings attached. I can accept it with no qualm of conscience.

Result: no conflict.

And no climax.

Shall we spell out the message? When we talk about an "easy way," it's easy from a *material* standpoint only. On a *moral* level, it must nail your focal character to the cross. Though "practical" considerations back it 100 per cent, it should bear an emotional price too high for your character to pay.

   (c) The alternative to the easy way isn't sufficiently disastrous.

The way to make a focal character sweat in climax is to build his alternative to sheer catastrophe.

Thus, in (b)'s example, Hero stands to lose not just Mother, but Girl too.

Partly, this is because it's too easy on a hero to center the climax on his saving or sacrificing someone else's interests. All of us do wonders with rationalization in that area. If Mother is old, already dying, and I can make a show of virtue by refusing whisky money—well, maybe it won't be so hard to stand on principle, at that.

When my own neck's in the noose, on the other hand; when I'm set to lose not just a dying mother but the girl I love so desperately as well, I perhaps tend to think a bit more realistically. The temptation to take the easy road is stronger.

But over and beyond this, you build tension higher if, to stick with principle, your hero must throw himself completely and utterly into the teeth of fate. Then, a "right" decision sacrifices everything; gains nothing. All common sense, all logic, all self-interest, bar his way.

   (d) The focal character's goal isn't important enough and/or attractive enough to him.

A man seeks a goal—something he yearns to attain or retain. His pursuit of it brings him face to face with a situation that reeks of potential calamity, disaster. One step more, and he'll plunge over the brink.

What does he do then?

He backs off. Fast.

That is, he does so unless the something he seeks is ever so important to him, subjectively. The casual, the trivial, the transient—as motivations, they just aren't strong enough.

What constitutes a good goal?

It's one which, in the character's eyes, stands as his key to future happiness.

Consider the child who doubts his mother's love. If only the basket he makes can be the best in all the kindergarten crafts class, perhaps she'll take him in her arms.

Life without those arms is too terrible a thought to bear. It colors the child's whole picture of world and future.

Therefore, construction of a superior basket is a good goal. Q.E.D.

An old man sits writing his memoirs. He has no hope that the scrawl will bring him fame or money. But if he can only explain the things he's done and why he's done them, perhaps his son will some day read, draw insight from the words, and cease to sneer.

There can be happiness even in the dream that someone dear may understand you after you're long gone.

So, what constitutes a good goal?

Any objective that your focal character envisions as shaping his future, his chances for happiness.

What doesn't?

Anything he *doesn't* see as affecting, and affecting substantially, the life he'll lead and the way he'll feel in days and years ahead.

    (*e*) The situation isn't built up sufficiently.

The climax is the biggest moment of a story; its peak of peaks. To dismiss it casually is to throw all your other work away.

So much for climactic situation. Now, let's move on to our second point:

    (2) You force the character to choose between the two courses available to him.

To make a choice between self-interest and principle is difficult for any of us, in any situation, at any time.

Especially if catastrophe hangs over us like the sword of Damocles.

Part of your job in climax, therefore, is to show precisely how hard such decision-making is.

How do you do this?

You prolong the agony for your hero.

Sometimes, that means breast-beating and hair-pulling. Others, merely a moment of aching tension, with flashes of significant detail against the silence.

In any case, your focal character must sweat and suffer, whether we watch the scene from inside his skin or out.

And then, at last, he decides.

Decision itself involves two problems:

(a) How do you force it?
(b) What tips the scales in the right direction?

Where (a)'s concerned, urgency is of course the answer. The girl turns to leave. The villain raises his gun. The friend cries out for help.

Whereupon, your character must decide . . . *right now*.

In (b), however, the question itself tends to be misleading. For there's no trick to making your character go the way you want. You just hit the right keys on your typewriter!

More critical is an unstated, implied issue: How do you make your reader *believe* that Hero would choose emotion over logic?

Phrase it that way, and once again the answer is simple: You use a gimmick.

Understand, a gimmick is by no means the *only* way to get your character to react as you wish. But it's certainly one of the most practical and useful devices for so doing. By all means, master it.

Actually, a gimmick utilizes the principle of conditioned reaction, much as the Russian physiologist-psychologist Pavlov used a bell to train dogs to salivate on demand. In fact, we may define a gimmick as some material object or sensory phenomenon made to serve as an emotional bell.

Your first step in developing a gimmick is to choose such an object or phenomenon—one that evokes a strong emotional reaction in your hero.

You also demonstrate that this emotional reaction is linked to adherence to principle where said character is concerned.

You do this early in the story. Preferably, you do it several times.

Then, at the critical moment in your climax, when the focal character hangs on the verge of taking the easy way, you reintroduce the gimmick once more.

Promptly, your character reacts, precisely as he did before—with emotion; with a sudden upsurge of passion for principle.

On the crest of that upsurge, he makes his "right" decision; and it's instantly logical and believable to your reader that he should do so.

Why?

Because he, the reader, has been conditioned to expect an emotion-based reaction from the character whenever the gimmick comes on stage.

Thus, let's say that, early, you make your reader aware that Hero wears a silver St. Christopher's medal on a chain about his neck. In some passing incident, it's brought out that Hero's mother gave it to him, and that he wears it not only because it was her last gift, but because it makes him feel closer to her . . . reminds him to live up to the standard of rectitude that she set.

Other such incidents follow, at intervals through the story. Each time, Hero responds similarly, with deep feeling for his mother and her virtue; with quickened pulse and heightened conscience.

Now comes the climax. Hero stands at the fork in his private road, torn between right and wrong, good and evil, principle and self-interest.

Which way will he go? What course will he follow?

The villain buffets him. Hero's shirt tears open. The chain breaks. The medal sails across the floor.

The medal. Symbol of all Hero's mother meant to him.

For an instant, Hero stares at it; and in that moment lies decision, surging up on the tide of emotional response and past conditioning a simple silver trinket brings.

Do you see how gimmick operates? You can use it in almost any story, crudely or subtly according to your tastes and skill. Here, it takes the form of a wedding ring . . . there, a strain of music . . . a battered bullet . . . a broken doll . . . a wisp of fragrance that reminds someone of a half-forgotten girl's perfume.

So small a detail, the gimmick.

And so big.

Because it holds the power to explode climax into decision.

So: Hero's mind now is made up. We're ready for the third step in our climax pattern.

(3) You make the character translate his choice into an irrevocable climactic act.

There's a saying very pertinent to climax: "Don't just stand there. Do something!"

Doing something, in climax, means translating decision into an irrevocable climactic act.

Next to decision itself, it's the most important facet of your climax.

Why?

Because decision remains meaningless till you act upon it. The road to hell is paved with good intentions. All of us are quick to come forth with well-meaning resolutions. We promise to be kinder, to stop smoking, to put our dirty clothes in the laundry hamper, to mow the grass each and every week.

A day or a month later, we're back yelling at the wife, making like a chimney, leaving the bedroom a litter of soiled underwear and smelly socks, and blithely ignoring the shaggy yard.

So it is in climax also. Decision alone won't do the job. What you seek is a road to resolution of your story—one that will pave the way for release of your reader's tension.

That demands a change in the situation set up by the climax. Further, said change must be wrought by your focal character, not luck or blind fate.

To that end, the peak of climax is a pivot. It flips the situation over. The rest of the story, the resolution, hangs on it.

Such a flip demands motive force. The climactic act provides it.

So, let's lay down an axiom: A climax is always an act.

That act is performed by the focal character. Until he moves, nothing happens. And virtuous thoughts are not enough.

The earlier portions of the climax are merely build-up to this moment. The climactic act itself stands as a pinnacle, like a burning glass that brings the rays of the sun into sharp focus in order to start an all-consuming fire to follow. For in the instant that he makes his play, your character changes the whole balance of the story situation.

As an added bonus, such an act saves you all sorts of explanation. Your character's decision, as such, may never be verbalized. Hero probably won't even be aware of his mental processes. He just does the thing that conscience and feeling tell him he must do, and the act itself says more than words.

What, particularly, characterizes the climactic act?

Its irrevocability.

Caesar, crossing the Rubicon, burned his bridges behind him. Once the knife is thrust or the trigger pulled, the murderer never can return life to his victim.

A climactic act should be like that: an ultimate commitment. When your hero signs the paper or throws the switch or spits in the villain's eye, it should close the door forever on the possibility of his turning back.

Consciously or otherwise, your focal character knows this. Acting, he waives the privilege of changing his mind later.

Such a move sends tension soaring. Before, your man had a choice. He could abandon principle and take the easy road to his objective. He didn't have to lay out his hopes and dreams as a burnt offering.

Now, however, all chance to choose is thrust aside. There remains only the hard road, the road of sacrifice and suffering, with its apparently inevitable disaster.

Acting, Character challenges fate and the villain to do their worst. In so doing, he distills the story question down to essence: Will the course he's chosen crucify him?

Tension hangs at a peak while Reader awaits answer.

Why?

Because Reader's own heart is in it. Whether he can put it into words or not, he knows that in the climactic act he has seen man rise above self-interest. And that, to most of us, comes out as heroism.

* * *

So, at long last, your focal character has demonstrated that he deserves to win. What now?

Specifically, what does the focal character get?

How to resolve story issues

The resolution of a story is the payoff. It rewards or punishes your focal character for his decision in crisis, as epitomized in the climactic act.

In the process, it releases tension and leaves focal character and/or reader with a feeling of fulfillment.

The steps by which you trigger this release and create this feeling are three in number—the fourth, fifth and sixth points listed when we began our discussion of how to end a story:

(4) You reward or punish the focal character for his climactic act, in accordance with poetic justice.

(5) You tie up any loose ends.

(6) You focus fulfillment into a punch line.

Now, let's consider each of these items in detail.

(4) You reward or punish the focal character for his climactic act, in accordance with poetic justice.

Given a correct decision, what the focal character wants determines what he gets.

Thus, his desire to attain or retain something launches the story. It's his goal. In his eyes, at least, his future happiness depends on said attaining or retaining.

Because this is so, he fights whatever forces threaten this objective. Increasing jeopardy and tension only increase his efforts.

This conflict between desire and danger finally focuses into a climax, in which the focal character must choose between principle and self-interest.

If, in that moment, the character stands on principle despite all hazard, and thus demonstrates that he deserves to win, you reward him with attainment or retention of the thing he wants, the goal he seeks.

In other words, cause leads directly to effect. Deed brings reward. As soon as you know your hero's goal, you also know how your story is going to end.

But knowing a destination and working out the route to reach it are two very different things. Practical problems have to be faced along the way . . . problems which you, the writer, must solve.

So, how do you move your focal character from decision to reward?

Again, three steps are involved:

> (a) Let your focal character suffer through a black moment of anguish after climax.
> (b) Reverse his situation with an unanticipated development.
> (c) Give him his reward.

Each of these three items is important. Slight any one of them and you're in trouble.

Further, none of these issues are quite as simple as appears at first glance. To handle them effectively, you need to understand them in terms both of dynamics and mechanics.

Take (a):

> (a) Let your focal character suffer through a black moment of anguish after climax.

The reason your reader reads, we've said, is so that he can worry.

In the moment immediately after climax, that worry comes to its sharpest focus.

Why?

Because the focal character, acting, stands convinced that he's lost; that the seemingly inevitable doom the course of principle threatened is about to destroy him. It's a moment when, to him, all hope is gone.

Experiencing with the focal character, your reader shares this feeling. It brings his fear to its highest pitch.

Therefore, you don't dare hurry or slight that moment. Let your reader chill to—and thus enjoy—it to the full! The blacker things look, the longer the moment hangs. In consequence whereof, the higher your reader's pitch of tension rises, and the greater will be his sense of release and relief when the flip finally comes.

> (b) Reverse the focal character's situation with an unanticipated development.

The story is a western. Or science fiction, or mystery, or adventure. Now, in the climax scene, while minor characters stand by in aching silence, Villain gives Hero an unpleasant choice: Let Hero betray the cause for which he fights, and Villain will let him live. Let him refuse, and he'll die. Messily.

Hero chooses: He'll die. In the process, he'll try to take Villain with him.

Not that he has a chance. The odds are far too long for that. But at least he'll go down fighting.

He starts forward. Villain tightens a finger on the trigger of his weapon.

It's a moment that lasts an eternity. The chill breath of death seems to freeze the scene.

Only then, as Hero makes his play, and Villain bares teeth in a sadistic grin, a voice cries, "No!"

Whose voice it is, and why the cry is uttered, are unimportant here. The vital thing is, something happens. Something unanticipated. Something that upsets the balance of the situation.

So, here, someone cries, "No!"

In the brief moment that the Villain hangs distracted, Hero drives in hard. Villain's shot goes wild. And Hero is on his way to victory.

There, in its crudest and bloodiest form, stands the secret of story resolution: An unanticipated development has reversed the focal character's situation.

Not that triumph follows automatically or without effort, you understand. Hero still may have to bleed and battle. But his sacrifice of self in climax opens the way to a reversal.

"The art of life," Justice Holmes once said, "consists in making correct decisions on insufficient evidence."

How better can you describe the focal character's plight at a story's climax? Seeing only part of the picture, he still must make his choice—his sacrificial decision—and act upon it.

Whereupon, you the writer reveal the rest of the picture: the things which have a bearing that your character didn't know. The variables, the unperceived factors. Like what's going on inside the villain, or how another character will react, or the fact that somebody's gun is loaded or empty, or that there's water instead of poison in the hypodermic needle.

Nor is this any falsification of reality, even remotely. Life is full of shocks and twists and flips. Every man Jack of us has ever so often feared, but still plowed straight ahead; and, plowing, found our fears were groundless. Not a day passes but someone startles us with his reaction. A hundred times we face disaster, only to find that the blackest cloud can indeed have a silver lining.

A good reversal demands three things:

/1/ It must be *desired.*

If your reader doesn't want—want desperately—to see the focal character saved, even the best of twists is unlikely to impress him. You *must* make Reader care what happens to your hero.

/2/ It must be *unanticipated.*

You lose half the impact, at least, if your reader guesses in advance what's going to happen. The obvious just won't do.

/3/ It must be *logical.*

Believability is the payoff for proper preparation: planning and planting. An effect without a legitimate cause spells disaster every time.

Given these three elements, however, reversal will prove effective in a story on any level. Don't allow the fact that we here use an action-type example to prejudice you. No matter what kind of fiction you prefer to write, once a sacrifice is made, the climactic situation changes: Father revises his estimate of Son's potential. Girl recognizes Suitor's worth. Monster backs down before raw courage. Executive takes new cognizance of Subordinate's sense of duty. Wife sees that Husband really loves her.

Desired yet unanticipated yet logical developments, one and all.

Such a development, in turn, is what starts release of reader tension. It begins the answer to the story question: Will this focal character survive the hazard that threatens attainment of his goal, or won't he?

Specifically, the reversal demonstrates that the course of principle your hero chose in crisis isn't really going to crush him.

In so doing, it cuts fear sharply.

Result: a matching drop in tension . . . a drop that relieves and satisfies your reader.

How do you lay the groundwork for a reversal?

Herewith, five hints:

/1/ Know every detail of your climax situation.

—And that means, know them precisely! Even go so far as to draw a map or plan of the setting if it's not completely clear to you. The general is your worst enemy. In terms of pure mechanics, Hero may need a window that isn't there, or an electric cord, or a text on astrophysics.

/2/ Know your characters.

List them, every one. Then, ask yourself what each is doing at this particular moment, and how each will react to the fact of your character's decision.

/3/ Remember that audacity often carries the day.

Tonight's paper carried a story about a householder who saw a thief stealing the tires from Householder's pickup truck. So, Householder went out with a shotgun to stop the theft. Thief promptly pulled a "small pistol," ordered Householder back into dwelling, and then drove off with tires *and* shotgun!

/4/ Bear in mind that people react favorably to unselfishness.

If the man I detest displays moral courage, I may conclude that he's more worthy than I thought him. Whereupon, I may act upon that belief to help him.

Further, an act of principle and courage can sometimes free your hero himself from the bondage of his own fears. Once he's taken the first step, inertia's paralysis breaks. Committed, he has nothing left to lose. So, like a berserker, a Moro run amok, he rises above what he always imagined were his limitations.

/5/ Above all, remember that your role of writer makes you god within the boundaries of your story.

In time of need, a change in circumstance—anything from weather to locale to the villain's attitude—will *always* solve your problem.

(c) Give him his reward.

How do you reward a character?

You let him attain his goal, in letter or in spirit.

✸   ✸   ✸

Beginning writers seldom pay enough attention to the nature of reward.

Because this is so, too often they also talk cynically about the "hypocrisy" of fiction and the eternal need for a "happy" ending.

Actually, the *happy* ending is infinitely less important than the *satisfying* ending. Given reader fulfillment, you don't necessarily have to close with a clinch, the Marines landing, or the villain snarling, "Foiled again!"

Forget the phony, therefore. Distortion of reality will get you nowhere. What your reader seeks is less nirvana than the feeling, "This is as it should be."

How do you create this feeling?

The first step is to release tension.

Source 1 for tension, already discussed in detail, is danger. It culminates in the climactic moment, with its threat of disaster for your hero.

To release tension stemming from this source, you eliminate the hazard. In so doing, you dissipate character's—and reader's—fear that some specific something will or won't happen. Whereupon, tension ebbs.

Source 2 is desire.

Desire, you'll recall, is the ground-swell from which all danger springs. It precedes peril. For what trouble can you give a focal character who doesn't care what happens to him? Implicitly, desire to live must exist before there can be a fear of death. How can you worry about what a woman does, if she means nothing to you? Does money matter, when you've already taken a vow of poverty?

Whether we're consciously aware of it or not, desire is in all of us, every moment. Somewhere deep inside, we ache; we yearn; we hunger.

Out of such desire, in your focal character, springs goal . . . a goal so vital to him, subjectively, that early in your story he commits himself to fight to achieve it against all odds.

Specifically, he wants to attain or retain some particular something.

When you want anything badly enough, the wanting creates tension in you. A continuing tension that gnaws and churns and burns.

Until your focal character gets the thing he wants, therefore, this desire-born tension roils inside him—and, vicariously, inside your reader.

To release that tension, you give Character what he wants. You allow him to attain his goal.

It's at this point that a host of writers go astray.

Why?

Because they assume that the thing the focal character gets must match to the letter the goal he seeks. If he wants a million dollars, a million dollars he must have. Does the heroine yearn for a red dress? Then give it to her! And so on down the line, all the way to the ruby from the idol's eye, the banker's house, violent vengeance against a hated rival, and Cleopatra reclining on a tiger skin.

This isn't reward or poetic justice. It's nonsense.

The reason is that often there's a vast difference between *stated* goal and *true* goal. Though they may be the same, frequently the gap between them is as wide as that between sentimental and intrinsic value, where the kerchief or tintype or lock of hair an old man treasures may be thrown out by his heirs as trash.

In the same way, physical goal is primarily a symbol.

As a symbol, it represents an emotional need. And it's this need which the symbol represents that reward must satisfy.

Such a need is like a hunger, an inner thirst. It makes its host a driven man.

Often, however, the man doesn't even realize the need is there. He only feels an unrest, a dissatisfaction.

Whereupon, consciously or unconsciously, he picks a goal to strive for, in the belief that once he attains it he'll be happy.

Frequently, he's mistaken. What he really needs is to satisfy his inner hunger. Such satisfaction is more vital by far than acquisition of fame or girl or gold.

Take the man above who claims he wants a million dollars.

Actually, his need—the thing the million dollars represents to him, on an unconscious level—may be to feel an inner sense of his own worth and, with it, the self-confidence to tell his arrogant boss to go to hell.

Give him that confidence, and he's happy even though he still stays broke.

Likewise, the girl who longs for a red dress may not truly care about the dress at all. It's love she's seeking, actually. But deep inside, she sees herself as far too drab and unattractive ever to win the man she wants. So, the dress is only a means to her emotional end. Let her once find love, and she'll blissfully forego the garment.

The ruby from the idol's eye, in turn, may be the verbalized target of someone who seeks a sense of power; for who but a brave and dangerous person would ever dare to try to steal it? The banker's house, likely as not, stands as a status symbol, and the man who wants it really seeks proof that he's as good as anyone in town, despite the fact that his father was the local drunk and his mother took in washing. A drive to violent vengeance can grow from a need to impress a girl who disdains you as weak and ineffectual. The fantasy of wooing Cleopatra on a tiger skin speaks of loneliness and deep-seated yearning for affection. Quite possibly it's less sexual craving than it is hunger for tenderness and warmth, embodied in a living woman.

So much for the distinction between stated goals and true goals. Now, how do you use that variance to help resolve your story problem and reward your hero?

/1/ You determine the emotional need behind your focal character's stated goal.

Here, the issue is one of character dynamics. We'll discuss it at length in the next chapter.

/2/ You devise a way to satisfy that emotional need.

How do you satisfy an emotional need?

You so change your character's outlook that he achieves fulfillment.

Fulfillment is a feeling, a state of mind. State of affairs runs a poor, poor second.

To change a character's outlook means that you let him see what he really wants.

That is, you allow him to perceive and achieve the true goal that lies behind his stated goal. You help him to understand that work or adventure is more important to him than girl or money, or that success isn't always suburbia and Brooks Brothers' suits. Facing up to the fact that you don't have the talent to be a concert star can free you. Some marriages are better broken than mended. There can be happiness through the tears when a son or daughter finally finds the strength to leave home.

Even death can upon occasion be a triumph. If you don't believe me, take time out some day to read Talbot Mundy's fine story, "The Soul of a Regiment."

How do you change a character's outlook?

You show him the negative side of his stated goal and the positive side of his true goal.

Let's say the issue is vengeance. All through your story, Character has lived for the moment when he could plunge his knife into the villain.

Now, that moment's here. Evil, arrogant Villain lies at Hero's mercy.

To slay an evil, arrogant man can be a triumph. It gives you a sense of power and virtue.

But suppose this proud figure now breaks and cringes . . . crawls in the dirt and begs for mercy. What does that do to your stated goal?

Before, you saw Villain as strength and menace incarnate. As such, he was a challenge to you.

Now, his mask is torn away, his façade shattered. What lies revealed is fear and weakness.

With that change in Villain comes an end to challenge. You're really the strong man; he, the weak. To kill him now would serve only to degrade you. His humiliation is enough.

That's the negative side of your stated goal.

Simultaneously comes realization that the fear and self-doubt that earlier drove you on have vanished, and it dawns on you that those flaws in your own self-image, not Villain, were your true opponents.

Because this is so, from here on out you can face the world serene and unafraid. Never again will you need to question your own stature.

That's the positive side of your true goal.

Add positive and negative together, and you have tension released, desire attained . . . fulfillment; resolution.

Or suppose your fondest dream has been to marry a girl with a million dollars. —Not just any such girl, you understand; one particular one.

To that end, you've gone through hell in terms of the rising action of your story. But the climax turns the trick. At last Girl stands ready to accept you. You're about to attain your stated goal.

Now, however, you discover that her idea of marriage is to keep you as a sort of house pet—and that's certainly a negative aspect of your stated goal.

Nor is this totally her fault. She's the product of her background, her upbringing. Her view of the world is something that she takes for granted.

Seeing this, you reconsider your own motives . . . realize at last that what you've felt for Girl isn't love, in fact, so much as it is a drive for status, which you've misinterpreted as the quickest road to independence.

Independence: That's what you really want; that's your true goal.

And you can achieve it better without Girl than with her . . . besides which, she deserves more than a parasitic husband who doesn't really love her.

A positive angle on true goal, right?

Girl faces the facts, when you explain it. She can't change; neither can you. Your differences are too great to resolve.

The parting scene is tender, touching. And you go off fulfilled, even though sans girl.

How do you resolve a story?

You know your focal character.

Then, you let him know and be true to himself.

As a writer, you have no higher duty, to yourself or to your reader.

And this in spite of the fact that said reader may never realize the source of his satisfaction. —Which is as it should be, of course. Story technique is the writer's business only. It's like plastic surgery: The best nose-bob or face-lift is the one that goes undetected.

* * *

What about the negative character . . . the weak man, the evil man, the man who can't or won't make the right decision at a story's climax? How do you resolve *his* story?

You punish him.

That is, you deny him his goal, in letter and/or in spirit.

You do this because such a character prizes self-interest above principle. He proves this in climax, when he chooses the easy road instead of standing firm for right.

In so doing, he demonstrates himself to be unworthy of reward.

If, then, in spite of his misdeed, you *do* reward him, you create a conflict in your reader.

How?

Your reader, too, has emotional needs. One of the deepest of these, as we've pointed out, is his desire to believe that there is order in the world; that life holds meaning.

In reading, Reader seeks reaffirmation of this belief. He wants to feel that cause leads to effect; that deed influences reward.

Deny this, in your story, and in effect you tell him that his whole philosophy is wrong; that he's a fool for all the sacrifices he himself makes daily.

Result: frustration. So, tension doesn't slack; it builds. And Reader loses his precious sense of story satisfaction.

This is why adolescent cynicism proves such a blind alley as a theme for fiction. The clever criminal who gets away with crime, the man of principle made a fool of or destroyed by circumstance, the woman who cheats successfully on her husband, the triumph of the ruthless and the evil—they mark your work as amateur. In life, such people stand as the exception, not the rule. In fiction, almost invariably, they draw a quick rejection.

As a matter of fact, even the so-called "biter-bit" story (in which the central character receives richly deserved punishment at the climax) has only the narrowest of markets. Make your "hero" a murderer who's trapped because he overlooks one tiny clue and, count on it, the yarn will prove twice or three times as hard to sell as the story with a positive central character.

Part of the reason for this is because the pattern itself has grown so worn and trite.

More important, however, is the established fact that most of the time, most readers would rather read about the worthy man who wins.

* * *

So much for the mechanics and dynamics of reward.

Once reward is bestowed, the story question is answered. Suspense drops sharply. Most reader tension is released.

But you still need to round out your story, briefly, and bring it to a neat conclusion.

With that in mind . . .

(5) You tie up any loose ends.

Face one fact: The moment your story question is answered, your story itself ends, for all practical purposes.

Therefore, don't hold your reader any further past that point than need be. Stall a bit too long, and you may lose him. Your job from here on out is to say good-by, in as few words and pages as you can.

At the same time, you don't dare move too fast, or you'll lose emotional impact.

Ordinarily, a few pages—certainly not more than a chapter, even in a novel—of denouement should be enough. Long explanations will prove unnecessary, if you've snipped off subordinate threads early, in accordance with instructions.

So, work for a *short* concluding section.

On the other hand, be careful not to leave characters unaccounted for or loose ends dangling.

How do you avoid such?

You go back over your work. Painstakingly. Check plot development, point by point. Ask yourself if there are questions that you've left unanswered.

Often, too, a reading by someone who doesn't know the story will bring holes and loose thinking to your attention.

Be careful, though. What you need is honest appraisal, not flattery or half-baked critical opinion.

Finally . . .

(6) You focus fulfillment into a punch line.

How do you write a proper punch line?

You strive for euphoria.

Euphoria may be defined as a sense of well-being and buoyancy. It's the feeling that follows the draining off of the last vestiges of reader tension.

To create it, you hunt for a final paragraph, and a line to end it, that will epitomize your character's or characters' fulfillment.

Since a story is the record of how somebody deals with danger, this final paragraph and line should make clear to your reader that said danger—and the tension and trouble it created—are at an end, so far as the characters are concerned. Completely.

On the other hand, ". . . and so they lived happily ever after" isn't quite enough. Life goes on, and your reader knows it.

Therefore, you need to include some indication that your characters still have a future. Other troubles may come. In fact, assorted woes may be hanging fire right now. But they're not yet on stage, so your people can still glow happily in the relief and release of this moment's triumph.

The actual writing of a good punch line can be a nerve-racking, floor-pacing, time-consuming job. The most common approach, perhaps, is simply to jot down each and every idea that comes to mind, no matter how remote. Then, settle for whichever one seems best.

Beyond this, here are three tricks which may help:

(a) Try, earlier, to establish the idea that a particular event, a significant detail, represents fulfillment to your hero.

Throughout the story, Hero's been striving to make time with Girl, without success. You conclude, "This time, *she* was kissing *him*."

Conceivably, your reader may decide that Hero has indeed attained his goal.

(*b*) A comic or apparently pointless line may turn the trick
—if only because it demonstrates conclusively that trouble and tension are over.

Exhibit A: "Words came through the tears: 'Steve . . . oh, Steve, you're *home!*'

"The steeldust kept on grazing."

Actually, no one gives a hoot about the horse. It's just that by shifting attention to him, we confirm that danger is dissipated.

(*c*) Ignoring the present for the future may carry the implication that all's ended and all's well.

"Seth cut in: 'I'll take care of it soon's I can, Ed. But right now, Helen and me need to run over to Red Rock. We got some things to take care of.'"

* * *

Thus do you write the ending to your story. The key issue to bear in mind is that the thing your reader remembers best is what he reads last. In consequence, a strong ending may save a weak story. If the ending disappoints, on the other hand, Reader quite possibly will feel that the story as a whole is a failure.

* * *

Beginning plus middle plus end equal story.

Here in this chapter we've chopped them up, dissected them, dealt with each almost as if it were a separate entity.

They're not. Except analytically, as here, story components have no life separate from the whole, any more than a hand or a head or a stomach can survive apart from the parent body. To allow atomistic concepts to rule your thinking when you write is as futile as to try to assemble a living cow from hamburger.

"What's wrong with my third act?" a playwright asked dramatist George Kaufman.

"Your first," Kaufman answered.

That's a lesson every new writer needs to take to heart. A successful story is always an integrated unit. Treat it as a mishmash of bits and fragments and it disintegrates.

Neither should you accept a breakdown such as this chapter offers as attempting to establish a set pattern. The purpose of fragmentation is to show you what makes a story tick . . . devices with which you create effects; a few of the tools you use to manipulate reader feeling.

Each story, however, is unique and individual. Tricks and techniques must be adapted to its special problems. No universal blueprint is worth the paper on which it's reproduced.

That's the reason I put such stress on function and dynamics . . . the *why* behind the superstructure. For the thing a beginner needs is understanding, not a copy camera. A rule is a rock around your neck, if you let it dominate intelligence and imagination.

Especially is this true when you set out to create people to populate your stories . . . which same is the subject of our next chapter.

CHAPTER 7

The People in Your Story

A story is people given life on paper.

A character is a person in a story.

To create story people, you grab the first stick figures that come handy; then flesh them out until they spring to life.

This process of character creation is no more or less difficult than any other phase of authorship. Yet the mere mention of it fills too many would-be writers with all sorts of trepidation.

Why?

Because we spend our lives with people, but we seldom pay attention to them. As the late Sir Arthur Conan Doyle once caused Sherlock Holmes to comment, "You see, but you do not observe."

Which is just another way of saying that the human animal is really a mystery to us. We don't know what he looks like, we don't know how he behaves or why, we don't understand what it is about him that bores us or excites us.

The unknown is always frightening. To be forced to deal with it, face to face, sends us into panic.

No such consternation is warranted. You learn to build characters the same way you learn anything else in this writing business: You take the job a step at a time, working in terms of function and process and device.

What specific points do you need to master? You'll find them in the answers to five questions:

1. How does a character come into being?
2. How do you bring a character to life?

3. How do you give a character direction?

4. How do you make a character fascinate your reader?

5. How do you fit a character to the role he has to play?

So much for generalities. Now, let's get down to cases.

How does a character come into being?

To what extent is a character like a real person—a living, breathing human being?

At a generous estimate, about one one-thousandth of 1 per cent.

The reason this is so is because a living person is infinitely complex. A story person, on the other hand, is merely a *simulation* of a living person. So, he's infinitely simpler. Space and function limit him.

Thus, even the longest book can capture only a tiny segment of any human being. To try to get down the real person would demand a library at least. The cortex of a man's brain has more than ten billion nerve cells. The Empire State Building couldn't house a computer with that many tubes, and a scientist says that a machine to play unbeatable chess would have to be "slightly larger than the universe."

What's more, there's no need in fiction to go into all the facets of a living being. A story is the record of how somebody deals with danger. *One* danger, for a simple story; a series of inter-related dangers, for one more complex. In neither case can you possibly involve the full range of a personality.

So?

So, you develop a character only to that limited degree that he needs to be developed, in order to fulfill his function in the story. You give an impression and approximation of life, rather than attempting to duplicate life itself.

To that end, you oversimplify the facts of human personality, since to do otherwise complicates your task to the point where it becomes completely impractical, if not impossible.

And that brings us back to our original question: How do you bring a character into being?

You plan a story.

Sometimes, in so doing, you begin with a character. But sometimes you don't. For despite a host of literary folk-tales, a story may start from anything—the most evanescent of fragments in a writer's mind.

Sometimes, that fragment may be a person, or some aspect of a person. But it may equally well be a mood, a situation, a setting, an object, an incident, a conflict, a complication, a word, a flash of imagery or sensory perception.

Once you have this fragment, you begin to build your story. By *accretion*, as mystery writer Fredric Brown once phrased it. By gradual addition, bouncing your idea around in free association until other thought-fragments, magnetized, cling to it.

Eventually, it adds up to a story.

Your characters, too, come into being gradually. Often, in the early stages, they may be faceless; mere designations of role— "hero," "villain," "girl," and the like.

Then, a little at a time, you find yourself individualizing them. Pictures begin to form in your mind—vague at first; then sharper. The girl becomes a redhead, the hero has a habit of gulping and staring blankly, the villain beams cordially at the very moment that he twists the knife.

Where do you get these fragments?

From observation. From thought and insight. From imagination.

Take *observation*. All your life long, automatically, you store up a reservoir of impressions. Impressions of people are among them. You see what they look like, how they behave, the way in which they think. Then, when you take to writing, and need characters, you find yourself selecting and juggling and recombining these components.

And there stands a major source of writer trouble. For observation isn't always an automatic process. Soon, if you're at all perceptive, you discover that your eye for detail tends too often to be sloppy, inaccurate.

Whereupon, you take to paying closer attention to people . . . seeking out types and individuals that intrigue you . . . studying them consciously in an effort to enrich your store of raw material.

Particularly, you stop taking so much for granted. Instead of accepting vague impressions, you hunt for specifics. You break down behavior into cause and effect, motivating stimulus and

character reaction. You search out significant details—the trivia
that create or betray feeling.

But observation alone isn't quite enough. We have to supplement it with *thought and insight*.

Why?

Because, in day-to-day living, we tend to accept rather than
analyze; to take for granted, more than understand.

Consequently, when we try to build story people, we find that
we lack a grasp of mental mechanisms; motivations.

To remedy this demands conscious study.

Sometimes, that study takes us to the library. But life itself
may prove a better teacher. Even psychiatrists admit that novelists pioneered the behavioral area before them.

Certainly, in any event, you need all the understanding you
can get. Character, human personality, is a subject no writer
ever masters completely. But with a little effort, you can broaden
your discernment enough to satisfy your reader.

Enter *imagination*.

A human being is more than observed fragments; more than
mental mechanisms too.

Specifically, each of us is an entity, a personal and private
whole that transcends its components.

To understand a man, you have to grasp the essence of that
wholeness . . . its *Gestalt;* the totality of its configuration.

So also with story people. The parts just aren't enough. You
have to integrate them into a larger pattern. Until you do, they
won't coalesce into what appears to be a living person.

Conceptualizing this *Gestalt*, this wholeness, is imagination's
task. It brings the character to life.

To claim that this is always simple would be to lie to you.
Character creation can be a complex operation . . . one that
calls for every bit of skill and inspiration you can muster.

Further, each character constitutes a separate problem, individual and unique. Some demand much labor, some little. Some
spring to a semblance of life full-grown, with virtually no conscious effort. Others require endless floor-pacing. And still others,
for no perceptible reason, never come through clearly, fully believable, no matter how much you sweat or strain. You simply
can't seem to tune in on their wave-length.

Which means?

You too are human and have private limitations. And that's good. The writer who sees himself as a surrogate of God is on the road to paranoia.

* * *

It's question time again:

   a. How many characters should you have in a story?

No more than absolutely necessary. Each takes extra words, extra space, extra effort. Throw in too many, and you may even lose or confuse your reader.

   b. How do you decide whether or not a character is necessary?

The best rule is to bring in no one who doesn't in some way or other advance the conflict . . . which is to say, the story. If a story person isn't for or against your hero, leave him out. Every character should contribute something: action or information that helps or harms, advances or holds back.

   c. Can't this still leave you with more characters than you can safely handle?

Of course. The trick here, however, is to consolidate. Ask yourself if waiter and bellhop and room clerk can't be combined; if the contributions they make can't be attended to as well by one person as by two or three.

   d. Are good characters really as contrived as this would make them seem to be?

They are. A story isn't facts or history; it's the product of a writer's imagination.

Consequently, *everything* about it is contrived. The only issue is, do you contrive skillfully, so that your reader doesn't detect that element of contrivance? Or, is the job inept and awkward, with your hand as obvious as that of a bumbling puppeteer?

   e. Wouldn't it be better to write about real people?

No; and for three reasons:

(1) A real person may recognize himself in your story.

He can resent this, in terms of a—for you—disastrous lawsuit.

(2) A real person seldom fits your story needs precisely.

So long as you write fiction and not fact, you need to work with people exactly suited to their tasks. Create a character, and you can tailor him to fit the situation. Pick one from life, and more often than not reality gets in the way.

(3) A real person is hard to work with.

Frequently, your contact with or knowledge of a real person blocks you when you try to write about him. You grope, trying to remember exactly how he does a thing. You draw back from making him behave the way he should.

These reactions may not even reach a conscious level. All you know is, all at once you just can't write.

Therefore, your best approach is to make no attempt to pattern your character after anyone you know, except perhaps in the broadest terms. You should *avoid* detailed copying, in fact, even if it takes conscious effort.

f. How do you shape development of your characters?

Stress is the formative factor; the thing that makes or breaks a man.

So, plunge your people into conflict. Let pressure strip away the gloss and reveal them as they really are.

In so doing, don't hesitate to play the tune by ear. The inspiration of the moment, the heat of your own fervor, may produce results that startle you!

g. What about character growth?

Here we have a point much beloved and belabored by the critics. But most stories occupy a brief time span. The action runs no more than forty-eight hours, say; or twenty-four.

How much growth do you yourself, or your friends, exhibit in such a period?

On the other hand, in the novel that covers years, your characters do indeed grow. Or, to put it more precisely, they learn by experience.

Which means that if you show them living through the specific events that teach them their lessons, there's no problem.

> *h.* Don't some writers claim that their characters come alive and themselves control a story's direction, despite the writer's contrary wishes?

They say so.

What such a writer means, however, if he only realized it, is that he becomes so fascinated with the personality he's created that he prefers to write about that personality instead of the story he originally had in mind.

This can be good, or it can be disastrous.

Fascination with anything makes work easier and, in fiction, results in a more vivid product.

On the other hand, preoccupation with a character seldom substitutes for sound story structure. The personality run wild too often throws everything else off balance.

As a general rule, therefore, the character who stays within the framework of his function turns out best.

> *i.* Doesn't such a limitation make many characters shallow and superficial?

Actually, despite all screams of anguish from the literati, many characters have no depth, and need none.

Such characters start as "John" or "Mary," and go no further.

The trick in this is to weigh each character as you build him. Ask yourself how much attention he warrants. If the role he plays is only a walk-on bit, deal with him in the simplest terms. You pay little heed to the man who drives your cab, in life. You pay a great deal to your wife. In most cases, the same principle applies to fiction.

> *j.* What do you do if a minor player completely captivates you?

This offers the same hazard we discussed in question *h*, above. When it happens, you have to decide whether to reshape the story to fit the character; or, cut the character back to fit his original function. There's no way to avoid the choice.

This is *not* to say that you shouldn't make a bit player colorful and intriguing, you understand, so long as you hold him within the framework of his role.

    k. How much should you flesh out your not-so-minor characters?

Give them precisely as much attention as their importance in the conflict needs and warrants.

    l. Is it a good idea to set up dossiers on your characters—detailed biographies and the like?

This too is a matter of degree. Carried too far, it can be dangerous, simply because it's so time-consuming. If you follow the routine some books suggest, down to whether or not your heroine likes pineapple ice, you may very well end up with fine background studies of your people—but no hours or energy left to write the story.

    m. Should you group characters into such categories as "simple," "complex," "flat," "round," "in relief," and so on?

Such labels are tools of the critic, not the writer. They're arbitrary, analytical, and after the fact. Slap them on in advance, and they tend to paralyze creative thinking.

    n. How can you be sure that you understand the psychology of your story people correctly?

Difference of opinion is what makes horse races. Behaviorists work on one set of assumptions, Freudians another. A detective and a social worker and a clergyman may each draw different conclusions as to the motivation of a given act.

Your ideas about why a man takes a certain path can quite possibly prove as valid as another's. In characterization, as in anything else, you have to act on the courage of your convictions. If you intrigue your reader with your concepts, he'll go along.

How do you bring a character to life?

"A 'living' character is not necessarily 'true to life,'" declares poet-dramatist T. S. Eliot. "It is a person whom we can see and hear, whether he be true or false to human nature as we know it. What the creator of character needs is not so much knowledge of motives as keen sensibility; the dramatist need not understand people; but he must be exceptionally aware of them."

What do you say about a character and his behavior to make him seem vivid and credible to your reader?

You make him look and act like a living person. Which is to say, you give him an *appearance* of life.

To this end, you use learned tricks and techniques of presentation.

The key to effective character presentation is *contrast*. The world's population today is numbered in the billions. Yet each individual remains different. There still are no two fingerprints alike.

Story people must be thus differentiated also. Continuously, from start to finish. Otherwise, how can your reader know who's who? How can he decide which characters he likes?

Liking characters is vital to your reader. So is disliking, and feeling pity and contempt and respect and tenderness and sexual excitement.

Why?

Because without such variations of emotional reaction, the reader can't care what happens to your people.

If he doesn't care, he can achieve no sense of inner tension when they're endangered.

It's to gain such tension, remember, that your reader reads. Therefore, you must give him vivid, contrasting story people . . . men and women who strike sparks in him, and in whose moccasins he can walk.

To differentiate between your characters, you do five things for each:

> *a.* Determine dominant impression.
> *b.* Fit impression to role.

c. Modify the picture.

d. Match character to cast.

e. Assign appropriate tags.

What does each point involve? Let's take them one at a time:

a. Determine dominant impression.

Consider what happens when, in life, you meet a person for the first time. One way or another, whether you will it or not, he makes a dominant impression on you.

That is, you find yourself labeling him as a *dignified* person, or a *cruel* man, or a *sexy* woman, or a *flighty* girl, or a *rowdy* boy, or what have you.

Precisely the same process takes place in fiction. So, to shape your reader's reaction to a story person, you decide what image you want said reader to receive.

b. Fit impression to role.

Suppose you're directing a play. You want to pick an actor for the hero's part.

Immediately, the question arises: Should you cast *to* type or *against* type?

This merely means that, in life and in fiction, each of us has certain preconceived notions as to what certain categories of person are like . . . stereotypes, as it were. Thus, most of us think of a hero, a leading man, as tall, dark, handsome, physically prepossessing, and so on.

If, as director, I pick an actor who *matches* this stereotype— a tall, dark, handsome, physically prepossessing man—I'm said to be casting *to* type: I'm fitting actor to audience preconception.

If, on the other hand, I choose an actor who *contradicts* this audience preconception—an ugly man as hero; a gawky, awkward girl as heroine—I'm casting *against* type.

It goes on the same all down the line. Maybe I pick Mother to fit Whistler's picture, complete even unto rocking chair. Or, perhaps I visualize her as a beady-eyed, gin-guzzling, vitriol-tongued old bitch. Child may be sweet innocence personified; or, she make take form as an evil-minded little monster or a ragamuffin tomboy.

Partly, of course, your decision on such issues will be a matter of personal taste. But there are also a few objective facts you should take into consideration.

Any stereotype has familiarity on its side. It makes for easy reading . . . demands no thought, no readjustment. Though you run some minor risk of reader boredom, *Abie's Irish Rose* and the strong, silent heroes of ten thousand TV westerns stand on your side.

When you contradict stereotype, on the other hand, you lose familiarity but you add realism and interest. Readers know that not all policemen are Irish, not all gangsters gorillas, not all girls beautiful. They're excited by the very novelty of a Huck Finn or a Philip Carey.

Now, back to story:

When you write, you're in the position of the director above. You have to decide whether the dominant impression you pick for a given character fits or contradicts your reader's stereotype of the figure who should be assigned such a role.

If you decide to contradict said stereotype, you must be prepared also to devise ways to get Reader to accept that contradiction.

Yes, it can be done—witness Rex Stout's use of ponderously obese Nero Wolfe as a mystery hero, or the hypocrisy that stands as the trade-mark of Elmer Gantry.

But thus to go against the tide demands that you attack the task with open eyes and forthright recognition of the problem.

c. Modify the picture.

Here stands your character, suited out in the armor of dominant impression.

Now, ask yourself a question: Is this a true picture?

Consider the dignified person. Is he really dignified—or is the appearance of dignity merely a mask he's adopted to hide stupidity? Is the cruel man totally cruel . . . cruel to certain people only . . . or using the appearance of cruelty to hide the fact that he's really so sentimental as to be a pushover for any appeal? Is the sexy woman in fact eager to go to bed with all comers, or does she hold sex in such fear that she must hide her panic behind lewd talk and pretense of promiscuity? Does the flighty girl's appearance of flightiness conceal cold calculation? Is the boy's rowdiness a mask for shyness?

All of us are, in truth, a maze of inconsistencies and contradictions. That's what makes man interesting. Capture the paradox in print, and your characters will be interesting also.

Obversely, the person or character who's all black or all white, all good or all bad, all honor or all lust or all servility, may do very well in a bit part. But he lacks the depth to hold sustained attention. If you don't believe me, try reading a year's *Dick Tracy* strips at a single sitting.

The more effective character possesses both strengths and weaknesses. They modify the dominant impression. The scholar, irked at a poor haircut, reveals a human touch of vanity. The drunk turns down a drink because his young son is standing by. The concert pianist cancels an engagement to help care for her sister's newest baby.

Of such are actual people made. They don't want just one thing. They aren't limited to a single feeling. Despite surface consistency, conflicts and contradictions upon occasion rage inside them.

Your story people should show the same range of inner contrast.

One warning, though: Dominant impression should remain dominant; major modifying elements limited in number. Too great complexity blurs the picture for your reader.

d. Match character to cast.

Ordinarily, a story involves people, plural.

Each person should make a *different* dominant impression. If three characters all pulse dignity at every turn, each will detract from the impact of the others. What you want is variety, not sameness.

e. Assign appropriate tags.

A tag is a label.

You hang tags on story people so that your reader can tell one character from another. An impression, dominant or otherwise, is created by the tags a character bears.

Black hair is a tag. It helps distinguish the raven-tressed girl from another who's a blonde.

A stutter is a tag. It sets apart one character from others who speak without impediment.

Shuffling your feet is a tag. It keeps people from confusing you with your friend, who strides along.

Pessimism is a tag. It marks its victim as different from the joker.

Tags also may translate inner state into external action. Each time the brother in *Arsenic and Old Lace* shouts "Charge!" and dashes up his imaginary San Juan Hill, we're reminded that he lives in a private world.

What types of tags are there?

Most fall into four categories:

(1) Appearance.
(2) Speech.
(3) Mannerism.
(4) Attitude.

Appearance is obvious. Some men are tall, others short; some handsome, others ugly; some blue-eyed, some brown, some black. Women may be well-groomed or sloppy, old or young, with good posture or bad.

Speech, too, individualizes. Most college professors talk differently than most truck drivers. Most prostitutes have a vocabulary miles apart from that of most preachers' wives. A Texas drawl is distinct from New Yorkese. Each of us has habitual expressions, from "Well, now . . ." to "Looking at this business-wise. . . ." We fumble, grope, speak precisely or pedantically or slangily or to the point. Our use of language reflects background, experience, occupation, social status, psychology, and a host of other things

Mannerism? Some men scowl. Some women flutter. You know hand-rubbers, ear-lobe tuggers, eye-dodgers, buttonholers. The doodler, the nail-cleaner, the pipe-puffer, the gesticulator, and the seat-squirmer all are commonplace.

Tags of *attitude*—sometimes called *traits*—mark the habitually apologetic, fearful, irritable, breezy, vain, or shy. Obsequiousness is an attitude, and so is the habit of command. Here, too, are found the men and women preoccupied with a single subject, whether it be golf or babies, business or yard or stamps or fishing. For all preoccupations, in their way, represent habit of thought or view of life.

The key thing to remember about tags is that their primary purpose is to distinguish . . . to separate one character from another in your reader's eyes.

Therefore, it's important that you don't accidentally confuse said reader. Don't duplicate tags. One fat man, one lush blonde, one profane engineer to a story is enough.

Same way for names. Jack, John, and Joe in the same scene will mix up readers. Likewise for Hanson, Thomson, Johnson. There are worse rules than to check off each initial letter and terminal syllable as you use it, just so no careless scanner goes astray.

A second function of the tag is to characterize. To that end, fit label to personality. If a man is timid, let it show in handshake and diffidence and speech. A woman who glances sidewise at a stranger and hitches her skirt above her knees as she sits down tells more about herself than a paragraph of author comment.

Again, names enter. While "John Strongheart" and "Tess Truelove" have gone out of style, it still doesn't hurt to choose John's cognomen with an eye to its connotations of vigor and/or masculinity. As for Tess, styles in girls' names change. "Agatha," "Beatrice," and "Chris" each tends to point to a different decade of birth.

Now, three points of application to remember:

(a) *Do* use enough tags.

Sometimes, one or two tags for a given character are enough. "Now the door opened, and a heavy-set, crew-cut man poked his head in. 'Hey, anybody here drive a blue Buick?'" may prove entirely adequate for someone with only a walk-on bit.

But if a character is going to play a major part, constant reference to his wavy hair or bulging eyes or grimy nails eventually will get to be a bore.

Solution? More tags. Often, you'll find it desirable to use labels of all four types for a single individual . . . maybe even several of each. Thus, our man may be burly, black-haired, and stubble-chinned . . . fumble for words and speak in incoherent fragments . . . lick his lips and scratch his chest and shift from foot to foot . . . combine belligerence with a tendency to beat around the bush whenever he's asked a direct question.

(b) *Do* bring on tags in action.

"He had blue eyes" is the worst possible approach. "The blue eyes glinted coldly"? Better!

Often, the best trick is to try to find some bit of stage business on which to hang the tag. Thus, for a proud woman: "She stood there for a moment, the violet eyes ever so steady. Only the slightest trace of heightened color showed in the smooth cheeks.

"Then, with a quick, deft movement, she snapped the purse shut, turned still without a word and, blonde head high, left the room."

An irascible character? " 'Get out!' he roared, jowls purpling." A haughty character? "Kurt brought up the monocle, studying Frances as if she were some sort of bug." An awkward character? "A strange, shambling figure, he moved to the chair. But as he reached it, something seemed to happen to the too-large feet, and all at once the drink was flying one way and the ashtray another while he and the chair crashed to the floor together in a tangle of gangling arms and legs and ill-fitted clothing and shaggy hair."

Well, you get the idea.

(c) *Do* wave tags often.

Don't assume that your reader will remember a character from page to page. Focus attention on your man's tags, his labels, whenever he appears. If a girl has dark, wavy hair, let her run her fingers through it, smooth it, brush it back, complain how it won't hold a permanent, or the like, at virtually every turn.

* * *

So much for the five steps of character presentation.

Of course, in applying such a guide, you won't necessarily follow the order in which the steps are set forth here. A character ordinarily takes form a little at a time, as I've pointed out, so you don't want to limit yourself to any set procedure.

But the basic principles are those outlined, and if you use them as a checklist, working and studying and experimenting as you go, they'll help you create realistic, believable story people, with the appearance of life stamped on them.

How do you give a character direction?

Though contrived by a writer, a good—that is, effective—character should appear to move under his own power. He needs to act without ostensible prodding from his creator.

To that end, you provide a pattern of rationalization for said character . . . an excuse for him to behave the way you want him to.

The simplest way to do this is to make the goal a character seeks symbolize, to him, satisfaction of personal, private inner needs.

To make a goal symbolic of such needs demands that you supply your character with two elements:

　　a. Lack.
　　b. Compensation.

Which means?

Each of us wants to feel adequate to his world . . . in control of his situation and, thus, of his destiny.

Anything that endangers a character's sense of control indicates a *lack* in him . . . an inadequacy. If my wife nags, or my jokes fall flat, or the promotions I seek go to other men, I may eventually come to doubt myself.

When a man becomes aware of such a lack, and even if he can't figure out precisely what disturbs him, he grows tense and restless: unhappy, discontented, ill at ease.

To relieve this tension, he takes some sort of action . . . escapes from the nagging wife in work, abandons humor for books, eases the sting of disappointment at failure to get ahead by taking refuge in gossip or sullenness or hobbies. Defeated, emotionally speaking, he substitutes one kind of behavior for another, in order to achieve a private victory. He pays for what he lacks, his inadequacies, with conduct designed to make up for them.

As a psychologist would phrase it, he *compensates* for his deficiencies.

Your character's need to control destiny, to feel adequate to each developing situation, is what gives him his strength, his drive, his motive force: in a word, his *direction*.

His goal, in turn, reflects that direction. If he can attain it, he feels, his sense of inadequacy will vanish, never to return.

In other words, to your character, goal is a symbol of fulfillment.

To you, as his creator, it's the ultimate product of lack plus compensation . . . the objectified, finely-focused essence of his inner needs.

So much for the general pattern. It constitutes a perfectly respectable, if limited, theory of personality. And where the psychiatrist frequently must deal with people who stubbornly refuse to fit into his diagnostic rule-book, you can make your character behave as if your theory were well-nigh absolute.

Further, you stand free to deviate at will. —Which you'll do, have no doubt, as you gain self-confidence, insight, and experience.

In the interim, this approach provides you with a basic structure—a skeletal hypothesis to work from while you learn the ropes.

Now, let's consider each factor in more detail.

* * *

Any feeling of *inadequacy*, it should be obvious, is an individual matter. The stimulus or situation that creates a sense of lack in one man may leave another utterly untouched.

In the same way, there are as many ways to compensate as there are human beings.

This is because a person—or a character—is primarily a point of view. His attitudes are the dynamic aspects of his being. The direction he takes and the road he travels depend on them. They constitute his private, subjective, individual mode of adjustment. They're the reason one man runs from the threat of violence, and another tries to talk his way out, and a third reaches for the nearest club.

A point of view is the sum of how a character sees and reacts to:

(1) Himself.
(2) His story plight.
(3) His world and life in general.

To establish a character's point of view, you first must provide
a background that will logically evoke it.

Much of that background may never get down on paper.
Much of what does get down will be for your eyes alone. Your
reader needn't know it. But if it doesn't exist—if you yourself
haven't thought it through—then count on it, the day will surely
come when your character won't behave the way you want him
to. Or, if he does, his reactions will prove so wildly inconsistent
and out of character as to shatter the picture of him that you've
tried so hard to build.

So, you give your character a history.

Because Character learns by experience, even as you and I,
his patterns of thought and feeling and behavior will be dis-
tilled from the totality of his past lacks and compensations. Each
successful or unsuccessful attack upon a problem shapes and
molds his way of dealing with new crises. So does each failure,
each frustration . . . each effort, each hurt, each false start, each
withdrawal.

To create a character's background, you can do worse than to
start with a survey of his areas of uniqueness.

Specifically, consider what he, as an individual, has to work
with, in terms of:

(a) Body.
(b) Environment.
(c) Experience.
(d) Ideas.

Take *body*. A woman is different from a man. The fact of that
difference, in our society, may make her feel frustrated, inadequate, inferior . . . deprived of opportunities that should right-
fully be hers. In her mind, at least, because of her sex, a lack
exists that tends to strip her of control over her own destiny.

A small man, in turn, may be intensely, bitterly aware that

he lacks the physical strength of his larger rival. An ugly girl reacts differently than one secure in beauty. A clumsy boy envies his brother's better coordination. The bald head, the big nose, the withered hand, the crossed eye, the slow wit, the stiff knee, the weak heart, the ulcer—all are notorious for their effect on the person whom they afflict; all may constitute lacks that shape the attitudes and patterns of their hosts.

Nor need any such add up to a handicap by objective standards. It's not the physical fact that counts; but, rather, the way the individual views it. No one else may notice the drooped lid, the sagging stomach, the minor deafness. But if *you* resent it, it may color your whole approach to others. The slight freckling that charms a girl's friends still may grow in her mind to sheer disfigurement.

Environment? The slum child and the country boy aren't the same. Neither are the resident of the sleepy college town and the New Yorker. East and West each molds its people. So do Maine and Mississippi. Wilshire Boulevard may loom broad and deep as the Grand Canyon to an aspiring actor who lives two blocks on the wrong side. Gopher Prairie breeds rebellion and resentment in the nonconformist. The girl at home on Chicago's Rush Street finds she feels uncomfortable and ill at ease when, jerked out of context, she's forced to live in Keokuk. The boy from Painted Post has trouble adjusting to Greenwich Village. The Louisiana Cajun or the West Virginia mountaineer may not fit into life at an army post.

Experience differentiates factory hand from cowman, preacher from peddler. Lack of it may petrify the virgin on her wedding night, or panic the new recruit under fire for the first time. The man perfectly at home at a banquet can feel hideously out of place in a cheap bar . . . and so can the waitress who now enters the Waldorf dining room as guest.

It's the same with *ideas*. Among old friends, I may do well. But a glibly contemptuous son, fresh home from college, makes me feel inadequate and inferior. Son, in turn, may writhe in helpless fury when a Communist trained at the Lenin Institute exposes him as a babe in arms politically. The boy who's lost his religious faith feels acutely uncomfortable and aware of difference under the accusing eyes of his devout family. And so does the woman who thought her taste impeccable until, today, a visitor laughed at the table setting.

Needless to say, all these analytical entities tend, in life, to overlap. Each of us is a compounding of complexities. No one can say for sure that a man is the way he is primarily because he was born with a tongue-tie that minor surgery corrected, or grew up on a Grosse Pointe Farms estate, or nearly drowned at nine when a sailboat overturned, or went from Michigan to Harvard Law School, or served as a naval officer before he took an executive post with Chrysler Corporation, or married a girl from Lake Forest and had two children by her, or chose to espouse the Democratic cause in a district solidly Republican. But add them all together, and you have a personality that's individual and unique. Each factor colors our man's feelings, his thinking, his behavior. Know him in terms of those factors, and despite all surface similarities he stands out in marked contrast to other men.

He is, in brief, a character you can work with in a story.

And that's why it's so well worth your while, in building characters, to survey each person's areas of uniqueness. From them, you can project some of the secret fears and lacks and feelings of inadequacy that drive your man or woman, and thus determine individual direction and make each appear to move independently, under his or her own steam.

Beyond this, it also helps if you'll take time to consider your character's involvements in:

(a) Love.
(b) Work.
(c) Society.

Here, the issue is simple: Man doesn't exist in a vacuum. A character without relationships to his fellow men is bound to prove flat as a cardboard cutout.

Take *love*. How does your man feel about women? Why? Is he married? If not, why not? If so, does he love his wife? As much now as when they married? Even more? And again, if not, why not?

In the same way, how does a child feel about his parents? His brothers and sisters? His playmates? His neighbors? His teachers? How do these experiences and reactions color and shape his attitudes?

Work, in our society, offers equal opportunities for study. Failure to take it into account can bring into being such ridiculous figures as the cowboy who always has cash to hang around the town saloon, yet never is observed actually punching cattle.

Further, employer and employee view the world from separate angles. Banker and grocer and farmer and office manager operate in different frames of reference. Union and non-union painter approach their problems in marked contrast. The attitudes of lawyer and engineer are miles apart.

Society? Whom does your character associate with, and why? Are his close friends on a level with him—socially, educationally, in terms of income? If not, why not? Does he relax alone or in company? Are his companions chosen from the stable or unstable, the homebound or the rovers, the beatniks or the suburbanites?

Again, such information is of little value per se. It offers you no magic key to character dynamics.

What it *does* provide is an additional method, more or less systematic, of tracking down possible areas of inadequacy and lack.

* * *

Now, what about *compensation?*

Compensation, as stated earlier, is what your character substitutes for what he hasn't got . . . the price he pays to make up for his lacks, the behavior with which he attempts to ease the sting engendered by feelings of inadequacy.

Compensation breaks down into two basic reaction-patterns:

(1) Fight.
(2) Flight.

Thus, if I feel sufficiently at a loss about something, I may attempt to counterbalance this feeling by striving toward some specific goal and/or way of life which, to me, symbolizes superiority.

Or, overwhelmed by my own frustrations and sense of weakness, I may withdraw from the battle and try to preserve my ego from further bruises by refusing to strive, on one excuse or another . . . denying the worth of striving in general, or focusing on a side issue, or developing physical or psychological symptoms which prevent my taking action.

The fighter is a familiar figure. We see him daily in the ninety-seven-pound weakling who becomes a Charles Atlas . . . the small man who makes up for his size by developing such drive and ambition that he amasses a fortune . . . the homely woman who achieves the charm of an Eleanor Roosevelt . . . the stutterer who rises to the heights of a Demosthenes.

Those who resort to flight are with us too. Here's the woman who forgets her fading beauty in a bottle . . . the boy who thwarts successful parents' pressure by failing in school or on the job . . . the girl, secretly frightened by the sheer enormity of life, who plays it so cool as to reject all emotional involvement . . . the man who masks present failure with tales of college football glory . . . the hypochondriac female, fearful of pain and responsibility alike, who claims her heart's too weak for her ever to bear children . . . the hoodlum whose sense of inferiority is so deep-seated that he lives outside the law . . . the coed who makes up for an unsatisfactory love-life with continual overeating.

Your character, too, forever seeks release from his frustrations.

Like other men, he finds that release in either fight or flight. How he achieves it should be part of the past history you assign him.

If he's a fighter, he seizes upon some specific thing, some act, the performance of which will, he believes, give him the sense of fulfillment that he seeks.

If flight's more his habit, he'll dodge the issue—duck responsibility or involvement, chase women, abandon ambition, go in for sweet lemons or sour grapes.

Or maybe, like many of us, he'll combine the two: sometimes fighting, sometimes running, in accord with circumstance and his own impulse.

* * *

Lack plus compensation equals rationalization of behavior equals a character who appears to move under his own power.

Create your story people on that basis. Experience and experimentation will do the rest.

As for specifics, here are a few miscellaneous points to bear in mind:

(1) Pay attention to self-image.

Consciously or otherwise, each of us sees himself in a particular light—as attractive or honest or dashing or ugly or what have you.

Then, we react *as if* this subjective image were an accurate and objective picture, and attempt to live up to the role in which we've cast ourselves.

When you write, you need to take into account this self-concept your character has built up. If Ed considers himself first of all a gentleman, and if his idea of gentlemanliness precludes loud or boisterous behavior, then hold his activities within the limits of that image.

Often, the image itself is false, of course. A woman may still think of herself as the "cute" girl she was twenty years ago. A child tries to live up to adult comments that he's a "little devil" instead of a normally mischievous boy.

Regardless, the image remains important. The psychic dividends the woman's self-concept originally paid her may have been so high that now she can't break the chains of her own conditioning. A loosely tossed-off label can blight a child so badly that it casts a shadow across reality.

Consequently, whether a character's mind-picture be true or false, you can't afford to ignore the image.

(2) Keep each character consistent.

Habits, William James once said, tend to become habitual.

Characters' reaction patterns operate on the habit level. The volatile girl stays volatile, the stolid man stolid. Overreaction or underreaction or irrational reaction often amount to a way of life for the individual concerned.

Recognition of this fact is your most useful tool where keeping a character consistent—and thus believable—is the issue.

(3) Make behavior tell the story.

In life, you judge a man more by what he does than what he says. His powers of rationalization may make his self-image sheer delusion—witness the familiar figure of the "great lover" who's seen by the girls in his office as a filthy-minded, foul-mouthed, clammy-handed old lecher.

Therefore, be sparing of psychological analysis and conducted tours of the unconscious. Implication can be golden. Let your reader draw his own conclusions as to the forces at work within your story people. For your own part, most of the time, your best bet is to *show* your man, in characteristic action, and let it go at that.

(4) Deduce cause from effect.

This is a plea that you *not* conceive characters by the numbers. Rather, play by ear wherever possible, especially when you first start work on a story.

Then, later, ask yourself *why* Eugene tore up the fifty-dollar bill, or Kitty begged Blake to take her back. Hypothesizing from possible lacks and compensations, you may come forth with startling—and effective—insights.

(5) Integrate inner and outer man.

Tags and impressions mirror dynamics. If Marie is punctilious or Andy sullen, it says a great deal about what's going on inside them.

Therefore, match external behavior to dynamics, and vice versa. Ned's fussiness about perfect grooming may reflect doubts of inner worth. Linda's secret guilts and hostilities may reach the surface in a tendency to take more than her share of blame.

Understand, you don't need to talk about or explain such. But you'll write better if you yourself have a pretty good idea of the motive forces behind everything each character does.

(6) Strive for contrast.

Inside your characters as well as out, your reader likes variety. So, no two story people should have inner drives that match precisely. If Alex cringes over his lack of education, let Howard draw direction from loss of a mother who ran off when he was

only ten. Does Laura build her ego by sleeping around? Then
it might prove effective contrast if Vivian takes pride in her
competence at work.

(7) Don't overbuild.

Even in a novel, there'll be only half-a-dozen people you or
your reader need to know in depth. Where the rest are concerned, type casting and surface freshness via tags will do the
job nicely.

Which is to say, you waste time and energy when you overbuild. Beware the temptation to make every spear-bearer a major project. More likely than not, it's just an unconscious excuse
to avoid getting on with the story.

(8) Learn your craft.

No writer can ever know too much about people.

Much of this knowledge can be gained from thought and
careful observation. However, a little preliminary reading may
help to orient you to the task.

Two simply written books that will add to your insight are
Understanding Other People, by Stuart Palmer, and *The Importance of Feeling Inferior,* by Marie Beynon Ray. Both are
available in paperback.

In addition, if your library has a copy, you should check out
Modern Clinical Psychiatry, by Arthur P. Noyes. Since it's a med-
ical text, and fairly heavy going, I'd suggest that you read just
Chapter 4: "Mental Mechanisms and Their Functions." It describes briefly the various ways in which people try to adjust
to problem situations, and the things you'll learn are well worth
whatever effort you expend.

How do you make a character fascinate your reader?

When a character excites and fascinates a reader, said reader
wants to read about him . . . experience with him.

Or, as an editor would phrase it, the reader *identifies* with
Jack or Susie.

If your characters don't thus intrigue readers, your stories won't
sell. Therefore, it's worth your while to learn how to inject the

elements that excite and fascinate, just in case they fail to develop spontaneously as you characterize by ear.

How do you persuade your reader to identify?

You shackle him to the character with chains of envy.

That is, you make the character someone who does what your reader would like to do, yet can't. You establish him as the kind of person Reader would *like to be like* . . . a figure to *envy*.

Further, and no matter what you may have heard to the contrary, Reader identifies with *every* truly successful character, not just one per story.

Why?

Because envy knows no limits. You may envy one man his wealth, another his poise, a third his success with women. In one way or another, in one degree or another, consciously or unconsciously, and whether you admit it or not, you envy a host of other writers their achievements. The fact that you focus on one in particular at a given moment doesn't mean that you can't feel just as strongly about another, instants later.

What is envy?

Webster's Collegiate Dictionary speaking: "To envy is to be discontented at another's possessing what one would like for oneself."

What do exciting, fascinating, successful story people possess that your reader would like to have?

Courage.

Courage to do what?

Courage to attempt to control reality.

What is reality?

Reality is limitations. It's law, natural or man-made . . . physical, statutory, psychological.

What opposes reality?

Imagination. Fantasy. All the things that man conceives of, yet cannot or dare not do.

Specifically?

The impossible. The unattainable. The forbidden. The disastrous.

This isn't to say your character must *achieve* such things, of course. The issue is courage, not victory. Conflict is what counts:

man's struggle against the world and all the overwhelming odds it mounts against him. The exciting character is the one who challenges fate and attempts to dominate reality, despite all common sense and logic.

Now I know this doesn't sound like what editors mean when they talk about identification. The word is used so loosely that it's become a sort of meaningless literary catchall, into which people throw anything and everything for which they lack a proper pigeonhole.

Actually, identification is a specialized psychological term, variously defined: "A method of tension reduction through the achievements of other persons or groups or in some cases through the merit of inanimate objects." "A process by which an individual imagines himself behaving as if he were another person." "A mental mechanism by which an individual endeavors to pattern himself after another."

When an editor uses the word, what he really means is—and here we complete the circle—that a particular character excites and/or fascinates him to the point that he lives through the story with that character, enthusiastically.

Because Editor fails to recognize the true issues, he develops a series of private rationalizations as to what constitutes identification. These fall into three major categories:

> *a.* He decides that you identify with the *recognizable* character.

What makes a character recognizable?

The *familiar.* That is, the character chews tobacco or likes cucumbers or spends all his spare time fishing or takes great pains with his dress.

All this is good. As pointed out earlier, when we dealt with techniques of character presentation, it adds reality to your story people.

But it has little to do with identification as such.

> *b.* He claims that you identify with the *likable* character.

What makes a character likable?

The *similar.* Or, to put it even more simply, the likable person is someone who agrees with us. If you're a Baptist deacon, you'll have difficulty *liking* a character who's an outspoken atheist. If you're a staunch Republican, you probably won't *like* a Communist character.

And while this has some small bearing on identification, it still isn't the heart of the matter.

> c. He decides that you identify with the *interesting* character.

What makes a character interesting?

The *contradictory*. In fiction as in life, we tend to take the totally predictable for granted. If you know in advance that Good Old Joe always will react to trouble with a temper tantrum, or to good news with an order for another beer, you quite possibly may find him pleasant enough, but you're unlikely to pay too much attention to him. Your interest and attention are saved for the man who, while consistent in his inconsistencies, has elements of the paradoxical in his personality that keep you guessing.

John D. MacDonald's burly soldier of fortune, Travis McGee, is a good case in point. He's kind and sensitive. Yet when a girl is sufficiently upset, he may slap her face instead of trying to console her. Why? Because he sees she's drawn too tight to benefit from solace. What she needs is an excuse to break loose, to cry. The time for gentleness comes later.

Is this behavior consistent with McGee's character? Yes. But it's also unanticipated and, at first glance, contradictory. Consequently, it sharpens interest.

But though close to the target, interest in a character won't necessarily make you identify with him.

* * *

Actually, the factor on which identification rests, and the thing too many editors miss, is a concept called *wish-fulfillment*.

What is wish-fulfillment?

Break it down for yourself: A wish is a desire. To wish is to want, to yearn for, to crave.

Fulfillment, in turn, is satisfaction. To fulfill a person is to gratify entirely his desires in a particular area.

Put the two together, and you get wish-fulfillment: the satisfaction of a craving.

How does this tie in with fiction, and identification?

Let's take it a step at a time, starting from reality itself.

Reality frustrates us. We cannot or dare not overstep the various laws laid down for us by man, nature, and practicality.

Frustration, as pointed out earlier, is anything but pleasant. Therefore, emotionally, we yearn for a world more to our liking. We crave to control our destinies. Yet by and large, day to day, most of us are afraid even to try to do so.

A fictional character, on the other hand, knows no such limits. He's free to acknowledge forbidden impulses, gamble with disaster, challenge the impossible, reach for the unattainable.

By living through a story with such a character, your reader shares these experiences. Vicariously, his repressed desires come out into the open. Emotional needs find satisfaction. Without endangering himself, he gets to expand his horizons . . . do things he'd never dare attempt in life.

Thus, to a degree, he relieves tensions built up by life's frustrations.

And there stands the real reason you find a character exciting and fascinating: His story activities help to satisfy some aspect of your own emotional hunger.

Or, as we put it to begin with, you identify because, unconsciously, you envy the courage of the character who challenges world and fate.

To create a character who'll fascinate your reader, then, you must give said character the opportunity to display such courage.

To that end, make him attempt:

(1) The impossible.
(2) The unattainable.
(3) The forbidden.
(4) The disastrous.

The *impossible* is the stuff that dreams are made of . . . pure fantasy; man's revolt against natural law itself. When you visualize yourself walking through walls, or flying across the sky without benefit of aircraft, or rising from the grave, you take this route.

The *unattainable* lies closer to hand. Here we confront The Clerk Who Aspires to Marry the Boss's Daughter. Close beside him stand The Detective Who Must Find the Murderer before His Beloved Is Executed Tomorrow Morning . . . The Young Entrepreneur Who Must Translate $100,000 in Liabilities into $10,000,000 in Assets by the Time the Bank Opens . . . The Aging Housewife Who Must Delight Daughter's Rich Fiancé with Life as She Is Lived in Ye Olde Family Hovel. Whatever the issue, somebody must reach for something that appears to be beyond his grasp.

The *forbidden?* Deny me even a wormy green apple, and in my thoughts it will taste indescribably sweet; for as any psychologist will tell you, no nice girl would dream of doing the things that every nice girl dreams of doing. So, in fiction, your minister may read delightedly of murder, your banker of theft. Adultery has a tantalizing flavor to a host of suburban housewives who'd be truly horrified to learn that the girl next door had kissed the milkman. Which explains, in large part, the success of *Lolita* as a novel, *Playboy* as a magazine.

Disaster constitutes a challenge epitomized in our fascination with the human fly and the airplane-wing walker of the 1920s. We thrill to the hideous threat of atomic war. Our excitement feeds on cataclysm. The narcotics addict, the racing driver, the rebel, the surgeon fighting death—all hold us spellbound because they flirt with calamity.

*   *   *

The impossible, the unattainable, the forbidden, the disastrous: These constitute the raw materials with which you combine courage, in order to create story people who excite and fascinate.

Conversely, you cut deep into your chances for any broad success if you choose your major characters from the ranks of the weak and passive. Nothing is drearier than the story that centers on dull, apathetic people borne down by trivial problems, without the strength or imagination—the courage—to rally and fight back. As Howard Browne once phrased it, "Readers want heroes, not victims."

Even a minor character acquires allure when he steps out

of his rut and in some way defies fate. Here, you have the girl who's sexually promiscuous. There, the man who overextends himself financially in order to promote a new housing project. Another man tries to maneuver political favors from an old enemy. A woman dreams that her crippled child may somehow be made whole.

Because the girl toys with the forbidden, your reader reads about her eagerly. Man Number 1 gambles with disaster—again, you have a fascinating character. Attempting the unattainable, Man 2 grips your audience. Poignancy vibrates in the mother's impossible dream.

Some of these people may play mere bit parts. But because they hazard so much; because they face such odds, your reader finds himself striving with them for the moment as they challenge fate, however casually or briefly.

It's entirely possible, of course, that reality will overwhelm such characters. The girl may end up dead in an alley or a cheap hotel room. Man 1, gambling so desperately, might lose and jump out an office window . . . Man 2 go down into humiliating oblivion . . . the woman with the crippled child fade to a tearful, heart-broken specter.

But that's all right too. For the moment, each of them played his role and held your reader, because they dared to fight against all odds.

Is this a device for melodrama only?

No, it isn't. Macbeth is here, and also Nelson Algren's *Man with the Golden Arm* . . . Robert E. Lee Prewitt of *From Here to Eternity*, and Walter Tevis' *Hustler*.

There's nothing about the character who dares that isn't true to life. You meet him every day. The difference between him and other people is that one way or another, in one degree or another, as saint or sinner, crook or chancellor, he insists on trying to stand up on his own two feet like a man and control his destiny.

Which is what makes anyone worth writing about.

✦ ✦ ✦

What else is there to say about how to make characters fascinate your reader?

Three things:

(1) Pinpoint the emotional needs of your specific reader group.

When an editor tells you that his teen-age public has trouble identifying with your eighty-year-old heroine, he means that this particular coterie of readers finds little about said heroine to envy. Her situation is so remote from theirs that, courageous or not, she isn't a person they'd like to be like.

Which is to say, at least one character in any story should in some way show and satisfy needs that parallel those of your reader. And the more specifically this is done, the better.

Such a character needn't necessarily be like your reader on the surface, understand. Differences in age and sex and background can, to some degree, be overcome. You don't even have to cast your man as a dominant figure in the story.

But it's well-nigh essential that he possess and satisfy *specific* reader emotional cravings. The general is not enough.

Why?

Because emotional response isn't something you, the writer, can impose. The hunger is there first, always, deep inside the reader.

The focus of that hunger varies from reader to reader and group to group. Wish-fulfillment, control of destiny, may center on curiosity about and desire for sexual experience, in an adolescent boy. In his father, the issue perhaps is escape from a drab world of routine work. Loss of status and fear of death quite possibly preoccupy his grandmother. His mother longs for an end to poverty . . . some touch of grace and beauty; glamour.

To appeal to a given member of this family, your story must provide some character who challenges fate, and who does so in an area and manner that fits the specific reader's special needs.

In other words, to bring a reader's emotional hunger to the surface, you must give him a character who reflects and projects it.

Take Mickey Spillane's Mike Hammer, with his violence and abuse of women. As a character, he'd prove a failure if the men who read about him didn't already unconsciously feel pent-up aggression and hate—much of it focused on frustrations created by the females in their lives.

In the same way, a young girl may yearn for affection, romantic love. So, you offer her some character who demonstrates the power to evoke such. The meek, the rebellious, the lonely, the withdrawn, the fanciful, the cautious, the power-hungry—all have their private patterns. And each searches fiction for the character whom he'd like to be like, in some specific way or other.

Because this is so, there can be no true universality of appeal in fiction. The story or the character who fascinates everyone is a myth and non-existent. The writer must pick a target audience and shoot for it—with a rifle, not a shotgun. Sir Arthur Conan Doyle had the right idea when he prefaced his famous adventure novel *The Lost World* with this verse:

> I have wrought my simple plan
> If I bring one hour of joy
> To the boy who's half a man,
> Or the man who's half a boy.

But even when you find the character or characters who spark the needs of your particular reader group, often there are other matters that you must consider—feelings of guilt, for instance.

These spring from the very pleasure the reader derives from a character's violation of taboos. To ease these qualms, you may have to insert punishment for misdeeds, or provide your hero with a private morality that justifies deviation from established codes.

How do you decide just what to do, in the face of such a host of problems?

You study your reader group. Learn to understand its members, collectively and as individuals. Talk with them face to face, every chance you get—not as a writer, but as a casual acquaintance. Search out their interests, their problems, their favorite topics, their enthusiasms, their feelings.

Then, design characters to fit these readers' needs.

Does all this sound difficult?

It is.

But it also can prove—pardon the word—fascinating, to the writer eager to achieve control of *his* own destiny.

(2) Don't try to make virtue take the place of courage.

Admirable qualities are fine as subordinate characterizing elements. But fascination is born of valor, not virtue.

You may loathe Harry Diadem, in Calder Willingham's *Eternal Fire*. Probably you despise his goals. But he continues to fascinate, even if with horror, simply because he moves ahead so ruthlessly in his defiance of all that most of us hold dear.

A saintly character, on the other hand, may fall ever so flat—not because he's saintly, but because he doesn't, *in addition*, challenge fate.

(3) Have faith in your own judgment.

One of the most successful characters I ever created was hero of a story written on assignment and paid for in advance.

The editor, previous purchaser of at least a quarter-million words of copy from me, bounced the yarn because, he said, no reader could identify with my man.

Later, the story was published in another magazine, and as a paperback by American, British, and German houses.

The lesson here is as stated above: Have faith in your own judgment.

Obversely, don't confuse the editor with God.

Editors used to say that American readers couldn't identify with oriental characters. —Then, Pearl Buck came along with *The Good Earth*.

They also claimed that a character had to be physically attractive. —Enter Clarence Budington Kelland with Scattergood Baines.

They insisted that characters to any degree amoral or immoral would outrage the public. —Check your corner newsstand on this point.

Editors have their prejudices and preconceptions, even as you and I. But you don't have to accept their ideas as gospel. If a character fascinates *you*, then take it for granted that someone else also may be intrigued, regardless of any rules a given market lays down.

After all, there's always another editor around the corner!

How do you fit a character to the role he has to play?

Certain people perform such vital functions in a story that often they determine its success or failure. Others, though perhaps less important, offer special problems.

Such characters rate a little extra attention, so that you'll know how to make them effective in their roles.

These characters are:

   a. The hero.
   b. The villain.
   c. The heroine.
   d. The sensitive character.
   e. The character-in-depth.

Next question: How do you deal with each?

   a. The hero.

Here, we'll limit ourselves to two points only.

   (1) *Do* have an individual hero.

Must a hero be an individual? Can't "he" be a group?
Both in theory and practice, the idea's weak.
Why?
Because a group is made up of individual people, and danger is subjective. The thing that constitutes a menace to me may prove of little concern to you. Loss of a particular girl or job or cherished object devastates Hero A, perhaps, only to be dismissed with a shrug of the shoulders by Hero B.

Thus, even though thousands or millions of people are affected—as by a war, a flood, a depression—your story becomes meaningful only as you zero in on individuals. The fact that a regiment marches into battle doesn't change the fact that each soldier will react in his own intimately personal fashion. His private involvements, his past conditionings, his aspirations for the future—these are what count; for it's through them that you focus the emotional responses of your reader. He needs someone to cheer for. The old Hollywood attack, "Which is our ball team?" remains valid in the vast majority of cases.

Give your hero associates, therefore, if you will. But don't so submerge him among them that he gets lost. He *must* remain the center of attention and of interest. For without a clear and obvious hero, a story is liable to end up a pastiche—a patchwork of anecdotes and character sketches, intriguing as an experiment, but so diffuse as to be of doubtful appeal to most readers.

(2) *Don't* let your hero resign from the story.

Where your hero's concerned, the big problem is to keep him heroic.

A hero's primary characteristic is indomitability. He has a goal he seeks to attain or a way of life he wants to retain. Even if he changes direction somewhat along the way, the road he follows is his very own. He sticks to his guns, no matter what. For in the words of Robert G. Ingersoll, "When the will defies fear, when duty throws the gauntlet down to fate, when honor scorns to compromise with death—this is heroism."

When a hero fails you, ordinarily it's because your reader comes to realize that your man is, or should be, willing to abandon the fight and quit the story, even though you as writer continue to hold him on stage.

Solution? Give Hero strong motivation, both outside and in.

That is, let circumstance or the villain trap him so that he can't run.

Then, in addition, make what's at stake symbolic of Hero's whole pattern of being, his style of life. For if the internal issue is vital enough, he's left with no choice but to fight on, regardless of the odds against him, or forfeit his status as a man.

Exhibit A: Heroine is in dire peril. If Hero backs down, she'll die for sure.

That's *external* motivation.

In addition, Heroine has often expressed her doubt that Hero is capable of really loving anyone. He knows that if he abandons her to her fate, he'll automatically prove her right and thus damn himself forever in his own eyes.

That's *internal* motivation.

Put the two together, and you create a character who'll fight, fight, fight.

At the same time, don't confuse indomitability and idiocy. As a writer, you're supposed to be able to think realistically and devise *believable* situations. There's no virtue in the totally incredible hero who stands in the middle of Main Street, waiting for six sinister gunmen to shoot him down. Anyone in his right mind would run for cover like a scared rabbit, and your reader knows it.

So, *do* have an individual hero, and *don't* let him resign.

Nor is there any rule that says you can't use all other characterizing tricks and techniques in order to help said hero come to life.

b. The villain.

Psychologically, a story's villain is ever so important. He constitutes a stranger figure—a scapegoat on whom your reader may concentrate unconscious impulses to hostility and aggression.

Your reader needs such a scapegoat. For through him, Reader releases feelings that conscience forbids him to purge in real life.

Further, and despite sociological theorizing to the contrary, villains do exist. A man with vested interests—whether these be economic, political, romantic, or otherwise—can defend said interests ruthlessly. If you don't believe me, try telling your immediate superior that you're out to get his job.

To develop a villain properly, you need to understand three things:

(1) The villain's role.
(2) The villain's characteristics.
(3) How to make a villain effective.

Role-wise, the strength of the villain is the strength of your story.

Why?

Because a villain is the personification of the danger that threatens your hero. If the danger—that is, the villain—is weak, then your story's bound to be weak also.

Why should danger be personified?

For two reasons:

(*a*) Personification concentrates the danger down to a single source and thus gives unity to a story.

(b) The personal villain can *react* to your hero's efforts and, through continuing attacks, sharpen and intensify conflict.

The primary *characteristic* of the villain, in turn, is ruthlessness.

Which means?

The villain is determined to have his own way, without regard to other people's needs; and he's uncompromising in this determination.

Must a villain be an unattractive person?

Far from it. A villain may very well be utterly charming. Given half a chance, he may quite possibly steal your story. His villainy lies in the fact that, where one specific issue is concerned, he also is utterly ruthless. A sweet and loving mother, determined to prevent a daughter's marriage to a man said mother deems unsuitable; a brother set on forcing his aging sister to give up her apartment and come live with him, so that he can look after her properly; a wife pushing her husband into ambition and advancement even though he much prefers his present rut—these are villains, every bit as much as the murderer, the traitor, the rapist, the thief.

It follows that the villain is unlikely to be ruthless in everything. His compulsion to control often may be limited to a single area or situation.

The reason this is so is because the villain is a human being like any other. Consequently, he's the product of his own background and lacks and compensations. When his self-concept—as conscientious mother, as solicitous brother, as adoring wife—is endangered, he acts to protect it; and circumstance forces relentlessness upon him.

Nor does this necessarily make him evil. In his own eyes he's completely justified . . . as all of us justify ourselves in our own rigidities of behavior. Each of us, in some area or other, is a villain.

How do you make sure your villain will prove *effective?*

(a) You lay out a private plan of action for him—a "villain's plot," so-called, that sets him in continuing opposition to the hero.

(b) You think him through as a person, so that he'll fight
uncompromisingly to the bitter end.

Beyond the obvious steps you'll take to do this, the central
factor is, in large measure, timing. Ordinarily, danger has already
confronted the villain before the story starts. His goals, his self-
concept, have been threatened. He's made his decision as to how
to deal with that threat. Now, he carries out said decision. Ruthlessly.

How does that make him a villain?

The course of action he's chosen endangers your hero; and
this is the hero's story.

Isn't the hero ruthless also, in fighting back?

He may become so, as story pressures mount. But because we
can see and feel those pressures with him, he remains heroic in
our eyes.

Further, when you finally reach your story's climax, you make
the hero demonstrate that he deserves to win, in terms of adherence to principle, selflessness, and sacrificial decision. —Which
same also helps to convince Reader that any prior misdeeds on
Hero's part are inconsequential and justified.

Isn't it possible to have a satisfactory story without a personal
villain?

Of course it is. Any number of such stories have been written,
about heroes striving against nature or social forces or a hostile
universe. Your hero's foe may be a mountain, or time, or injus-
tice, or the emptiness of outer space, or a machine that won't
work, or life itself.

So?

Ordinarily, these stories are a good deal harder to write than
are those in which the villain is human. In fact, and because
of this very problem, a writer frequently personifies such an impersonal foe as if it were a human being. That is, he conceives
of or represents it as a person; gives it human attributes.

How do you give an impersonal object or force human attributes?

You write in such a manner as to give the impression that the
object or force behaves *as if* it were a human being, with implied
or explicit human feelings, human motivations. It's an easy trick,

and one that brings to life robots and ghosts, mountains and rivers, gods and animals, houses and towns, torpedoes and Tiger tanks—all the thousands of inanimate and subhuman and super-human entities that have played roles in fiction down through the years.

But be your villain human or inanimate, his guiding principles remain the same: ruthlessness, and uncompromising determination.

   c. The heroine.

How do you create a heroine who comes alive?

   (1) You make her human.
   (2) You develop her in conflict; that is, give her goals and opposition.

A heroine's prime characteristic is desirability. Her main function in a story is to serve as part of the hero's reward for being indomitable.

She's *not* always essential. Many stories without female characters have been written. But most of today's fiction does include her.

The main problem arising where the heroine is concerned is to prevent her deteriorating into a beautiful nonentity.

Solution: Give her direction in her own right. Make her just as much a dynamic character as hero or villain.

To that end, let the heroine have her own ideas as to the sort of world in which she wants to live . . . a self-concept which she seeks to maintain, compounded of lacks and compensations and reactions to external pressures. Only as you permit her to choose her own path and to fight to achieve or maintain her independence will she come alive. Only as you develop her in conflict will she play an integral part in your story. And though she'll be harder to handle when developed thus, she'll reward you for your efforts by doing her part to help intrigue and hold your reader.

   d. The sensitive character.

The particularly sensitive or perceptive character doesn't appear in every story, by any means. But when he does pop up, it helps if you have some notion of how best to develop him.

Three tricks put you in free:

(1) Let the sensitive character show more awareness than
do your other story people.

This means, let him observe his world in shades of gray,
rather than just black and white. He sees a smile or a frown as a
thing of infinite subtle variations . . . draws conclusions from it.
Small deviations from the norm attract his notice. Perhaps he
exhibits a tendency to self-analysis. If a girl's fingers tremble as
she lights her cigarette, he spots it and guesses the reason for
her reaction. Is he a kindly person? He compliments the old
woman at the corner fruit stand on her hideous new hat, instead
of laughing. Or, if hatred drives him, he knows precisely where
to sink the knife in his adversary's psyche.

The way he phrases his interpretations, in turn, reveals
whether he's illiterate, intellectual, or poet.

(2) Contrast the sensitive with the insensitive.

This old favorite of too many novels of army life plunks down
one gentle soul in a barracks-ful of crude, crass, callous types.
While the rest of the boys talk things over in four-letter words
and leap to profane conclusions with no heed to evidence, he
teases out nuances to half the diameter of a spider-thread.

Because the difference between him and his fellows is so
marked, he sticks up like a sore thumb.

Though this procedure can descend easily to the ridiculous,
its principle is sound. Contrast makes anything stand out more
sharply.

(3) Set up situations which allow for a difference in reaction.

Fast action and violent conflict give little opportunity for you
to establish a character's sensitivity. The job needs to be taken
care of earlier, *before* the explosion comes. Otherwise, your man
is likely to register as foolish, inadequate, or a coward, instead
of discerning or insightful.

Therefore, plan a scene or two in which nuance is important,
so that your reader will see Ben or Horace as at least remotely
understandable and justified in his habits of intuition or percep-
tiveness or analysis. Give him excuses to appraise people or be-

havior . . . reasons to notice small, vital differences. Then, when the big scene comes, our sensitive friend will be accepted for what he is, instead of appearing a mere buffoon.

In other words, decide in advance on the *effect* you want your character to create, and devise ways to achieve it.

e. The character-in-depth.

What factors help to round out a character and give him depth?

(1) Involvement in a wide variety of situations.

You don't know a man in depth till you've seen him against diverse backdrops.

Thus, at home, he may be the soul of probity . . . in New York, a woman-chasing drunk . . . at the office, a quiet and respectful worker . . . in the army, a rank-happy martinet. His mother sees him as a dutiful son . . . his children as an erratic combination of cruel disciplinarian and fawning sentimentalist . . . his poker friends as a sucker for a bluff.

To round out a character in fiction you need, above all, space. That's why you so seldom find the character-in-depth in anything short of a novel. In the more compact forms, you simply don't have the room to display and integrate his conflicting images and expose his assorted attitudes to view.

But depth is a matter of degree, and our heading states one device to help you approximate it: Give your man as broad a range of situations as you can. Then, let him react, so that your reader gains insight into assorted facets of Character's personality.

Further, all this must be *shown* . . . not merely talked about. Long-winded statements of appraisal by an author accomplish little.

(2) Careful development of sequels.

A bit-player can act, and your reader will pretty much accept what's done, even if motivation and/or explanation leave a good deal to be desired.

Depth treatment imposes greater demands on you. Reader wants to know *why* your man does the things he does and feels the way he feels. Attitudes, reasoning, background elements—all may need to be brought out into the open.

To that end, it's to your advantage to develop sequels in considerable detail when you build a character in depth. For it's in sequel that you reveal the factors that influence your character in his choice of goals, his selection of direction.

Why, for example, should Leo put up with his alcoholic wife? Does he see her as the cross he has to bear for earlier sins? As a social or financial mainstay that he doesn't dare abandon? An excuse for martyrdom and self-pity? A convenient scapegoat for his own failures? Reaffirmation of his concept of himself as a man not to be swerved from duty?

Well, sequel's a good hunting-ground for answers to such questions.

(3) Fragmentation of motivation and reaction.

To understand a man, break down his behavior to its root components.

Thus, how does Gil react to a sneer? With violence? With panic? With disdain? With hurt? With logic?

Or, does he simply ignore it?

Further: Is the panic revealed in quivering voice, or stiffened face? The disdain, in caustic words, or contemptuous glance, or turned back?

Whatever the answer, it helps to give your character depth.

*   *   *

So, this chapter ends; and with it, our analysis of the major elements that go into fiction: words, motivation-reaction units, scenes, story patterns, and character.

But there still are a number of things you need to know about the actual preparation, planning, and production of a story.

You'll find them in the next chapter.

CHAPTER 8

Preparation, Planning, Production

A story is the triumph of ego over fear of failure.

The best observation anyone can make on preparation, planning, and production is that everyone has a God-given right to go to hell in his own way—and don't let anyone kid you out of yours.

The greatest talent in writing is nerve: You bet your ego that your unconscious has something in it beside dinner.

Ignorance must be defeated in the process, and inertia also. The true recipe for writing success is that laid down by dramatist Jerome Lawrence: "You've gotta get up very early some morning five years ago."

So, now, the alarm clock is ringing. What do you do about it?

1. You learn what it means to be a writer.
2. You learn how to recognize good story material.
3. You learn how to prepare to write a story.
4. You learn your own best way to plan it.
5. You learn how to get out copy.

Each of these aspects of creative work involves a variety of problems. Taken a step at a time, however, none of them is too difficult to master.

Shall we dive in?

On being a writer

To become a writer, you first must be capable of emotional involvement.

That is, you must feel, and feel intensely. Though you work with language, the words you use are only symbols . . . means to the end of communication of emotion.

You can't communicate that which you yourself lack. No feeling, no story.

To feel, in practical terms, means to react . . . to desire to behave in a particular way. Given the right stimulus, things happen inside you. Awareness vibrates—assorted gradations of like, dislike, surprise.

If no such response takes place, or if it comes through on too low a level, give up. You'll never make it as a writer.

On the other hand, don't cross yourself off the list of candidates for authorship too quickly. *Everyone* feels, to some degree. Further, the very fact that you *want* to write is a good omen. To desire, to yearn, itself demonstrates a capacity for involvement. Restraint, indifference, apathy—in major measure, they're all learned responses; habit patterns. With sufficient perseverance, and at least in part, you can break them down.

Which brings us back to where we started: Writing springs from feeling.

What comes next?

To succeed as a writer:

a. You must be enthusiastic.

Why is enthusiasm so important?

Because writing is murderously hard, lonely, frustrating work, upon occasion. Unless a project excites you to begin with, odds are you'll stand ready to slash your wrists before it's done. —Maybe you will anyhow, as a matter of fact. But at least, with enthusiasm, you improve the percentages a little.

How do you acquire enthusiasm?

Enthusiasm is an emotional response, a feeling. Outside stimuli spark it.

These stimuli come from your story's topic, its subject matter—

love in Manhattan or Okmulgee, murder in a hospital, war in Vietnam, smuggling in the Big Bend country, ambition and jealousy in business.

To build enthusiasm, you search for aspects of your topic that excite you . . . immerse yourself in factual raw material till you find some unique something about which you can be fervent. Inspiration springs from saturation. No one can write for long out of his own unsustained unconscious. Emotion is an element which that unconscious can supply, virtually without limit; but it must have stimulating facts—about people, about events, about setting, about objects or what have you—upon which to feed.

b. You must be sincere.

Sophistry is a subtle poison. The story that falsifies your emotional standards, your convictions, does you infinitely more harm than any editor's check can compensate.

Why?

Because a story is in essence a parable. Though you set it on Mars and cast it with bug-eyed monsters, the message it conveys is deepest truth.

That truth is you. On an unconscious level, it reflects your innermost feelings.

The story which by implication proves that promiscuity is good clean fun, or honor a fraud, or duty and honesty outmoded, when you really believe the opposite, makes you one with the prostitute who simulates ecstasy for money. Hypocrisy moves you over into the ranks of the constitutional psychopath, the con man.

Result: emotional conflict. Conscience joins battle with creativity.

Then, one day, you freeze up so tightly that you can't write at all, and another career goes down the drain.

c. You must be self-disciplined.

No one really gives a damn if you don't make it as a writer. No one, that is to say, except you yourself.

Further, no one's going to pay you for the stories you don't write.

This means you have to be your own taskmaster. If you're not up to the job, you can always sack groceries for a living, in a store where someone else tells you what to do and when to do it.

To succeed as a writer means getting up in the morning, even when you'd rather sleep.

It means working when you'd much prefer to take in a movie or go swimming. —*Really* working, too; not just staring, trance-like, out the window.

It's your decision.

   d. You must be yourself.

"I was surprised," Somerset Maugham remarks in *A Writer's Notebook,* "when a friend of mine told me he was going over a story he had just finished to put more subtlety into it; I didn't think it my business to suggest that you couldn't be subtle by taking thought. Subtlety is a quality of the mind, and if you have it you show it because you can't help it. It's like originality: no one can be original by trying. The original artist is only being himself; he puts things in what seems to him a perfectly normal and obvious way: because it's fresh and new to you you say he's original. He doesn't know what you mean. How stupid are those second-rate painters, for instance, who can't but put paint on their canvas in a dull and commonplace way and think to impress the world with their originality by placing meaningless and incongruous objects against an academic background."

It's hard to accept yourself for what you are, sometimes. No one likes to admit to inadequacy or limitation.

But a mask is difficult to hold in place, on paper. It keeps slipping out of line. The truth pops forth, in spite of all your efforts.

You're better off to face the facts at the beginning. Ben Hecht was no Virginia Woolf, nor was Woolf a Eugene Ionesco. Herman Wouk, Erle Stanley Gardner, and A. J. Cronin each found his place.

They did it by being themselves, not fakes or copyists.

Strength is in each of us, as well as limitation. Call your shots the way you see them, and you give the world a chance to rate you and your talents realistically.

Whereupon, your reader may like the way you write in spite of all your lacks, just because that way is individual and different.

Material, good and bad

Some years ago, a scholar at a leading university made it his hobby to translate French fables of an earlier day.

But hobbies have a way of getting out of hand. Soon Scholar yearned for a public for his efforts.

An acquaintance remarked that a certain magazine occasionally carried translations from the French.

Our man had never seen this publication. But he promptly sent its editor a batch of his best work.

Enter happenstance. The magazine was one of the most ribald journals ever to sully the nation's newsstands. The editor, with perverse humor, accepted the fables and ran one each month, sandwiched in between naughty nudes and bawdy ballads. Each carried the good professor's name and full academic pedigree, and mirth and embarrassment were the order of the day on his campus when word got round.

The lesson here is that material is neither good nor bad, per se. You must rate it in terms of the reaction it evokes from a given market, a specific reader.

Thus, this entire book has been designed to give you a standard by which you may judge story.

As you read current books and magazines, however, you'll soon see that not all fiction fits this pattern.

The reason is simple: There are two ways to acquire a reputation as a good marksman.

The first is to draw a target on some appropriate surface, then shoot at it and hit the bull's-eye.

The second is to fire at the surface to begin with, and afterwards draw target around the spot where the bullet hit.

In the same way, it has become the habit of the literary world to apply the term "story" to any pleasant or intriguing fragment of writing which involves fictional characters and/or situations. Sketches, vignettes, anecdotes, word photography, and all sorts of other *curiosa* are so described.

In consequence, we have good stories and bad, weak stories and strong, stories appealing to one reader and those appealing to another. So whatever you write, you quite possibly will find someone, somewhere—even a distinguished critic, perhaps—who'll proclaim it a story.

Further, there are complex non-literary matters which an editor must take into account: readership, available space, "house image," business-office pressures, and the like.

It follows that recognition of good story material involves much more than evaluation of how a given piece of fiction will shape up. For while such evaluation is ever so important, it becomes truly helpful only as it's related to market, with due consideration given to the editor's problems.

To this end, ask yourself three questions:

a. Is this material too diffuse and/or complex?

Here, the issue is length. Some stories may be told in few words. Some take many.

Each market, in turn, has its own standards. There are magazines that won't touch a yarn that runs over 1500 words. A hardback publisher is unlikely to boggle at a 100,000-word novel.

This being the case, it's only common sense to correlate material and market.

Factors to be considered include:

(1) Scope.

It's hard to deal with a whole war in a short story. The social movement of a family, shirt sleeves to shirt sleeves in three generations, is bound to demand wordage.

(2) Strength.

A girl worries about whether or not a particular boy will ask her for a prom date.

Will such an idea carry a short-short? Sure thing.

A short story? Probably.

A novelette? Weak.

A novel? Ridiculous.

(3) Complexity.

Rona Jaffe's *The Best of Everything* interweaves the romances of five New York career girls. Such an involved tale demands novel length.

Does your story make it essential that you use three different viewpoints? Each time you switch, you'll have to re-establish emotional tension . . . and such re-establishment eats up pages.

The more characters you use, and the more fully they're developed, the longer your story will run.

Same for settings.

(4) Passage of time.

A man dies at the age of eighty. To tell the story of his life adequately in all likelihood will take a novel.

How he in one day met and won the girl he married may make a 3000-word short story.

In general, the longer your story's time span, and the more events you deal with, and the more scenes you develop, the longer that story will have to be.

b. Does this material fit the philosophy of your reader?

Why does a story please one man and displease another, even though its subject may be a favorite of both?

The core reason is that the man displeased disagrees with certain of the author's basic assumptions . . . his personal philosophy, the way he views the world. Whereas, the man pleased agrees.

Often, neither reader nor author is even aware that such assumptions exist. They're things taken for granted, not even the subject of conscious thought.

Thus, this book jumps to all sorts of wild conclusions.

For example, I start from the idea that you write in large measure to please a reader.

Some people don't agree.

—And on that issue, I can't resist quoting a statement by John Fischer that recently appeared in *Harper's:*

Among serious fiction writers, one large group now seem (in the words of a veteran publisher) to be "more concerned with self-expression than with entertaining the public." [British novelist Geoffrey] Wagner defines them as the poetic novelists. With them, and with most of the critics who make "serious" literary reputations, storytelling has become disreputable. Their main concern is with sensibility, with the inner drama of the psyche, not with the large events of the outside world. Often they are accomplished craftsmen. Their style is luminously burnished . . . they write on two levels, or even three . . . their work contains more symbols than a Chinese band . . . it may plumb the depths of the human soul . . . it may be (in Felicia Lamport's phrase) as deeply felt as a Borsalino hat. But all too often it just isn't much fun to read.

If such exercises in occupational therapy don't sell very well, the author has small grounds for complaint. He has written them, after all, primarily to massage his own ego and to harvest critico-academic bay leaves. Since he isn't interested in a mass audience, why should it be interested in him?

Back to our point:

I also assume that readers like form. I think they prefer a story that has a beginning, a middle, and an end.

Most do. But not all.

Again, I take it for granted that said readers believe man possesses at least a degree of free will, that they like active characters better than passive, and that they think a cause-effect relationship exists between what you do and what you get.

Some voices would dissent.

This list could go on thus for pages. But the point, I trust, is already clear: Each market, consciously or unconsciously, represents a particular philosophy of life.

The stories it buys reaffirm that philosophy.

Further, the issue reaches far beyond mere literary technique. *McCall's* believes in premarital chastity. *Playboy* approves of sexual freedom. Grove Press takes the avant-garde view. Doubleday aims more toward popular appeal.

All of which is something to consider when you evaluate story material.

Does this mean you should tailor your own beliefs to fit a given market?

Well, hardly. It makes more sense to hunt markets that see the world the same way you do.

    c. Does this material fit your market's needs?

Shall we talk common sense for just a little while?

Closely related to philosophy, yet by no means precisely the same, each magazine has a personality all its own.

This personality is compounded of reader interests, editorial taste, and ad-department pressure.

Drop the advertising angle, and the same statement applies to book houses.

If you're eager to hit some special market, it's only good judgment to consider this personality factor. *Rogue* and *Secrets* and *Redbook* buy vastly different stories. The novel that bears Little, Brown's imprint isn't likely to be of a type to win a place at Gold Medal, or vice versa.

How do you familiarize yourself with a given market's tastes and rules?

You read what that market publishes.

In quantity.

Particularly, you pay attention to:

    (1) Age of characters.

Ordinarily, character age reflects audience and, even more important, the publisher's compulsive striving to build a readership.

The young adult is king in most magazines. Advertisers see him as a big buyer, not yet set in his spending habits.

The publisher reads this fact as an equation: Young-adult readers equal advertising equal profits.

Young-adult characters attract young-adult readers. Q.E.D.

Obversely, stories that feature older characters are notoriously hard to sell.

Though not to such a marked degree, the same pattern is found in the book field.

Why?

Because young adults tend to buy and read more books than do their elders.

There are exceptions aplenty to generalizations such as this, of course. And if you're good enough, you can throw any rule away.

But over-all, and whether you like the idea or not, it does pay to think young.

(2) Sex of characters.

It should be obvious to anyone, it seems, but I still find plenty of would-be writers who don't realize that male-viewpoint stories sell more readily in men's markets, female-viewpoint in women's.

Take the confession field. Sure, *True Story* or *Modern Romances* or *Secret Diary* buy yarns with male central characters. But they probably publish five times as many in which women play the leading roles.

(3) Settings.

Does your chosen market prefer exotic backgrounds, or familiar? Glamorous, or everyday?

Again, consistent reading gives you the answer.

One point of caution, however: Historical settings find few takers these days, especially in the magazines.

(4) Categories.

The western is always with us, and so is the mystery, the science-fiction yarn, the doctor-nurse story, the romance.

Such category fiction offers a special hazard, though: Readers of a particular *genre* frequently are fans.

That means they've read widely in the field. They know the clichés, the worn-out plots, the too-familiar patterns.

Consequently, unless you know the area equally well, you'll waste endless hours writing yarns doomed in advance to rejection because they feature the vengeance trail, the range war, the locked room, the biter-bit, atomic doom, the interplanetary travelogue, or the like.

Don't let the fact that old hands get away with such fool you, either. The long-time professional has other elements working on his side. Whereas the beginner is expected to come up with something fresh.

On the financial front, profitable pickings from the categories tend to be slim in the magazine field. Probably it's because the TV series have so largely taken over.

Hardback book publishers, in turn, seem more and more to give prime emphasis to the big literary and pseudo-literary novels, with their potential of fantastic profits from best-seller-dom, book club and movie sales.

Result: A high proportion of category material now appears under the paperback houses' imprints.

Finally, and unfortunately, when one category rides high, chances are that others are scraping bottom. Specialize too narrowly, and you may be in for a long hard winter.

(5) Treatment.

Scan the girlie books casually, and all appear to be much alike. Check more closely, and you discover that this one likes sex with a light touch, that one prefers clinical detail, and another works largely in terms of implication.

Crime equals violence, at some houses. In others, cleverness dominates. One builds up character; another puts its emphasis on plot.

In the same way, Ace and Berkley set different standards for their westerns. Random House buys one kind of mystery, Dutton another. The story heavy with technical detail that *Analog* features would fall flat at *Amazing*.

* * *

Does all this sound like a plea for rigid slanting?

It isn't.

To me, it seems that a writer should be intensely aware of the markets he hopes to hit. He needs to read them, study them, learn to recognize their tastes and strengths and weaknesses.

When he sits down to write a story, however, he ought to forget said markets, utterly and completely. The story itself should become his entire preoccupation. Because if that story is good enough, count on it, it surely will find a home somewhere.

That incredibly prolific fictioneer John D. MacDonald once summed up the matter, in a letter to *Writer's Digest* in response to a man who declared that a book written for one publishing house often had small chance of acceptance elsewhere.

Wrote MacDonald: "I agree heartily. I would even say that a book written for one publishing house has little chance of acceptance at that publishing house. A book written for oneself—to meet one's own standards, to gratify and satisfy and entertain the toughest one-man audience a writer can ever have—such a book has a good chance of acceptance anywhere."

* * *

So, what about material? —That's where we started, remember?

MacDonald's statement still applies. You judge by personal standard.

And, *personal* is the key word. You can't use someone else's yardstick. You have to shape your own, out of an intimate amalgam both of fiction principles and of market patterns.

Preparing to write a story

Preparation boils down to two issues:

a. Getting ideas.
b. Finding facts to back them up.

* * *

What is an idea?
An idea is something that excites a writer.
Will the same idea excite two writers?
Not necessarily.
Then why is it important that the writer have an idea?
Because only insofar as he experiences excitement—a sense of mounting, goal-oriented inner tension—will the writer be able to muster the enthusiasm and energy he needs to seek for meaningful relationships in his material.

Creativity, in turn, may be defined as multiple response to single stimulus.

Most of us, when we look at a doorknob, see a doorknob. It's a one-to-one relationship: one doorknob, one response.

But some day you may fall prey to a sadistic old writing teacher who removes that self-same doorknob from the door and commands that you list ten ways to kill somebody with it.

Now, suddenly, the doorknob is no longer just a doorknob. You find yourself dealing with it in terms of qualities and context, as well as appearance and/or function.

Whereupon, the laws of association take over.

Thus, the doorknob's shaft is *similar* to a dagger . . . the knob to a billy . . . the material to an electrical conductor.

What *isn't* a doorknob, by way of *contrast?* Well, traditionally, it isn't supposed to function as the trigger to a booby trap, or a clue to the existence of a secret room ("Look! If you just stick the shaft through that knothole—"), or a secret container for poison or dope.

How about *contiguity* . . . meaning *next to*, as one house is next door to another? Apply it to doorknobs, and soon you find yourself thinking about locks and windows, panels and pull-cords, handles and hinges.

Before you know it, ideas begin to flow: A doorknob is round, maybe. Metal, maybe. Or glass. Or porcelain. Or hexagonal. Or octagonal. Why would anyone want a square doorknob? Maybe the knob slips on the shaft, so someone can't escape. Take the knobs from a door, and it gives you a tiny window into the room, through which a bullet or dart or rapier might pass . . . after which, the knob could be reinserted. How about radioactive material inside the knob? Or a poisoned-needle mechanism—snake or spider poison? You could run a piano-wire noose through the hole for the shaft. Maybe gimmick the latch—substitute a spring-lock for it and, at the same time, put the regular lock out of action, so that whoever's in the room thinks the lock is locked and he's safe, when really anyone outside can open the door without a key. How about wiring the knob for electricity? Or piping the shaft-hole for gas? "Glass" knob made of ice melts when the room heat is turned on. Diamond might be concealed in glass knob. Metal knob might be made of gold or platinum. What if knob were a symbol of something or other, and possessing it made its possessor a target? Or, turning knob trips hidden camera. Or load knob with germs. China knob turns out to be an insulator. Knob given to villain. Or unique knob used as clue to betray hiding place of right or wrong person. Knob filled with explosives. Shaft thrust into electric socket to stop some vital device by blowing fuse. Knob dusted with fluorescent powder to reveal who's touched it . . .

The above, please note, tends to take the form of a wild, chaotic, and often barely coherent jumble. It's random. It's disorganized. It's without any pre-established plan or pattern.

It is, in a phrase, a product of *focused free association*—that is, free association centered upon a particular subject and/or related group of subjects.

Such focused free association is what gives you ideas.

Your prime tools, in this associative process, are a scratch-pad, a pencil, and a willingness to set down a multitude of utterly and completely impossible notions, until you find one that rings an emotional bell somewhere deep inside you. For if anything is certain in this world, it's that only out of a host of *bad* ideas will emerge the occasional *good* one. Censor your thinking, attempt in advance to limit yourself to a superior product, and you can count on it that you'll end up sterile, or paralyzed, or both, creatively speaking.

Whenever you need an idea, then, make a list. —Not just lists of story situations, either. Whether you're looking for an incident, or a setting, or a character, or a bit of characterizing business, or a title—make a list! Even if you feel you've already worked out a proper angle, jot down half-a-dozen more, just for kicks.

And when the list is done—what then?

You put it aside; then come back later. Main strength and awkwardness mean little, in this phase of a writer's work. You have to sneak up on ideas. To that end, you must learn to change your point of view . . . your approach . . . your routine . . . even yourself

The stimuli of daily living help to accomplish such change. Suddenly, out of nowhere, as you stand shaving in the morning, the problem is solved. Or you fall asleep brooding over it at night . . . wake up next day with precisely the answer, the idea, that you need.

In fact, a scratch-pad and pencil beside your bed prove invaluable, upon occasion. You can even learn to write in the dark, with the pad balanced on your chest. Of course, the vibration will shake the bed just enough to awaken your wife or husband; but what does conjugal felicity matter, so long as your muse smiles sweetly?

The more boring types of idleness often help to provide the incubation time in which ideas take form. So, cultivate bars and park benches and night bus rides. Dull concerts or bad movies sometimes help. So do especially dreary sermons. There can be virtue in a Mexican radio station that alternates between marimba music and Spanish newscasts—that is, if you don't speak Spanish.

Time spent thus "loafing" is, at the right moment, the most productive occupation in which you can engage.

It should also be pointed out that, in considerable part, successful ideation lies in the area of serendipity—the art or knack of finding desirable things not sought.

This is to say, frequently the idea you uncover will at first glance show no perceptible relationship to the thing you think you're seeking.

The trick is to take advantage of this faculty.

Thus, you may suddenly find yourself confronted by a remarkable character . . . then later realize that introduction of said character will bring your yarn to the precise climax you've been struggling to achieve, even though at the moment Character seemed only a distraction or an irritation.

In view of this, it's to your advantage not to let your thinking become too set, too rigid, in the early stages of ideation. Feel free to switch and juggle and change and reverse and reshape the fragments on your list. Would the Comanche chief have more impact if he carried a parasol and wore a woman's flowered hat —instant visual proof that he's already raided and killed that day? Can you combine your beetle-like alien monsters and your human villainess by giving the woman multifaceted insectile eyes? Is there more interest in someone trying to steal a million dollars, or in his trying to return it? Search always for the unanticipated twist, the fresh approach!

Establishing a process of continuing elaboration may help too.

Don't just sit and stare at your scribbled notes. Type them up, throwing in any new thoughts that come to mind as you go along. Then, later, check through the typescript, penciling in changes and additional ideas and second guesses.

Is this the only way to develop ideas?

Of course not. To explain creativity as multiple response to single stimulus is really to define it as alertness—alertness to all that takes place around you; alertness to the full potentialities of whatever comes your way.

To that end, maybe *your* best procedure involves floor scrubbing, or long solitary walks, or drawn shades and bubble bath and Scarlatti on the record player. Perhaps you'll discover special insight from a private version of Twenty Questions, or Ben Jonson's Topics of Invention, or a file of blurbs or magazine story illustrations.

The important thing, always, is not to sit idly waiting for the feathers to grow. Don't just hope for ideas. Hunt them down! Find a springboard! Develop a plan of action! Nothing is more subjective than an idea, and no canned approach ever can work quite as well for you as your own system—even if said system is merely a matter of grope, fumble, pace the floor, stare out the window, and snarl at your wife.

* * *

Where do you find facts to back up your ideas?

You engage in research.

Research comes in two sizes: too much and too little.

Unfortunately, a considerable number of would-be writers want to probe their psyches, not the encyclopedia. They assume that fiction is one field in which adherence to fact is unimportant, and so proceed to write with no regard whatever for reality.

To a degree, perhaps, they may be right. There have been successful western novelists who used such terms as "fen" and "gorse," and mystery writers who obviously didn't know the difference between a revolver and an automatic pistol.

On the other side of the fence, I still recall an adventure story of twenty years ago that was spoiled for me because the author had soldiers in the Seminole War playing stud poker—a game that didn't come into vogue until some years later.

But if too little research can render a story ridiculous, too much can stop a career before it starts. Ask any writing coach about the talented men and women who've postponed authorship year after year, because they never could assemble quite all the information that they thought they needed.

The trick, then, is to achieve a balance. How do you go about it?

Primarily, you limit yourself.

That is, you acquire only the information you need, insofar as possible. You don't pile up data just for data's sake. —After all, is it really essential to your story that you detail the exchange rates on Turkish currency in Genoa in 1540?

Hang onto that general principle.

Working from it, we find two favored ways to approach any given job of research.

One is to search out the facts you need.

The other is to use such information as you already have in your possession.

Thus, readers of westerns like authentic color.

Some writers, following System 1, spend hours without end tracking down details about specific people and places and events.

Others, devotees of System 2, insert fragments from favored source books into a story like cloves in a ham.

Obviously, these two modes of attack aren't separate and exclusive. System-1 men don't work out *everything* afresh with each new title. And System-2 writers do, upon occasion, go hunting some special bit of background.

It can't be gainsaid, however, that System 2 saves time, when quantity production is important. A single volume like Foster-Harris' *The Look of the Old West* can take the place of a small library, in skilled hands.

But approach is a matter of personal choice. Beyond it, research breaks down into three categories:

(1) Library research.

(2) Interview research.

(3) Field research.

Now, what's involved in each?

(1) You and printed matter.

Libraries are wonderful institutions. Especially if you learn to use them properly.

To that end, I strongly recommend that you at least scan a volume called *The Modern Researcher,* by Jacques Barzun and Henry F. Graff. It will help you both to find the facts you need and to organize them once they're found. In addition, you'll learn a host of things you should know about weighing and evaluating information.

As a fictioneer, however, you have special problems. It's these we'll deal with here.

A warning comes first: Beware the beguilements of the bookshelves. They fascinate. Before you know it, you may find yourself plowing through the thousand-odd pages of *The Trail Drivers of Texas,* when a single photo of Doan's Store would solve your problem.

What you need, most often, is atmospheric detail.

You find such in eyewitness accounts, on-the-spot reports of events, associated records, pictures, maps, instruction books, and the like. Though dull going sometimes, they reward you with specialized data you never could obtain from secondary sources or popularizers.

Where do you find this sort of information?

Here are five likely places to check:

(*a*) Newspapers.

How much did steak cost in New Orleans in 1920? Which Finnish names are common in Duluth? What are typical local issues about which characters might gossip in Elko, Nevada? When do lake freighters tie up for the winter at Buffalo? Does Baltimore have a city manager? What's the leading women's-wear store in Waycross, Georgia?

A few minutes with the right newspaper file can supply you with such information and, in the process, save you all sorts of letter-writing. As a bonus, you pick up the atmosphere and attitudes of the community, from news columns and ads alike.

(*b*) Magazines.

Here, the secret is to not limit yourself to generalized publications. While *Time* may give you succinct coverage of a news event, or *Saturday Evening Post* fill you in on a personality, the pictures in *National Geographic* or *Holiday* often provide more of the color you need.

Don't forget trade and specialty journals, either. *Hardware World* gives you a cross section of current products and problems and procedures among its group of retailers. *Boxoffice* provides you with topics for a theater manager to discuss. *Farm Journal* shows rural life as it is today, instead of the way you remember it from boyhood. *Grit and Steel* introduces you to the world of game birds and cockfighting.

(*c*) Government documents.

Since bureaucracy seems determined to have its way with all of us, try to benefit from the resulting flood of printed matter. Its range is incredible: child-care guides, navigational instructions, information on the operation of all sorts of small businesses . . . even an excellent criminal-investigation handbook.

Much of this material will already be in your local library. The librarian can tell you where and how to get items not on file.

(*d*) "How-to" books.

Do you need a character who can lay bricks or bind books or give a facial? Don't worry; somebody's written a book about it, with the kind of detailed instructions that add an air of realism to your story.

(*e*) Ephemera.

Good libraries have files that include all sorts of brochures, leaflets, clippings, pamphlets, and assorted miscellany, from book catalogues to travel folders. There may even be collections of maps or photos or telephone books or pioneer manuscripts.

❂   ❂   ❂

At this point, another question usually arises: How much of a personal library should you acquire?

There's no sensible answer to this, really. Some items you'll need and should have, simply because you use them often and they're not easily available elsewhere.

On the other hand, it's easy to go overboard. In my own case, things have reached that unhappy state in which I have only to come in the front door with yet another volume, and my wife cries, "But we've got a book!" in an appropriately anguished voice. The fact that you do a story with a Sumatran locale doesn't necessarily warrant acquisition of half-a-dozen tomes on the East Indies. Odds are that they'll gather dust on the shelves for twenty years before you need them again—and by then they'll be hopelessly outdated.

Besides, space soon becomes a problem. Every big fact job I've ever done has brought with it fat folders of printed matter, on subjects ranging from manure-spreader operation to mental health to oil-field pumping equipment. When the file overflows, there's no choice but to dump some out, or buy a bigger house.

Clippings offer an added hazard. For a clip is useless unless you can find it, and to find it you have to file it, and to file it takes time, and what do you want to be anyhow, a writer or a file clerk?

Well, every man to his own compromises!

(2) You and experts.

Fifteen years ago I took a job writing factual films.

The scripting of each such film, I soon discovered, is expedited if you insist that the sponsor assign a technical adviser to assist you.

The expert steps in where book research ends. He corrects your mistakes and calls your attention to developments too new to have reached the reference-shelf stage. Without him, you grope, flounder, and waste vast quantities of time.

To work with such an expert is simple. You need primarily a willingness to be thought a fool.

How do you achieve this happy end?

You take nothing for granted. You describe precisely what you propose to show in your film, step by step, so that error lurches out into the open. You ask every stupid question you can dredge up from the sub-depths of your brain, no matter how withering your expert's glances; no matter how biting his replies.

If you follow this principle, the expert goes his way convinced that you're a blithering idiot. You, in your turn, carry off the neatly-catalogued contents of the expert's head. A fair exchange.

There are worse tricks than to apply this same fact-film technique to fiction research.

To that end, dig out all the data you can from printed matter. *Do this first!* Any competent interview presupposes that the interviewer knows enough about the subject to ask at least a modicum of intelligent questions.

Then, background filled in, hunt around till you find someone —historian, homicide detective, marriage counselor, army colonel, zoologist—who has a strong track record in the area you're researching.

Make contact with this expert. Tell him your problem. Ask his aid. More often than not, he'll be flattered and happy to give it to you.

It also will help if you remember that an expert doesn't always look like one. Maybe, at first glance, your man appears to be only a sleazy beatnik type, unshaven and overdue for a haircut, playing guitar in a cockroach-infested coffeehouse. But if the data you seek concerns beatniks or coffeehouses or modern minstrels, he very well may prove an ideal source.

Further, an interviewee needn't know he's being interviewed. He may talk more freely if he thinks you're just an amiable screwball who likes to chase fire engines or noodle for catfish or gab about mining.

Charm radiated by the interviewer is no handicap. Neither is willingness to spring for an occasional drink or cup of coffee.

Quite often, your best leads come from people who themselves lack the facts you need, but are in a position to suggest someone who does have them. Chambers of Commerce, trade associations, local newspaper offices, public-relations men, county agents, motel managers—all are worth investigation.

You can even interview by mail, with luck, specific questions, brief checklists, and stamped, self-addressed return envelopes. However, it's my own feeling that such should be pretty much a last resort, for most people are reluctant to take pen in hand and their answers tend to be brief to the point of uselessness.

(3) You and the wide, wide world.

Field research is based on a simple premise: An ivory tower is a poor place to learn the facts about anything.

In many cases, the best way to find out the things you need to know is to go forth and poke around at first hand.

Thus, books and talk will tell you a lot about oil wells. But you add extra color and authentic detail if you walk a drilling floor yourself.

Similarly, what's wrong with working as a waiter for a week or two or three? Why shouldn't you ride a few nights in a police prowl car, if you can arrange it? Nurses' aides learn things. So do typists and dime-store clerks and door-to-door salesmen.

If such is too rich for your blood, that still shouldn't stop you from attending trials and loafing in bus stations and scraping acquaintances with jewelers and gunsmiths and carhops and rodeo riders, if these maneuvers suit your ends.

Get in the habit of handling the props you plan to use in a story. It sparks ideas and prevents idiotic errors. You discover that the barrels of two Mauser automatics can be switched in seconds . . . that a modern vinyl phonograph record can't easily be snapped in half . . . that most watches today don't carry Arabic numerals.

Finally, remember that every story comes alive in terms of sensory perception—the things some character sees or hears or smells or tastes or touches.

To describe such phenomena vividly, you need to experience them yourself, wherever possible.

Providing this sensory background is the function of field research.

The best-laid plans

By all means, plan your story.

But don't plan too completely, or the story may die before it's born.

Why?

Because a basic fallacy lies at the heart of all attempts to blueprint creative activity: Planning, you're one person. But by the time you sit down to write, you've become another.

You probably can see this most clearly if you're one of those methodical souls who goes in for journals, sketches of stories you hope some day to write, file cards listing plot ideas, and the like.

These efforts are laudable. But by now, if you've carried on such projects for any length of time, you've discovered that only on rare occasions do the notes develop into finished copy.

The reason is precisely as stated above: You yourself change, in the interim between the time when inspiration first becomes apparent and the later date when you attempt to reclaim the concept from your file.

In consequence, yesterday's idea strikes no spark today. Fervor has dulled to disenchantment.

Multiply this response by ten, and you get some small picture of what happens when you outline a story in too great detail.

For when you plan rigidly, in effect you nail down the road a story must take. You commit yourself to a mood and state of mind that no longer exist when you and your typewriter finally get together.

In so doing, you deny yourself the pleasure and privilege of following the impulse and inspiration of the moment.

Result: Writing flips from fun to drudgery. The idea lies dead as a skinned and gutted rabbit in a freezer, its only pulse that which you pump into it with sweat and dogged perseverance.

That's not what I'd call successful planning.

Let's try again, then, on a different tack. This time, we'll let things hang a little looser.

What elements do you really need in a story outline?

You should have:

  a. A focal character.
  b. A situation in which this character is involved.
  c. An objective Character seeks to attain.
  d. An opponent who strives against Character.
  e. A potential climactic disaster on which to hinge the resolution.

In other words, you require a starting line-up, such as was described in Chapter 6.

And that's all you need. For the line-up is a tool . . . its function, to pinpoint essential dynamic factors that drive a story forward, from page one to *The End*. Minor characters, tags, settings, incidents, bits of business—by comparison, these are trivial and unimportant. You can pick them up as you go along, if need be.

Next question: How do you acquire the elements it takes to build a line-up?

As with everything else in writing, each man must sooner or later develop his own tricks, his private system.

Right now, however, your problem is to find a starting point. So, try this one:

(1) Spend an hour in focused free association.

This period is to be spent in hitting the keys as fast as possible, describing the story you want to write. —Not actually writing it, you understand; not even organizing it, or attempting to go in a straight line; just doodling about anything that comes to mind related to your idea, from mood to characters, from moral to plot to incidents.

(2) Later, devote another hour to annotating the above material.

That is, take a pencil and go over your free-association typescript. Elaborate on your first thoughts. Cross out bits that have lost their charm. Change. Combine. Develop. Shape up. Flesh out.

(3) Still later, retype this annotated free association.

Again, switch and change and delete and elaborate as you go.

A few days spent with this routine will give you an amazing mass of formless yet promising material. You'll begin to see strong points, and weak; bad judgment, and flashes that excite you.

Included will be assorted fragments that hint of a potential starting line-up.

Don't force the process, though. Let "Hang loose!" be your motto.

Eventually, all this rambling will begin to bore you. Take advantage of it to draw up a list of incidents that strike you as essential to your story.

Some of these bits will loom larger and more important in your mind than others.

These may prove to be your story's crises: the big moments. Jot them down, each on a separate sheet.

Again, don't yet try to turn them into actual fiction. Just describe each in a paragraph or two or three of copy.

Shuffle these scene sheets as you go along. Put them into some kind of order. When holes appear, rough in additional scenes to fill them. Or, if scenes as first conceptualized don't seem to fit, reshape or consolidate or delete them.

Apply the same technique to characters. As each takes form, give him a separate sheet of his own. Then, use said sheet to doodle and hypothesize about him.

By now, count on it, restlessness will be upon you. You're ready to go; eager to start producing actual copy.

Fine. That's as it should be. But don't start writing. Not quite yet.

For this is the moment when you put an end to free association and loose thinking. —And I *do* mean, in terms of your starting line-up.

What you must have is a statement and a question, two sentences, nailed down tight precisely as described in Chapter 6:

Situation: Pursued by his boss's amoral wife, Linda,
Character: Steve Grannis
Objective: decides to seek a transfer, so that his home and career won't be destroyed.
But can he escape, when
Opponent: Linda
Disaster: swears that she'll have him fired and ruined if he tries to leave?

* * *

Situation: Reporting for her very **first** day's work, fresh out of college and the lone Negro teacher in a white high school,
Character: Loretta Kloman

Objective: stands determined to prove her competence.
But can she succeed, when
Opponent: Bucko Wilding, the Mississippi-born coach,
Disaster: urges her pupils to walk out on her?

* * *

Situation: Expelled from a Central American republic at the request of his Latin sweetheart's politically powerful father,
Character: Tom Reynolds
Objective: hitchhikes back to persuade the girl to run away with him.
But will he survive, let alone win her, when it turns out that
Opponent: Miguel Ortiz, the man who picks him up,
Disaster: is en route to assassinate *El Presidente?*

* * *

There are the elements. Thus succinctly do you formulate your story framework.

And then—?

Then, you're ready to start writing. Play it by ear, spontaneously, changing and adapting as you go along, to fit the ideas that pop forth moment by moment. Plan each scene as you reach it, and then only to the degree of pinpointing goal and conflict and disaster. Between scenes, free-wheel, so long as your focal character somehow ends up with a logical new goal toward which to strive. When you hit a snag—and you will—just pace the floor awhile, or resort to the list system: "Since Joe needs to show up as a selfish brute at this point, what are some of the typically selfish and brutish things selfish brutes do?" "How can Stella keep Len from investing in Papa's blue-sky goldmine, without revealing that Papa is a swindler?"

Stay with such long enough, and eventually you'll end up with a story . . . a *solid* story, because you worked within the framework of a starting line-up; yet a story that's free and spontaneous also, in that you didn't tie yourself to any rigid outline.

Is this the ideal way to plan, then?

Not at all. The ideal way is the one that gets the job done; and no two stories and no two writers are the same.

But at least, as stated earlier, this procedure offers you a springboard.

What comes after will and must be of your own making.

The organization of production

The beginner has a fond illusion: Once he learns to write a story, he thinks, everything will go swimmingly.

Professionals know otherwise. Writing fiction is like playing in vaudeville, except that you have to devise a new act for each performance. It's the only craft that gets harder as you go along instead of easier. Skill brings awareness of deficiencies. You grow more critical and strive—involuntarily, often—to do a better job; achieve a higher standard.

Thus, the difference between the beginner and the pro is less one of talent or knowledge than of endurance. The pro, having been over the road many, many times before, accepts the agony that goes with the journey in stoical silence, because he knows that if he perseveres long enough, eventually the way will clear and he'll get his story.

Consistent production starts with the presumption that you already have an effective grasp of story structure and fiction technique.

Beyond these, you must also work out methods to deal with routine problems of:

> *a.* Procedure.
> *b.* Revision.
> *c.* Polishing.
> *d.* Cutting.
> *e.* Production breakdown.

Each of these constitutes a subject in itself. Let's start with procedure.

> *a.* Getting out the work.

It has been truly said that, too often, writers hate to write, but love to have written.

Why should this be so?

Because writing demands that you put forth effort, and inertia is a hard foe to overcome. To muster initiative, to exert self-discipline—these are difficult assignments.

"There are basically two kinds of people in the world," says Jean Monnet, French founder of the European Common Market, "those who want to be and those who want to do. In the second category there is almost no competition."

How do you go about qualifying for Category 2?

Herewith, eight hints:

(1) Work.

Loss of a boss can be a dangerous thing.

Down through the years, you've grown accustomed to having someone tell you what to do and when to do it.

Now, abruptly, all that's changed. You've entered a field in which you not only do the work, but serve as your own supervisor.

On a job, you can dream through a spring day without penalty.

Dream as a writer, and your income stops. Physical presence or good intentions mean nothing. "Get the story written!" is the only thing that counts. You've got to drive yourself to work—and that means push as hard to turn out fiction as if a boss were breathing down your neck.

(2) Work regular hours.

Freedom is heady stuff. With it comes the temptation to postpone what must, upon occasion, be the drudgery of writing. —After all, you rationalize, you can always make up for it tomorrow, or tomorrow, or tomorrow.

But, as you soon learn, tomorrow never comes.

The answer, of course, is to set up a schedule of regular hours, *and stick to it*.

The hard part here is that friends and family very well may prove your worst enemies. The idea that writing must be dealt with as a job is alien to their thinking. They can't conceive that you must have uninterrupted hours. It never dawns on them that time is the only thing you have to sell, or that two minutes' conversation may, upon occasion, shatter your train of thought for half a day.

Further, you may not fully realize these things yourself. When it's a gorgeous morning and the kids plead for a picnic, you want to go along. Or old George comes by, and he's upset about this problem . . .

In consequence, you never give habit a chance to help you with your efforts. Always, there are errands to run or people to see or polite amenities to break up your time.

Then you wonder why you don't get out more copy.

If you're really serious about your work, you'll stop all this nonsense before it starts.

To that end, certain hours will be yours to write. You'll hold them for it, inviolate, complete with locked door and blunt refusal to be disturbed.

Does this mean you have to act as if you were a shoe clerk?

Of course not. If you really have good reason to break away and want to do so, go to it. But do it with your eyes open, in full knowledge that you must pay for that lost time later, in extra effort or lost income.

(3) Set up a quota.

A writer's unconscious is a sneaky thing. Give it half a chance, and it will devise a way to evade the grinding work of writing.

Thus, if hours spent in front of the typewriter are your only criterion of effort, you'll soon train yourself to sit, but not produce.

What's the remedy?

Make your standard the completion of a task—ordinarily, production of a certain amount of copy.

Here, the hazard is that you may set your sights too high.

That can be disastrous. Too stiff a quota freezes you before you even start. Pledge yourself to turn out three thousand words each and every day, and you very well may produce none at all.

A better way is to take smaller steps. Five hundred words may be enough, at first. Even seasoned professionals seldom complete more than a thousand words of finished copy, day in and day out.

Often, too, it takes as long to plan a story as it does to write it. A week of such preparation, for a short story, may prove none too much.

All this is an individual matter, though. Some writers are facile, others clumsy. This one works fast, that one slow.

So, find your own pace. Start with minimal demands; then work up.

But *do* produce. For a writer is, by definition, one who writes.

(4) Have a place to work.

There are books on the shelf next to your desk. Fascinating books, that you love to read. Outside your window, you can see white sails skimming down the lake, or watch the lights come on along the Sunset Strip, or marvel at snow sparkling on an Ozark hillside.

Is this your picture of a writer's workroom?

It's also a prelude to disaster.

Why?

Because, believe me, you'll read the books . . . gaze out the window.

What you really need is a windowless, bookless, distractionless gray room.

It will help if this room isn't even in your home. An office is a legitimate income-tax deduction. It frees you from family pressures and interruptions.

Keep its location a secret, and friends won't be tempted to drop by either.

Equipment? Desk, chair, typewriter, blank paper, carbon, pencils. Maybe a lounge chair, if you like to sit at ease while you scribble notes or edit copy. And lamps, since good lighting is essential to a writer.

Probably you should have a dictionary and thesaurus too . . . if you'll discipline yourself not to read them as an escape from writing. —Yes, a writer can read even a dictionary for entertainment. I've seen it done.

Most important of all, when you enter your workroom (or work area, if it's just a corner of the bedroom), it should be for purposes of production only. Again, habit is the issue. If you sit down at your desk only to write, you establish a conditioning that will help you.

(5) Eliminate distractions.

Some writers work nights, instead of days.

Why?

Because night offers fewer distractions. The noise and bustle of day are gone. Darkness closes in, like a protective mantle.

Result: more copy.

Schedule is a matter of personal preference, however. Some people work better in the morning, or the afternoon. The only way to find out your own best time is to experiment.

Whatever your choice, distraction still remains an irritating problem. It consists of anything that draws your attention from your work.

Thus, an uncomfortable chair constitutes a distraction. So does a too-low desk, or a flickering light, or a too-warm or too-cold room, or a typewriter with keys that stick, or squeaking floor boards in the hall outside your door.

Whenever you become aware of such annoyances, do something about them if at all possible.

Often, the solution is no more involved than purchase of a new ribbon for your old mill, or moving your desk into a corner so that you face blank wall instead of open window, or installation of a small electric fan to muffle encroaching echoes of sound.

On the other hand, there are things in this life you can't control.

When such arise, remember your grandmother's line about "What can't be cured must be endured," and condition yourself to ignore the situation. A newspaper city room resembles a madhouse, on occasion, but reporters still turn out their copy. Whole books have been written on subway trains, in ships' forecastles, or while bouncing a baby on one hip. If you want to write badly enough, you'll get the job done somehow.

(6) Don't push too hard.

Once upon a time there was a writer. Because he was a competent craftsman, he prided himself on his ability to deliver precisely what an editor asked, no matter how short the notice or great the pressure.

Magazines liked that attitude. Soon Our Boy was the man they called when, in crisis, they needed a 20,000-word cover piece by Monday morning.

Since such rush jobs often carried double or even triple rates, Writer felt very pleased with himself, not to mention prosperous.

That is, he felt thus until, one day, it dawned on him that maybe the pride was misplaced and the profit not quite so great, if you stopped to consider that he ended each story so knocked out that he couldn't work at all for two or three weeks after.

The lesson here is that, although you can outdo yourself on a short-time basis, you pay for it later.

In the same way, if you push yourself too hard, day in and day out, you become tired and bored.

Especially bored.

Boredom is born of conflict: You're doing one thing, but you wish—even if unconsciously—that you were doing something else.

How does this apply to writers?

Writing is hard work . . . work that makes strenuous demands on your unconscious.

Said Unconscious goes along. But it wants reward for effort.

If no reward comes . . . if you press too hard, if you drive too long, if you insist on labor without respite . . . Unconscious balks.

Try to force the issue then, and you may end up in real trouble.

And we wouldn't want that to happen to you, would we?

(7) Stay alive.

Life is a writer's raw material.

Successful writers immerse themselves in it.

To that end, you read. You travel. You shop. You loaf on street corners. You go to ball games. You visit friends. You attend parties. You work in church or civic club or Boy Scout troop.

In other words, you contact people. All kinds of people, without regard to age or sex or social stratum; the wider the range, the better.

No aspect of your work is more important. Ignore it, and you must face the unhappy plight met too often by the older person who decides he wants to write.

Frequently, this older person stopped reading fiction twenty years ago. Result: His ideas on style are hopelessly outmoded.

Worse, his friends, his attitudes, his allusions and his idiom all are drawn from his own age group. His world is one of age, not youth.

Yet to 71 per cent of our citizenry, World War I is something you read about in history books. Sixty-four per cent don't remember Prohibition. Even the Korean War is dead past to 22 per cent.

This creates a problem for the older person: How does he make contact with young readers?

Most often, he doesn't. The gap between him and them is too wide to bridge.

In fact, ordinarily you don't *make* contact with anyone, as a writer. You *keep* it. Every day.

And you do it by staying alive.

(8) Get enough exercise.

Writing is an appallingly sedentary occupation.

In addition, it builds nervous tension.

Put those two facts together, and you have a basis for all kinds of trouble, from obesity to the screaming mimis.

What do you do about it?

You exercise.

That doesn't mean pushups, necessarily, or handball. But it does mean getting out into the open . . . walking along the beach in early, pearl-gray morning . . . taking an afternoon off to sun and swim . . . venting your hostilities on the weeds, if you're a gardener . . . bicycling, fishing, hunting, golfing, riding, boating.

This is time well spent. Allow for it in your schedule. Your work will benefit, not suffer. You'll eat better, sleep better, relax easier. The plot problem that tied knots in your stomach before you dived into the pool will somehow have resolved itself by the time you sit down at the typewriter again. Raw-nerved touchiness and acid temper fade away as you chop wood or mow the lawn.

In fact, you might even come up with an idea for a new story!

b. How to revise; and when.

A first-draft story ordinarily is a lumpy, awkward thing.

To shape it up, you must rework it.

Mystery writer Margery Allingham states the issue this way: "I write everything four times: once to get my meaning down, once to put in everything I left out, once to take out everything that seems unnecessary, and once to make the whole thing sound as if I had only just thought of it."

Reworking a story involves two processes. One, here termed *revision*, deals with structural change. The second, to be taken up later, centers on language, and is called *polishing*.

Successful revision requires that you perform three operations, separately or simultaneously:

(1) See that the story goes in a straight line.

That is, make sure it centers on the story question.
You can check this with a little private quiz game:

(*a*) Does the story question define the issue?

"Can Loretta Kloman, lone Negro teacher in a white high school, prove her competence, when the racist coach urges her pupils to walk out on her?" is a good story question. It brings objective into head-on collision with opposition.

Leave desire (Loretta's determination to prove her competence) or danger (the fear that her pupils will walk out on her) vague and unformulated, and your whole story may grow weak and fuzzy.

(*b*) Can the story question be answered "yes" or "no"?

Let Loretta seek to "prove that Negroes are as good as whites," and you have a question that can't be resolved in fiction.
Why not?
Because you've shifted the issue from a test of individual worth to a debate on anthropological or sociological theory.

Similarly, if your story question deals primarily with process ("*How* can Loretta prove . . ." etc.), you switch emphasis from feeling to intellect, emotion to puzzle.

You're better off to stick with a pattern that focuses down to a definite "yes" or "no."

(*c*) Is the story question established early?

Loretta's objective, and Coach Wilding's opposition, and Loretta's decision to fight, should come on stage as soon as possible . . . preferably in the very first scene.

If they don't, the opening will drag.

> (d) Does each and every incident you include have some
> clear-cut bearing on the story question?

Discursiveness is a peril for all of us. Incorporate a love scene
between Loretta and her boy friend, with no reference to the
school situation in speech or thought or feeling on either side,
and you waste words better devoted to some aspect of the story
question.

> (e) Is development close-knit and logical from scene to
> scene?

If it isn't, it means that the disaster in the preceding scene
hasn't been devastating enough to preoccupy Loretta with the
need to find a new goal.

Thus, the theft of Loretta's lunch-box might rate as an irritation, but it won't force her to revise her thinking about her situation. Whereas Bucko Wilding's belligerent demand that other
teachers leave her table, when she sits down in the school cafe-
teria, and the other teachers' compliance, will increase her fears
. . . perhaps even tempt her to quit her job on the spot.

> (f) Is the question answered at the climax?

Your story needn't solve all of Loretta's problems. But if you
end with her still in doubt as to her competence, her ability to
meet and control her class, there's no release of tension, and your
reader has a right to irritation.

> (g) Does your hero's climactic act decide the issue?

We've reached the story's climax. The kids in Loretta's class
are on their feet to leave. She's floundering, in deep trouble.

Now, enter the principal. In a ringing speech on duty, toler-
ance, brotherhood and Americanism, he appeals to the class to
stay with Loretta. Whereupon, the kids sit down again.

O.K.?

No, no, no!

Why not?

Because God, in the shape of the principal, saves the day. Loretta herself does nothing . . . performs no climactic act to prove that she's worthy of reward.

And that, dear friends, is a cardinal sin indeed in fiction!

(*h*) Does the resolution tie up all loose ends?

The answer to any story question leaves an aftermath of minor issues. If you don't at least hint as to their outcome, your resolution won't completely satisfy your reader.

In our hypothetical story, for example, there's bound to be curiosity as to what happens to Bucko Wilding. So, don't leave it hanging.

And that's enough attention to the tricks of checking story line. Now, let's move on to the second aspect of revision:

(2) See that the story builds from beginning to end.

Here, the issue is proportion. A ten-page beginning to a twenty-page story is like opening a kids' cap-gun war with the blast of an actual hand grenade.

In the same way, a story whose big scene comes in the middle isn't likely to get you much; and neither is one that features two tremendous climaxes in succession at the end.

You *must* space your crises and keep your peaks of tension rising!

(3) See that your reader cares what happens to your hero.

The key to identification is desire, and it works two ways.

Thus, no one cares what happens to the character who wants nothing.

And if nothing stands between him and his goal—that is, if he faces no danger, no opposition—again, he's a dead duck so far as your reader is concerned.

Therefore, check force and counterforce in every scene. Build up the struggle. Emphasize what's at stake . . . its subjective importance to your hero.

In addition, remember that your reader looks for some element of personality in your hero that he himself would like to possess. It's your job to provide it.

* * *

So much for our three points.

Are they the only items you need to check when you revise?

By no means; for every story offers different problems.

However, our list does cover the key issues. And you can always fall back on Chapter 6: *Beginning, Middle, End,* and Chapter 7: *The People in Your Story,* if you grow confused.

* * *

Finally, there's one special hazard in revision: the tendency to substitute it for new stories.

Thus, too often, when a story is rejected, Writer decides that it must be revised.

Maybe he's right. Maybe it really needs reworking.

But if this happens more than occasionally, he should begin to suspect his motives.

Why?

Because writing, as before mentioned, can be devilishly hard work. For some people especially, playing with an already-completed product comes easier.

The solution?

Once a story is mailed, forget it. No matter how bad you decide it is, in afterthought, let it go out at least five times before you change it.

That is, unless an editor suggests that you rework it.

In which case, boy, get busy!

c. Polishing the product.

A story communicates emotion.

To that end, it uses language.

Whereupon, a question arises: Does the language used really say what you want it to say? Does it convey the precise nuances of meaning you seek to pass on to your reader?

Unless it does—and it seldom will, in first-draft copy—you need to give it further polish.

Specifically, you need to check and correct it, line by line, for:

(1) Clarity.

To be clear is to be distinct; plain; easily and correctly understood.

All of which is more simply defined in the abstract than it is put to use when you deal with the specific and concrete.

Thus, does your reader really know what "talus" is . . . how a harpsichord sounds . . . the function of a Zoomar lens? Because you visualize a girl as of a certain type, or picture a door in a particular place in your mind's eye, do you neglect to establish them as vividly for the audience with description? Are you sure each sentence is so written that the "he" refers beyond question to hero or villain, as the case may be?

If not . . . you need to clarify your meaning.

(2) Clutter.

In simplicity lies strength. Qualify anything too fussily, and you lose the forest in the trees. Explanation and interjection can bog a story down.

All those intriguing adjectives and adverbs! They lure us. We purr to the sonority of the convoluted sentence . . . rolling on, rolling on. Alliteration beckons, and so does metonymy, and a hundred other devices pressed into the service of self-conscious stylism. Why limit yourself to a simple statement, when fifty words will befuddle your reader so much more neatly and completely?

The remedy for clutter is simple: Get down to work with that blue pencil! Say what you have to say, briefly and to the point. Draw the picture cleanly and vividly, but don't embellish it with unnecessary words and phrases. Forego the purple prose. Your job is to tell a story!

(3) Consistency.

Does Rita have black hair on page three, brown on page seven? Is the sky overcast one moment . . . your character squinting against the sun the next? Have you planted the gun in the desk drawer on page twelve, so that its presence won't startle your reader when Babette snatches it at the climax?

These all are problems of consistency. Failure to check them out may spoil a story for your reader.

(4) Sequence.

"He turned, hearing the knock at the door."

Actually, of course, the knock came first.

Motivating stimulus *always* precedes character reaction, in proper copy. When it doesn't, you're faced with confusion of sequential order.

Correct it, or the passage will strike an awkward, jerky note.

(5) Flow.

"Standing there by the grave, he nodded gravely."

The repetition sticks out like a sore thumb.

"Standing there beside her in the cemetery, he nodded gravely."

Now we've come up with an inadvertent pun, and that's even worse than repetition.

"Standing there beside her in the polyandrium, he nodded soberly."

O.K., so the writer owns an unabridged dictionary. But does the reader?

All these examples represent disruptions of flow.

Your copy should read smoothly, and without attracting undue attention to your use of language. To that end, you try to select the right word, the right sound, the right connotation, the right combination for rhythm and pacing and balance. When too many long sentences fall together, you break them up. Are too many short? You check to make sure they don't sound choppy.

—Unless choppiness is the effect you seek, that is.

How do you train yourself to spot the literary awkwardness that breaks up flow?

You follow the same technique by which you avoid using barracks idiom at Aunt Matilda's tea: You cultivate awareness of language and its nuances.

(6) Impact.

Timing, word placement, makes a world of difference, whether in a joke or in a story.

Thus, "Sympathy is what one girl offers another in exchange for details" makes a good gag-line, because the punch, the unanticipated twist, is at the very end.

Would it be as amusing if you said, "When one girl offers another sympathy, the details of what happened are demanded in return"?

The technique of building impact is a fine art indeed. One wrong or extra word inserted, or one key word misplaced or left out, and what should be a bomb can sound like the backfire of a car a block away.

Perhaps the best way to learn timing is to practice telling jokes.

Don't just repeat; experiment with your phrasings endlessly. It may make your friends groan for a while, but every laugh you coax will increase your skill at adding impact to your copy.

(7) Idiosyncrasy.

To some teen-agers, everything is "swell" or "square" or "tough" or "cool" or "greasy."

Being people, writers too sometimes fall into bad habits.

—Dashes can become such a habit. So can elipses . . . not to mention unnecessary Capitals (or parenthetical insertions) or exclamation points!

How about you? Has "febrile" become your favorite adjective? Are "thickly" or "numbly" or "fiercely" adverbs too often used? Is the villain forever heavy-footed? Do the heroine's breasts rise and fall too fast on every other page?

It's something to think about.

* * *

A writer can devote a lifetime to mastering the tricks and techniques of polishing his copy.

He should.

He can spend days on end honing and burnishing a single paragraph or page.

And that's another matter.

How so?

Again, Somerset Maugham sums up the issue. "One fusses about style," he comments in *A Writer's Notebook*. "One tries to

write better. One takes pains to be simple, clear and succinct.
One aims at rhythm and balance. One reads a sentence aloud to
see if it sounds well. One sweats one's guts out. The fact remains
that the four greatest novelists the world has ever known,
Balzac, Dickens, Tolstoi and Dostoevsky, wrote their respective
languages very indifferently. It proves that if you can tell stories,
create character, devise incidents, and if you have sincerity and
passion, it doesn't matter a damn how you write. All the same
it's better to write well than ill."

   d. The not-so-gentle art of cutting.

   The letter says, ". . . so, we'd be most interested in having an-
other look at this story, if you can get it down to three thousand
words."
   What do you do now?
   You cut.
   What do you cut?
   You cut facts.
   More specifically, you do *not* cut emotion.
   This is the heart of the issue, believe me. As such, it's also
the reason why a great many revisions are rejected.
   When a beginner cuts, it's his tendency to lop out feeling, every
time.
   That is, he hangs onto his trees or his wharves or his buildings.
He clings to the routine incident in the railroad station, the
bit with the bootlegger, the explanation of precisely how a caril-
lon is played.
   What he throws away is character reaction.
   But a story isn't facts. Rather, the truly vital element is how a
specific somebody feels about the data; reacts to them.
   These feelings are what move the story forward. Eliminate
them, and the story stands still and dies.
   To cut, yet hang onto these so-essential feelings, the trick often
is to consolidate and regroup the facts. Maybe Character can
react to a mountain scene as a whole, a panorama, instead of to
trees and rocks and brooks and purple shadows separately. Dock
Street's wharves and fog and smells and murky alleys are less
important than the chill of fear your hero feels as he strides
along the broken sidewalk. You can leave out all sorts of descrip-

tion of glass and stainless steel, if you confide that the building is one of those that make the old man long nostalgically for 1890.

In the same way, if the railway-station scene represents little save passage of time and movement through space, it's possible that you can drop it altogether. Same for bootlegger and carillonneur, unless the parts they play are truly vital in the shaping of somebody's feelings.

So much for the general principle. Now, here are two specific rules:

(1) For limited cuts, trim words and phrases.

Blue-pencil an adjective here, an adverb there, an explanatory clause or rambling sentence or discursive paragraph on down the line, and two or three hundred words can be stripped from almost any manuscript. It's often well-nigh painless. And it's almost certain to sharpen up and so benefit your story.

(2) For major cuts, drop scenes or characters.

Carry a word-trim too far and your story thins, from loss of detail and imagery.

Elimination of a minor scene, on the other hand, may save you two or three pages, without affecting the color of the story as a whole.

In the same way, dropping a character takes out lines and paragraphs with a minimum of pain.

In either case, however, there *will* be a disruption of story balance. To remedy it often demands that you reappraise and rewrite most carefully.

e. The psychology of production.

"In the good hours when words are flowing well," remarks Herman Wouk, famed author of *The Caine Mutiny,* "it seems there is hardly a pleasanter way to spend one's time on earth."

How true. Production gives a writer his greatest satisfaction.

Only then Wouk adds, "Never mind the bad hours. There is no life without them."

Well, as a philosophical attitude, that's fine. But what a working writer needs when he's stalled is help; *practical* help.

Specifically, what's he to do when, for some mysterious reason, he can't get out the copy?

This is by no means an uncommon situation. Every professional has experienced it, at one period or another. Sometimes it lasts for weeks, or even months. Depression—both financial and emotional—comes with it, and panic . . . maybe even the end of a career.

Actually, the whole problem stems from one simple fact: Writers, too, are people.

Being people, the fear of failure lives in all of us, on one level or another.

Anything that frustrates us or makes us feel inadequate may bring that fear surging to the surface.

When that happens, self-doubt takes over. Consciously or otherwise, projecting your fears into your copy, you begin to wonder whether said copy really can be any good, when you yourself are such a failure.

A bad review can trigger such a mood. Likewise, a rejection. Introduction to a more successful writer may make you wonder if he hasn't some mysterious something that you lack. A sneer, a barbed joke, an inept compliment which Ego interprets as a slight—each holds the potential of undermining confidence.

Nor need the trigger be associated with your work. Inability to get proper service from a waiter can plunge you into a black mood. A child's question—"Why can't *we* have a new car, Daddy?"—or a wife's sigh over an expensive gown in a shop window have been known to start writers on a downward spiral. Divorce is notorious for its shattering effect.

Thus, you need not face *actual* disapproval or rejection. It's enough that you interpret what happens in derogatory terms, even on an unconscious level.

Whereupon, because you're already critical of self and unsure in your talent, you involuntarily question the worth of the work you do.

Consider, for example, the not-untypical case of a man with an overeager agent.

Writer has for years made a decent enough living from paperback science-fiction novels. Agent, aware of Writer's talent and dazzled by visions of greater profit, urges him to move over into the hardback field.

"This stuff you do is nothing," Agent presses. "A big book with literary quality—that's what you need to tackle."

Writer laughs it off. "I'm doing all right," he says. "Science fiction's fun. It's what I'm geared to."

But the laughter has a hollow ring: "This stuff you do is nothing." That's what the man said.

The words fall against a backdrop of irksome memory: snide remarks from an aging poetess . . . the disdain evinced by the young English professor who genuflects at the altar of the *Kenyon Review* . . . a tendency of friends to treat Writer as an amusing kook because his specialty is science fiction.

And now, his agent joins the pack.

On the surface, Writer shrugs it off. But a knot begins to tighten in his belly.

Finally, one day, he sits down at the typewriter—and no words come.

Why?

Because, without even being aware of it, Writer suddenly has become critical of his own work.

You can't be both creative and critical at the same time. They're opposing forces. Catch a writer between them, and they tear him apart.

And that gives us our first rule:

(1) Separate creative impulse from critical judgment.

How do you do this?

The first and most essential step is to recognize the human tendency to attempt to mix the two.

Then, walk wide around it.

To that end, adopt a working rule of "Create now . . . correct later." Promise yourself the privilege of being as critical as you like, as soon as the first draft of a scene or story is completed.

Until the draft is done, however, stick with impulse. Let yourself go in a heat of passion. Forget the rules. For as Balzac said, "If the artist does not fling himself, without reflecting, into his work, as Curtius flung himself into the yawning gulf, as the soldier flings himself into the enemy's trenches, and if, once in this crater, he does not work like a miner on whom the walls of his gallery have fallen in; if he contemplates difficulties instead of overcoming them one by one . . . he is simply looking on at the suicide of his own talent."

(2) Face up to your fears.

Writers as a group are notoriously hard to live with. They snarl, brood, take affront, pick fights . . . leap from heights of elation to depths of despond.

The reason is that they tend to project their fears . . . seek confirmation for their self-doubt in others.

Says Christopher Fry, playwright and poet, "An artist's sensitiveness to criticism is, at least in part, an effort to keep unimpaired the zest, or confidence, or arrogance, which he needs to make creation possible; or an instinct to climb through his problems in his own way as he should, and must."

So, you tend to be hypersensitive. What do you do about it?

First, recognize that most slights are matters of interpretation, not intent. Not every casual comment bears a barb. The sneer lies more often in your own mind than the speaker's.

Second, remember that to achieve, you first must stick your neck out; and that the jealousy of others, less able or less courageous or less insightful, is part of the price you pay for rising from the mass. When local literati jab, most often it's because they themselves can't write or sell. The fact that you deal in thoughts and feelings instead of shoes makes you different from your neighbors, and hence a trifle frightening to them.

Third, bear in mind that we all tend to expect our fellows to be perfect, long after we discover that we ourselves are not. Professional writers and professors have been known to cut beginners down, in order to inflate their own egos, or to vent frustrations, or from plain, simple fear of competition.

Will facing these facts eliminate your fears?

No, of course not. But given time and effort, they'll help you to live with yourself more comfortably.

(3) Build your self-esteem.

As someone has said, you don't have moods; moods have you. Resort to will-power isn't always the best way to combat them.

Sometimes, you get better results when you sneak in the back door.

If you're depressed, try to recall some action that in the past has lifted such depression—a simple thing, like being forced to put on a mask of cordiality and speak to people on the street, or joking with old friends over coffee.

Call it auto-suggestion if you want to. But the fact remains that if you take this route . . . if you act *as if* you were a competent, confident, successful person . . . then frequently, you'll become just that.

(4) Don't demand too much.

Frustration tends to block a writer's flow of copy.

Nothing frustrates more than too high a level of aspiration. You get nowhere when you try to force yourself to write today the way you *may* write ten years from now, if you're sufficiently talented and lucky and if you write and study every day for the next ten years.

Accept yourself as you are today, on the other hand, and work from where you are with what you've got, and you may develop beyond your fondest expectations. Skill is a thing you acquire a little at a time. It doesn't come in a flash of magic.

(5) Keep your own counsel.

Writing is a lonely business.

In consequence, there's always a temptation to discuss your latest story with your friends.

Don't.

Why not?

For two reasons:

To begin with, talking about a story—telling it, in effect— amounts to working through it for the first time.

Result: Your emotional need to write it is reduced. You're put in the position of the man who strives, in reminiscence, to recapture the thrill of a first kiss. No matter how hard you try, the sparkle's gone.

Secondly, you can't help but be affected by your listener's reaction. His slightest frown or misinterpretation may cast a pall over the whole idea, to the point where it becomes almost impossible to write.

Double that in spades if the "listener" is an editor to whom you've sent an outline or synopsis.

You're better off to write, not talk.

(6) Follow your feelings.

Writing isn't a logical process, thank heavens.

And consistency is the hobgoblin of petty minds.

Therefore, don't let what "ought" to be constrict you. Impulse may prove a better guide.

This is especially true when you're in trouble with a story and production breaks down.

At such moments, if something about your opus doesn't "feel" right—ditch the something!

Similarly, if it *does*, don't hesitate to drive ahead, regardless of any apparent violation of the rules.

Why?

Because myopia can ever so easily blind a writer. Wrapped in his task, he loses all perspective.

Feeling operates on a different level. It sorts out the variables . . . rejects the false . . . catches glimpses of the larger pattern. While it can be wrong, its verdict rates strong consideration.

(7) Fall back on free association.

To free associate, you merely spill out words on paper: any words at all, without regard to point or purpose.

Such a process cuts you loose from critical judgment. Creative impulse takes command. Disinhibition helps restore your sense of balance.

Soon, fragments—ideas, words, phrases, sentences—begin to strike your fancy. Your stricken ego revives.

So, try free association when you're stuck: one hour per day for a week; no other writing permitted.

By the eighth day, you'll be back to production of story copy.

(8) Draw confidence from knowledge.

Certain things you know: things like the relation of motivation to reaction . . . the pattern to which you build a scene . . .

story structure . . . character dynamics . . . a host of techniques and devices.

These things aren't original with you. Generations of other writers worked them out before you.

That means you can depend on them . . . write to them by the numbers, if need be, secure in the knowledge that they'll help pull you out of your production breakdown.

Thus, if you write down a motivating stimulus, however crudely, you know that your next step is to find the proper character reaction.

A scene, in turn, starts with a character's selection of and decision to attempt to reach a given goal. Conflict develops from this effort, and finally builds to a disaster.

A story comes into being when desire collides with danger. Its climax centers on how your focal character behaves when faced with a choice between principle and self-interest.

With the road so clearly marked, how can you go astray?

(9) Soak yourself in your subject.

In the scene ahead, Hero needs an unobvious way to disable Villain's car. How should he go about it?

That's something you haven't yet worked out. So you sit staring at your typewriter, frustrated and unhappy because the yarn's bogged down.

What you *should* do is go in search of facts. Dig up a mechanic. Ask him how *he'd* cripple a '62 Ford, in a matching situation.

Too often, too many of us boggle at research. We try to "think through" something that really calls for information.

Then, we excuse it with talk of "writer's block."

(10) Incorporate present interests.

I've mentioned boredom before, and the way it can bring you to a grinding halt when you have to do one thing despite your yearning to do another.

Closely linked to this pattern is the fact that, in writing, your interests often change as you go along.

Next step: You grow sick unto death of the story you're on,

especially if it's a long one. In consequence, your writing slows down.

Yes, there's a remedy. It's this:

One reason you grow tired of your story is because fresh new ideas keep pressing in. Yet you feel you must reject them.

Well, don't.

Accept them instead. Devise ways to incorporate them into your present copy.

Thus, maybe you find yourself intrigued by a slangy, loud-mouthed, belligerent old woman, real or imagined.

All right. Find a place for her. Substitute her for some drab, dowdy female already in the cast.

Are you suddenly fascinated by the lore of diamonds? Then let a character be captivated too. His preoccupation with precious stones can serve as a tag and thus add extra interest.

The same principle holds for any other topic, from sports-car racing to ancient armor. Use it skillfully, and you'll find it a first-class weapon against boredom.

(11) Take the bull by the horns.

"If you haven't got an idea, start a story anyway," suggests mystery writer William Campbell Gault. "You can always throw it away, and maybe by the time you get to the fourth page you *will* have an idea, and you'll only have to throw away the first three pages."

It's good advice. Such is the power of inertia in us that we hesitate to plunge into work. Like timid swimmers, we stand shivering beside the pool, urging ourselves to dive yet dreading the water's chill.

The remedy is the same both for swimmer and for writer: a quick-drawn breath, a shudder, and a leap.

Besides, once the initial shock wears off, you may find the water is warmer than you think!

(12) Stay with the cattle.

My friend Clifton Adams is a top western writer. To what does he attribute his success?

He answers: "Writing's the only way I know to make a living. I didn't have any choice but to go on."

Actually, of course, Clif understates his case. You can always quit. But in some people determination, dedication, commitment —staying with the cattle, in the old range phrase—are character traits too deeply ingrained to be brushed aside easily.

These are traits every writer needs. When you bog down, your best response may be simply to persevere.

To that end, force yourself to write, however badly. Work awhile; then take a walk around the block, have a cup of coffee, and come back and work some more.

When the dam finally breaks, you'll discover an interesting fact: The copy you wrote in agony isn't one tenth as awkward as you thought it was.

The reason?

Talent is something that you're born with. It doesn't evaporate or drain away.

Skill is an element you build, out of work and study and experience. It can't vanish in a puff of smoke.

That's why it pays you to stay with the cattle.

(13) Finish every story.

Years ago I shared an office with another writer.

One day, something went wrong for him. Though more successful than most free-lances, he decided that his copy just wasn't good enough.

From there on, he worked through story after story up to the final scene.

Then, despair would overwhelm him. Refusing to believe his work was anything but drivel, he tore up sometimes-brilliant yarns . . . pieces that would certainly have sold if he'd ever given them a chance.

Completion of any story, however bad, is in its way implicit proof that you're better than most people who talk of writing. Not to finish, on the other hand, conditions you to failure in advance.

Howard Browne summed up the issue for me in a letter he wrote when I was in a blue funk of my own: "You go ahead and do me a story the way I'm telling you. Finish it—BUT DON'T READ IT WHILE YOU'RE WRITING IT AND DON'T READ IT BEFORE YOU SEND

IT TO ME. I'll read the thing and if it's no good I'll reject it. But it's not your job to reject anything; who do you think you are—an editor?"

(14) Set up a private checklist.

You know more than you think you do, on an unconscious level.

So, when you stall, more often than not it means that something about the story itself is wrong.

Somehow, you sense this fact, even though you can't nail down the trouble on a conscious basis.

At such a time, it helps to have a private checklist . . . a compendium of your own literary weaknesses.

Why?

Because we all tend to repeat our errors.

Thus, quite frequently, you may let your heroes grow passive, or fail to motivate key actions, or allow a goal to remain abstract.

Each time you spot such a weakness in one of your stories, note it on a file card, one card per weakness.

Soon, you'll have a packet of such.

That packet can be your most helpful aid in spotting errors. When a story bogs down, turn to it.

More often than not, what really bothers you in your current work will stand revealed.

(15) Give yourself a break.

Too much time in his workroom can develop tunnel vision in a writer.

When that happens, words come harder.

What should you do about it?

One answer is to take a break. Abandon work for a day or two or three. Get out among people. Have fun. Go on a trip. Do some of the things you've planned and postponed too long.

The virtue of this treatment lies in the fact that it changes your perspective. Under reality's impact, you become to a degree a different person.

Whereupon, when you go back to work, your problems may not loom so large.

(16) Avoid crutches.

When a man's in trouble, he tends to clutch at straws, or even bottles.

In fact, *especially* bottles.

Why?

Because alcohol lowers inhibition. You forget self-doubt in a haze of bourbon fumes.

Catch is, alcohol also establishes a conditioning. Before you know it, you discover that you can't work *without* a drink. Or two. Or three. Or four.

Soon you may find yourself in the situation of a friend of mine. Each day when he sat down to write, he set a fifth of whisky beside the typewriter.

Finally he reached a point where story and fifth ran out together. One fifth: one story.

A night came when the story took two fifths instead of one. His wife found him dead in his workroom in the morning.

Moral: Drink socially if you want to. But don't drink while you work.

There are other crutches besides alcohol, from marijuana to LSD. All operate on the same principle, and each offers a throughway to disaster.

The smart writer sweats out his private hell without them.

*   *   *

So now the fiction factory is in operation.

But here, another question rises: How do you sell the finished product?

That's a subject dear to every writer's heart. For a succinct guide, turn to the next chapter.

CHAPTER 9

Selling Your Stories

A story is merchandise that goes hunting for a buyer.

This is going to be the shortest chapter on record.

To sell stories, do three things:

1. Study your markets.
2. Get manuscripts in the mail.
3. Keep them there.

And that's all there is to it.

          *   *   *

What about agents?

An agent is a business manager for writers.

If you have a business to manage—one that makes a solid, consistent profit—an agent can be invaluable to you. If you haven't, why should he waste his time?

One agent, Paul R. Reynolds, has written a book called *The Writer and His Markets.* It covers the waterfront.

Read it.

CHAPTER 10

You and Fiction

*A story is a larger life, created and
shared with others by a writer.*

So now you know how to write and sell a story: the tricks, the
techniques, the devices, the rules-of-thumb.

True, you still have plenty to learn. The creation of commercial fiction involves all sorts of twists and subtleties. A writer can
work at his craft for twenty years, yet continue to discover something new each day.

But such fringe fragments are largely a matter of individual
touch, and best assimilated through experience. They'll come
with time and work.

More important, now, is a different question: Where do you
go from here?

That depends on you, of course: your tastes, your talents, your
ambitions; above all, the depth of your inner need to write and
sell.

And that brings us to a crucial issue: Just what *is* the nature of
the need to write, precisely? Why does one man go on and on;
another not?

The answer, put briefly, is this: The writer is a man who seeks
a larger world.

When he finds it, he passes it along to others.

Believe me, this can be a vital matter to you. Once you truly
understand it and its implications, your most irksome problems
will be resolved.

Shall we move to the attack?

* * *

The true function of any teacher is to prepare his students to face the future and strike out on their own.

To that end, and whether he plans it so or not, he ponders said students as much as they ponder him.

My own chosen pondering-place is the University of Oklahoma, and the Professional Writing program in which I teach. It provides me with student writers to observe, and the fact of their talent is demonstrated by the success that they've achieved: more than three hundred books published; literally thousands of magazine stories and articles sold. Men and women like Neal Barrett, Jr., science-fiction specialist; Jack M. Bickham, now with more than a dozen novels to his credit; Bob Bristow, major contributor in the men's field; Martha Corson, top confessioneer; Al Dewlen, whose *Twilight of Honor* was a Book of the Month Club selection and MGM film; Lawrence V. Fisher, with *Die a Little Every Day* for Random House and Mystery Guild; Fred Grove, winner of Western Writers of America awards; Elizabeth Land Kaderli, author of assorted fact books; Harold Keith, whose *Rifles for Watie* claimed a Newbery Medal; Leonard Sanders—his latest novel is *The Wooden Horseshoe,* at Doubleday; the late Mary Agnes Thompson, one of whose short stories ended up as an Elvis Presley movie; Mary Lyle Weeks, another leading confession writer now moving into the hardback novel field, and Jeanne Williams, author of prize-winning books for young people, are among those with whom I've had the pleasure of working personally, at one time or another.

What do I find when I look back along the road that these writers and hundreds of others like them have followed, as they went through courses with me and various of my colleagues: Foster-Harris, Helen Reagan Smith (in the University's Extension Division), and the late Walter S. Campbell?

Typically, the beginning student (and in specialized professional courses such as ours, "beginning student" often means a man or woman far past usual college age) is eager to write, but has deficiencies and knows it. He can't make words or readers behave the way he wants them to. So, he comes to course or book to learn his craft.

The skills he needs are things that can be taught.

We teach them to him.

Very soon, however, Writer learns that tools and tricks alone just aren't enough.

Why not?

Suppose an accident occurs at a busy intersection, in the presence of a dozen witnesses.

If the police are very lucky, they may locate one person upon whose account of the wreck they can depend. The others catch part of the action only, or become confused, or simply see things that didn't happen.

Would-be writers, too, reflect a kind of private blindness. Give five of them the self-same training and raw materials, and it may be your good fortune to have one produce a story that's worth the reading.

Thus, whether you deal with writer or with witness, the individual is the vital factor.

Why?

Because each person "sees" things differently.

Further, a different *type* of seeing is needed in each case.

The man the police want as an accident witness is one who sees facts: the World That Is; what actually took place, without distortion or interpretation.

This kind of seeing constitutes a talent. To observe accurately takes experience and training and a special kind of person.

What the writer needs, on the other hand, is exactly the opposite: the ability to see *more* than the facts: to look beyond them; to hypothesize about them; to draw conclusions from them.

Above all, he must use his facts as stimuli to feeling: emotionalize them; give them a unique private life.

This, too, is a talent.

Why does one would-be writer see more than do his fellows?

Because one has it in him to *be* a writer. The others only wish they did.

And—now we're back to where we started—this is because the true writer seeks a larger world.

How so?

Because the World That Is can never be quite large enough to suit the writer. Hemmed in by reality, he feels restive, no matter how ideal his situation may appear to another eye. A rut gilded, to him, still remains a rut.

And just as each character in a story draws motive force from his need to make up for something that he lacks, so the writer is driven by his need to escape the limits of a too-small world, the World That Is. It's in his blood to range farther than life can ever let him go. The impossible intrigues him. So do the unattainable, the forbidden, the disastrous. Like the man who reads his stories, he wants to know what it's like to love, to hate, to thrill, to fear, to laugh, to cry, to soar, to grieve, to kill, to die, from inside the skins of a hundred different people.

Nor is it enough for him just to know. He must play God too; guide the hand of fate; somehow mold and control the forces that shape destiny.

These things can't be. The writer realizes it.

But that only sharpens his desire and whets his craving; for his need to reach out strikes deeper than the wildest dreams of other men.

And the writer *can* reach out, through the agency of his own imagination.

He does so.

Then, because the things he finds in the larger world that he creates so fascinate him, he yearns to pass them on to others.

He does that too, through the medium of the written word.

Do I make this plain? The writer's inner need is dual.

On the one hand, he's driven by his desire to live life in a larger world.

On the other, he feels a compulsion to share that world . . . to display it for others to admire.

Both these drives must coexist inside you, nagging and harassing, if you're to be a writer.

I stress this because it's so seldom understood. Too often, the would-be writer thinks that what he wants is fame or money or independence. He equates a taste for reading or a knack with words for talent.

Now none of these beliefs are wholly false. But neither are they wholly true. They evade the issue, for convenience' sake or lack of insight or unwillingness to accept the fact of difference, as the case may be.

Actually, what a writer seeks is a way of life, and that way constitutes its own reward. The criterion is never art for art's sake . . . always, it is art for self's sake. You write because you like to—need to, have to—write; there is no other valid reason.

Once let a writer recognize this; once let him understand his own dynamics, and uncertainty and self-doubt fade. You learn to face the fact that if your inner need is great enough, you'll write. If other needs surpass it—if your drives to adventure or security or love or recognition or family duties strike deeper—then you can turn away with no regrets. You won't have to kid yourself about fame or money or independence—those are bonuses for special skill and talent; fringe benefits. Convenient and desirable though they may be, on a basic level they're only status symbols; society's stamp of approval to mark your success in your chosen field.

More important by far is your own self-satisfaction. Build larger worlds of your private choosing; find the right readers to admire them, and you'll live content despite an income that would never rouse jealousy in a used-car salesman. Deny yourself your Worlds of If, your readers, and you can be miserable even with a Rolls-Royce and a Bel Air estate.

* * *

What is a story?

A story is so many things—

It's experience translated into literary process.

It's words strung onto paper.

It's a succession of motivations and reactions.

It's a chain of scenes and sequels.

It's a double-barreled attack upon your readers.

It's movement through the eternal now, from past to future.

It's people given life on paper.

It's the triumph of ego over fear of failure.

It's merchandise that goes hunting for a buyer.

It's new life, shared with readers by a writer.

A story is all these things and more. So much, much more . . .

For a story, in the last analysis, is *you*, transferred to print and paper. You: unique and individual. You, writer, who through your talent range a larger world than others, and thus give life new meaning to all who choose to read.

You: writer.

Attain that status, and you win fulfillment enough for any man!

Preparing Your Manuscript

Use sixteen- or twenty-pound white paper . . . black typewriter ribbon. Follow the general style of the sample pages that follow, with one-inch margins all around and plenty of space at the top of page one. Mail flat, first class, in a 9½×12½ or 10×13 kraft envelope. Enclose a stamped, self-addressed, 9×12 envelope for possible return. Address simply to the magazine's editorial department, unless you have reason to call the script to the attention of some particular individual. No cover letter is necessary.

For market listings, consult:

> *The Writer*, 8 Arlington St., Boston 16, Mass.
> *Writer's Digest, Writer's Yearbook, Writer's Market*, 22 East 12th St., Cincinnati, Ohio.

Finally:

1. *Do* keep a carbon.
2. Be *sure* you attach proper postage.
3. *Don't* use a ribbon so long that it types gray.

Dwight V. Swain   About 27,500 words

1304 McKinley Avenue

Norman, Oklahoma 73069

K I L L E R , H E R E I C O M E !

by

DWIGHT V. SWAIN

CHAPTER 1: HEAT FOR HOODLUMS

        The three men arrived at precisely four nineteen p.m.

They rode in a battered '58 Dodge sedan that had mud-smeared

plates and a motor that purred like a souped-up special job.

        The driver parked directly in front of Richter's

grocery. He left the motor running.

        The other two men got out -- one tall, one short. The

tall one had the dangling arms and gangling gait of a gorilla.

Pausing on the curb, they cast ever-so-casual glances up and down

the street. Then the head of the shorter jerked in a curt nod,

and they strode on into the grocery.

The knock sounded again. The voice echoed -- more strident, this time.

It left Clay no choice. Whipping out his gun, he prodded the fallen thug to his feet. "Open the door. Let him in."

The hood's face paled a little. Stiffly, he reached out. . .gripped the knob.

Clay fell back a step, to where the opening door would hide him.

"Zanzer! Hurry up!" the voice outside rasped angrily.

The hoodlum half-opened the door. Clay waited, braced and tense.

Popping sounds came: three of them -- quick, close together, flat, for all the world like the bursting of so many little paper sacks.

The hoodlum had bent forward a trifle as he grasped the knob. Now he rocked back on his heels. The left flap of his coat twitched, as if someone were slapping at it. His olive-skinned face took on a glaze of shock, of incredulity. Then his knees gave, simultaneously with a rug-padded whisper of running feet. Another moment, and he pitched to the floor.

Gaping, paralyzed, at first Clay couldn't believe it. Then, as the raw truth struck him, he leaped clear of the fallen man, out into the hall.

outside the door, drinking in its freshness. . .stared up at the
fading stars.

Death. Ashes of love.

Only the dead deserved to die, most of them. And the
love hadn't really been love; not unless a cobra's chill
fascination could pass as such.

Give Homicide twenty-four hours to tie things together.
Find a good lawyer to persuade the D.A. to listen to reason. . .

Yes, it might work out. Cobalt City would be a better
place to live. They'd need honest cops.

Clay let the hand that held the gun drop. . .sucked air
deep into his lungs. It tasted good.

Elm Street. Two ways to go. Two roads to travel.
Left: Trinidad. Right: Pueblo.

A girl with golden hair and softly shining eyes.

Again Clay sucked in the air. Turned right.

The roadster still stood waiting.

The End

Dwight V. Swain
1304 McKinley Avenue
Norman, Oklahoma 73069

For Further Reading

It does a writer no harm to read what others have to say about writing. Sometimes he even picks up a new idea!

The books here listed are among those I've found helpful and/or stimulating. As such, they represent personal taste and nothing more, but you may enjoy some of them too.

Included also are a few titles on such related topics as imagination, interviewing, psychology and research, plus key fictional works to which reference is made in the text.

The editions listed are those that happen to be on my own shelves.

Adams, Clifton. *The Dangerous Days of Kiowa Jones*. New York: Doubleday & Co., 1963.

Allen, Walter (ed.). *Writers on Writing*. New York: E. P. Dutton & Co. (Everyman Paperbacks), 1959.

Barzun, Jacques, and Graff, Henry F. *The Modern Researcher*. New York: Harcourt, Brace & World (Harbinger Books), 1962.

Bedford-Jones, H. *This Fiction Business*. New York: Covici-Friede, 1929.

——. *The Graduate Fictioneer*. Denver: Author & Journalist Publ. Co., 1932.

Brean, Herbert (ed.). *The Mystery Writer's Handbook*. New York: Harper & Bros., 1956.

Campbell, Walter S. *Writing: Advice and Devices*. New York: Doubleday & Co., 1959.

——. *Writing Magazine Fiction*. New York: Doubleday, Doran & Co., 1940.

Cowley, Malcolm. *The Literary Situation*. New York: Viking Press, 1958.

—— (ed.). *Writers at Work: The Paris Review Interviews.* New York: Viking Press, 1958.

Egri, Lajos. *The Art of Dramatic Writing.* New York: Simon & Schuster, 1946.

——. *Your Key to Successful Writing.* New York: Henry Holt & Co., 1952.

Elwood, Maren. *Characters Make Your Story.* Boston: The Writer, Inc., 1949.

Fink, David. *Release from Nervous Tension.* New York: Simon & Schuster, 1953.

Fischer, John, and Silvers, Robert B. *Writing in America.* New Brunswick, N.J.: Rutgers University Press, 1960.

Frankau, Pamela. *Pen to Paper.* New York: Doubleday & Co., 1962.

Fuller, Edmund. *Man in Modern Fiction.* New York: Random House (Vintage Books), 1958.

Gallaway, Marian. *Constructing a Play.* New York: Prentice-Hall, 1950.

Harral, Stewart. *Keys to Successful Interviewing.* Norman: University of Oklahoma Press, 1954.

Harris, Foster. *The Basic Formulas of Fiction.* Norman: University of Oklahoma Press, 1944.

——. *The Basic Patterns of Plot.* Norman: University of Oklahoma Press, 1959.

——. *The Look of the Old West,* New York: Viking, 1955.

Hayakawa, S. I. *Language in Thought and Action.* New York: Harcourt, Brace & Co., 1949.

Hull, Helen (ed.). *The Writer's Book.* New York: Barnes & Noble, 1956.

——, and Drury, Michael (eds.). *Writer's Roundtable.* New York: Harper & Bros., 1959.

Hutchinson, Eliot D. *How to Think Creatively.* New York: Abingdon-Cokesbury Press, 1949.

Jaffe, Rona. *The Best of Everything.* New York: Simon & Schuster, 1958.

Kerr, Walter. *How Not to Write a Play.* New York: Simon & Schuster, 1955.

Macgowan, Kenneth. *A Primer of Playwriting.* New York: Doubleday & Co. (Dolphin Books), 1962.

McGraw, Eloise Jarvis. *Techniques of Fiction Writing.* Boston: The Writer, Inc., 1959.

McHugh, Vincent. *Primer of the Novel.* New York: Random House, 1950.

Maugham, W. Somerset. *The Art of Fiction*. New York: Doubleday & Co., 1955.

——. *The Summing Up*. New York: Doubleday & Co., 1938.

——. *A Writer's Notebook*. New York: Doubleday & Co., 1949.

Mundy, Talbot. "The Soul of a Regiment." In *Adventure* magazine, November 1950.

Noyes, Arthur P. *Modern Clinical Psychiatry*. 4th ed., Chapter 4, "Mental Mechanisms and Their Functions." Philadelphia: W. B. Saunders Co., 1953.

Osborn, Alex. *Your Creative Power*. New York: Charles Scribner's Sons, 1948.

Palmer, Stuart. *Understanding Other People*. New York: Thomas Y. Crowell Co., 1955.

Peeples, Edwin A. *A Professional Storyteller's Handbook*. New York: Doubleday & Co., 1960.

Ray, Marie Beynon. *The Importance of Feeling Inferior*. New York: Ace Books, 1957.

Read, Herbert. *English Prose Style*. Boston: Beacon Press, 1955.

Reynolds, Paul R. *The Writer and His Markets*. New York: Doubleday & Co., 1959.

Smith, Helen Reagan. *Basic Story Techniques*. Norman: University of Oklahoma Press, 1964.

Trask, Georgianne, and Burkhart, Charles (eds.). *Storytellers and Their Art*. New York: Doubleday & Co. (Anchor Books), 1963.

Vale, Eugene. *The Technique of Screenplay Writing*. New York: Grosset & Dunlap, 1972.

Yoakem, Lola G. (ed.). *TV and Screen Writing*. Article, "The Opening Scenes," by Frank S. Nugent. Berkeley: University of California Press, 1958.

Index

Special thanks are due my good friend-by-mail, Phyllis A. Whitney, fine author of romantic novels of suspense, for generously allowing me to use her notes in preparing this index. She is, of course, in no wise responsible for its imperfections.

Books listed in Appendix B (For Further Reading), pages 321–23, are not included in this index.